UNDERGROUND LITERATURE
DURING INDIAN EMERGENCY

UNDERGROUND LITERATURE DURING INDIAN EMERGENCY

Edited by :

SAJAL BASU

 South Asia Books

SOUTH ASIA BOOKS
Box—502 : Columbia, Mo. 65201 : U.S.A.
in arrangement with
Minerva Associates (Publications) Pvt. Ltd.
7-B, Lake Place, Calcutta—700 029 : INDIA

Printed in India by Narendra Chandra Roy at Anulipi,
180, Bipin Bihari Ganguly Street, Calcutta-700 012 and
published by T. K. Mukherjee on behalf of South Asia
Books, Box-502, Columbia, Mo. 65201, U.S.A.

PREFACE

FOR THE first time in recent history perhaps, floating rumour could be so authentic and illuminating to the masses. In fact, the Emergency solemnised the role of rumour in public life. The cold wave of emergency flooded, temporarily, all the democratic channels. But the unprepared bureaucratic machinery could hardly contain the underground media that rose spontaneously with the promulgation of emergency. News circulated, from mouth to mouth, or in print, the news of the awakening of the sleeping President and of making him sign the declaration of internal emergency, of complete breakdown in Patna, of the house arrest of Jagjivan Ram (then Minister of Agriculture and claimant for Prime Ministership after the judgement of the Allahadad High Court), of the imposition of a black-out in the newspaper area of Delhi, of strikes in Bombay, of the dissent of some military personnel and what not !

The last uncensored news-telegram of 26 June 1975 afternoon broadcast to the world of the midnight swoop on all prominent non-communist opposition leaders. Within the next 24 hours, the news of arrests in the States were in the air. Still, a few leaders could slip away from the police and they became the leaders of the underground movement and the fount of its news.

At the time of the mid-night swoop by the Indira police, George Fernandes (GF) happened to be in a small town in Orissa. He somehow, through a hitch-hike, managed to reach Calcutta and on 29 June night met a small group of people at Calcutta. In that closed meeting he said, 'at this moment all the political parties stand irrelevant. We shall have to fight this dictatorship tooth and nail, even if possible through precipitating pockets of disturbances. In our struggle we should use Gandhi as a shield'. Possibly that was the first significant underground meeting after the emergency was declared. He tried to get in touch with the Communist Party of India (Marxist) leader Shri Jyoti Basu. On 31 June a meeting could be arranged between the leaders at a place at Park Circus. But due to police vigilance, GF had to leave Calcutta, narrowly escaping arrest. Though in the meeting no programme could be discussed in detail, subsequently his underground notes were like sparks of fire, urging people to rise for an all out struggle against dictatorship. Gradually, an information network was set up. Leaflets, cyclostyled and printed, blowed in from different sources. Individual and political groups organised their production. In most cases the police failed to prevent them since they bore either fictitious names or the names of the Jana Sangharsh or Lok Sangharsh Samitis (Resistance organisations) !

Soon the first spell of emergency was over, and the Lok Sangharsh Samity could be activised by underground leaders like Nanaji Deshmukh, Surendra Mohan, Ravindra Verma and others. In the meanwhile, during July-August, large inflows of banned foreign journals and typed copies of Lok Sabha and Rajya Sabha proceedings inspired the spirit of the underground. The lectures of Mohan Dharia, A.K. Gopalan, Krishna Kant, N.G. Goray, Umasankar Joshi and others were circulated in typed or printed forms. Xerox copies of foreign clippings bearing articles on India and Mrs Gandhi's rise to dictatorship were also circulated in private amongst intellectuals and political activists. In Bihar, Karpoori Thakur was active, and the members of the Chhatra Sangharsh Samity (Students Fighting Front) took the lead in circulating underground literatures even in the remotest villages. Gujarat became a safe pocket for the underground activists. The Dravida Munnetra Kazhagam (DMK) party in Tamil Nadu also stood for anti-emergency activities.

Bombay remained the headquarters of the underground literature movement. Foreign materials (news, articles, in photostat or xerox) were being circulated from a centre at Bombay through unique devices. Sometimes they were posted in printed envelopes bearing the name and post box number of knows firms. They could thus easily reach the address without causing any concern to postal or police vigilance. The roles of

Sm. Mrinal Gore in the underground and of Shri S.M. Joshi, G.G. Parikh, Pannalal Surana, Rajaram Patil and others were, indeed, commendable. In overground publications too, Bombay based journals like *Janata, Sadhana, Quest* were most militant to uphold the spirit of resistance. Other journals of resistance were *Seminar, The Radical Humanist, Freedom First* in English, *Nireekshak, Sadhana* and *Bhumiputra* in Gujrati, and *Kolkata* and *Juger Dak* in Bengali. Most of those journals were either banned or forced to close down.

At the outset, the sources of underground news were mainly radio broadcasts from the VOA and BBC. Subsequently, liaison between the leaders in jails and the activists outside could be made ; and news of various states came through the despatches of the underground leaders. These news were then readily compiled, printed and circulated. The primary base of underground literature being thus built up, the news elements were used for producing leaflets and bulletins in various Indian languages. The letter of George Fernandes addressed to Madam Dictator, and the letter to his son from Gour Kishore Ghosh, and the lectures and letters of Jayaprakash Narayan were published in almost all Indian language bulletins.

Documenting a book of this style involves risk since it is not possible that all groups active in the underground movement find space and acknowledgement, which could do justice to them. The materials reproduced here stand as they were published, although the background forces or men involved in various stages cannot be documented, for obvious reasons. Only the actual group involved, behind a fictitious printer and publisher, has been mentioned for the purpose of history. The materials have been selected with a view to projecting the multi-dimensional character of the underground movement. It would have been better to compile materials from all languages, with the hope that in regional languages too, persons interested would come forward to publish books on underground literature, but this has not been possible so far. I have selected materials mostly from English language publications, although some leaflets in Bengali have also been translated. Though we have in store volumnious foreign materials, in the shape of clippings.

I have not used them since a book is already there only with news and articles published in foreign newspapers.

The documentation of underground literature can perhaps never be complete. I have only initiated the process. Much of the material still remains unexplored or is lying secretly among piled-up papers. Many significant papers might still be in such a state. With this book, I wish I can add some historicity to such papers. In getting these papers, I am much indebted to Shri CRM Rao and Sujit Deb of the Centre for the Study of Developing Societies, Delhi, Shri Niranjan Halder, Asst. Editor, *Ananda Bazar Patrika*, Shri Sukumar Ghosh of the Socialist Party, Shri Bimal Banerjee of Hind Mazdoor Sabha, Citizens Committee, Calcutta, and Shri Amitava Chatterjee of *Samachar*. I must thank Sushil Babu (Mukherjea) of Minerva Associates for taking the risk of publishing this book, and Oroon Babu (Ghosh) of Minerva Associates for kindly going through the manuscript and offering suggestions. Lastly, I should also thank friends of the Committee for the Exhibition of Underground Literature which remains a basic source of materials published here.

7 Nandy Street   Sajal Basu
Calcutta-700 029
7 April 1978

CONTENTS

CONTENTS

CHAPTER I

LEAFLETS AND BULLETINS

WHY THIS EMERGENY ?

Mrs Gandhi has proclaimed special emergency measures to formalise dictatorship. The opposition parties have been held responsible for precipitating chaos and disrupting democracy. As we all knew, the opposition parties' combined strength lags far behind the Congress. Still Mrs Gandhi says that measures were taken only to save the country from the right reactionaries. Actually, it has become open that division in the Congress Legislature Party is sharp. More than half of the MPs were of the view that the Prime Minister should pay respect to the judgement of Allahabad High Court. To silence this voice of dissent the emergency has been proclaimed and many of these Congress MPs are arrested. Not to speak of Jaiprakash, Morarji Bhai, Asoke Mehta, Atal Behari Bajpai, Madhu Limaye, Samar Guha, Basava Punniah and other opposition leaders also were arrested on the same night.

JP's call to Military and Police was taken as a plea to confer dictatorship on the nation. What are the contents of JP's call. Has he ever asked to deny the cause of protecting national security ? In Bihar the youth-students have coined a now slogan —'Policemen are our brothers, our fight is not against them'. Congress government's practice of requisitioning Military's service in combating peoples' movements has excited serious controversy amongst the Military men regarding its legitimacy. Central Police Forces are also employed in provinces, as a practice CRP or BSF of other provinces are posted to meet the challenge of peaceful democratic movements. It only provoked provincialism and is dangerous to the cause of national integrity. JP's appeal to Military and Police is actuated to negate this evil. Before firing on the peaceful demonstrators who are their own brothers, Police and Military are requested to consider the justice of such orders. Such call is nothing new in History. It is in the Hague

Convention, the Status of Universal Human Rights of UNO also carry similar implementations. Military and Police, who are led by the people to protect the security of the nation, should consider whether it is just for them to open torture on their fellow countrymen on any plea, only to serve the wishes of the rulers.

21-point economic measures have been declared as if the measures could not be materialised in democratic conditions. Most of the 21-points are in the electoral commitments of Congress (R). Why they could not implement any of these GARIBI HATAO measures ? The opposition parties never hesitated to extend support to measures like Bank Nationalisation or Abolition of Privy Purse. Mrs Gandhi ousted the Syndicate Congressites in 1969 with the support of those parties. Her GARIBI HATAO measures could be materialised with the support of the capitalists like K.K. Birla. They are all hog with the Congress. Newspapers and parties never said that they would back a Birla or Tata to meet the challenge of GARIBI HATAO. Then why this censor and virtual ban on party activities ? Even Congress MPs and leaders opposed to official leadership are not spared. They are either arrested or under threats.

The whole thing has been machinated with a long term view. Serious grievances within the Congress against too much involvement with Russian economy impairing national interest, and growing strength of the anti-CPI lobby within the Congress, have invited this conspiracy. No sincere Congress man would tolerate the ugly nose of pro-Russian elements who are out to divide Congress and present the nation to Russian interest. The un-called for support of the CPI and its meddlesome offer to work with Congress unitedly expose the intention. As if Mrs Gandhi has declared emergency only to gain support of CPI and Congress as an organisation is ready to merge with Russian dictates. For this reason, the nationalist Congress men are sensitive about the whole affair and very much anxious to defeat this Russian conspiracy. Like the ordinary people they have become stunned lest that arrest or tortures may fall upon them. CPI men may feel victorious in the situation, but they should re-collect the history of dictators. Setting parties against each other is the primary step, ultimately liquidation measures come upon all to stabilise one man's rule. Congressmen are aware of this, so they did not rejoice the situation as the CPI do. The Russian lobby is over sanguine of their victory, but history is unpredictable to be dictated in one's own terms. Of late, Parliament has been prorogued to ratify the emergency measures. Some of the parties and the vote-seekers are over ambitious about restoration of normal democratic atmosphere. They do not read the situation objectively since their outlook have been one of getting elected in anyway and serve the nation. Two and half a decades' parliamentary politics has bring forth all these vested groups in all colours, left right alike. Indira knows it well. They should realise that their term of nation-serving has been terminated sine die. Some face saving device of democratic show, either a Russian or Bangladesh type or new one may come. We would be careful not to be camouflaged by such device. Voicing the demands for realese of arrested political workers, withdrawal of censorship on newspapers, combating the pro-Russian conspirators and their anti-national propaganda, rousing the sentiments of Congressmen against the conferring dictatorship, these are the tasks we can take at this moment.

JANA SANGRAM SAMITY.

N. B. This leaflet was published and circulated by the cadres of Socialist Party during second week of July, '75. Written by this Editor, the name of Jana Sangram Samity was given only to confuse it with Jana Sangharsh Samity.

INTELLECTUALS ! ATTENTION PLEASE
POINTS FOR YOU TO PONDER !

Is it a fact that the chiefs of the three services of Army, Navy & Airforce refused to attend the meeting convened yb Indira Gandhi ? Is it a fact that the three chiefs refused to attend the meeting not because the President of India who is the Supreme Commander of the Defence forces happened to be absent from the meeting, but because two Russian Generals were to be present at the meeting to give Directions to the Chiefs of our Defence services on how to meet the Emergency and thus boss over our Defence apparatus ?

Is it a fact that on the evening of 26th June '75 the day on which the Emergency was declared a Soviet aeroflot plane touched down at Dum Dum Airport under heavy security Guard, on the way to New Delhi ? Is it a fact that the heavily guarded Soviet plane was carrying a few Russian Generals and Ministers to mastermind the operation of the emergency ?

Is it a fact that with the proclamation of the Emergency all the living Ex-Army Chiefs, including Field-Marshal Shri Maneckshaw have been interned ? Is it a fact that as many as forty senior Army Officers above the rank of Colonels, officers of the Airforce, and the Navy of equivalent rank have been purged by way of being forced to go on compulsory retirement ? Is it a fact that this compulsory retirement was not due to their inefficiency (in fact they are veritable gems & pride of our Defence Forces) but due to their patriotic fervour for which Russian advisers of Indira Gandhi considered them to be inconvenient and sought their removal to establish Russian hegemony ?

Is it a fact that India's dictator Indira Gandhi is being dictated by two Russian Ministers since the proclamation of emergency ?

Is it a fact that Sri N. A. Palkhiwala, who argued before the Supreme Court on behalf of Indira Gandhi in order to obtain an absolute stay order, has since returned the brief and refused to appear on behalf of Indira Gandhi out of sheer disgust at the grossly unethical and undemocratic manner with which his client, namely Indira Gandhi, violated all standards of decency and decorum by running burserk, immediately after the proclamation of the Emergency ?

Is it a fact that Indira Gandhi refused to bow out of the office of the Prime Minister in favour of even a puppet of her choice (not to speak of Jugjiwan Ram, Y.B. Chavan or any other leader with an independent bent of mind) as she had a genuine fear that all the skeletons in her cupboard, like Maruti scandal, removal of Rs 60 lakhs from the Treasury of State

Bank of India and the murder of Nagarwala, physical liquidation of honest CBI officials and murder of L.N. Mishra will come to light and be exposed to the broad gaze of the public?

Is it a fact that important leaders like Jugjiwan Ram and Chavan are being kept surrounded by Security Guards to keep a watch on their movements, resulting in their virtual arrest?

Is it a fact that Indira Gandhi has lost faith in her party colleagues and placed as many as 89 Congress MPs under house arrest and thrown a few dozen behind prison bar?

Is it a fact that Indira Gandhi is under the absolute control of and in the confidence of her Russian advisers and their stooges in our country?

Is it a fact that the President of India was roused from sleep at the dead of night by Indira Gandhi and her pimp Sidhartha Shankar Ray, Chief Minister of West Bengal, (Who is made to do nasty jobs on her behalf) and was forced to sign the Emergency proclamation on the dotted line which was broadcast by Indira Gandhi herself on the next morning over the All India Radio hook-up?

Is it a fact that eight Cabinet Ministers who felt outraged over the grossly undemocratic behaviour of Indira Gandhi were made to keep mum under threat?

Is it a fact that J. P. Narayan & Morarji Desai have been on fast since the day of their arrest and the situation is very grave.

Is it a fact that the office of Ananda Bazar Patrika, the leading Bengali Daily and the allied periodicals and the house of Sri Ashok Sirkar were searched by a large force of Police for sixteen hours on 27th June '75 and valuable records were siezed by the Police to punish the authorities of Ananda Bazar Patrika for daring to write against Indira Gandhi. Is it a fact that celebrated columnists like Barun Sengupta, Gorey (Gour) Kishore Ghose, Ranjit Roy and others are being manhandled by Police?

N. B. This was published by R.S.S. Approximate date of circulation 18. 7. 75.

Pabanaco Bulletin No. 11

"AMNESTY INTERNATIONAL NEWS RELEASE

53 Theobald's Road London WCIX 8 SP   Tel : 01-404

Telegram : AMNESTY LONDON   Secretary General : Martin Ennals

FOR IMMEDIATE RELEASE   Friday 27th June 1975

AMNESTY INTERNATIONAL URGES INDIA TO FREE ARRESTED OPPOSITION LEADERS

"Mrs. Indira Gandhi,   1st July 1975.
Prime Minister,
New Delhi.

"The undersigned,

"*expressing* their deep concern at the measures taken by the Government of India, which have led to the suspension of fundamental Civil Rights guaranteed to Indian Citizens by their Constitution, the imprisonment of a large number of political leaders of almost all opposition parties ; the complete censorship of Press and news media, and a ban on all forms of protest and demonstrations,

strongly deploring these developments as undemocratic and as a step towards totallitarian rule by the Government,

Call upon you to put an end to the state of emergency, to release all political prisoners particularly Jaya Prakash Narayan, the internationally known and respected pacifist leader who is reported to be on hunger strike and whose condition is reported to be very serious.

Philip Noel-Baker, Martin Ennals, Hens Janitschek, James Cameron, E.F. Schuhmecher.

Evading the Censor's scissors an obituary was published in a Bombay newspaper :

"O" Cracy : D. E. M. O' Cracy, beloved husband of T. Ruth, Father of L. I. Berty, father of Faith, Hope and justicia, on June 28." That means, democracy, truth and liberty have been murdered on 28 June, 75.

N. B. PABANACO Bulletin was published by West Bengal Citizens Committee. This issue was published in the last week of July, 1975. The Committee is organised by dissident Cong (O) people led by Miss Abha Maity.

GLEANINGS FROM THE
LAST SESSION OF THE PARLIAMENT

Smt. Indira Gandhi had convened the Monsoon Session of the Parliament at a time when 39 of its important members were rotting in jails. Her object was to ratify the illegal Emergency and to show the outer world that democracy is still alive here. But in spite of her best attempts she could impress none by her stage-managed pseudo-parliament. Not a single line of what the opposition members said in the Parliament was allowed by the Govt. to be reported in the press. The Chief Censor of New Delhi imposed the restriction that nothing except the Ministers' speeches would be published. Reporters were not allowed entry into the sessions. The public had to remain content with what the Information Dept. of the Govt. dished out to the Pressmen. Such is the travesty of democracy that Smt. Indira Gandhi gave us an occasion to witness.

Perhaps many are not aware that on the third day of the Session (23rd July, 75), being exasperated by the policy of strangulation adopted by the Govt., all the opposition members excepting C. P. I., A. D. M. K., Republican Party and Muslim League, boycotted both the houses of the Parliament after reading out a note of protest, which was signed by 101 members. We quote below the note of protest as well as excerpts from the speeches of some of the renowned opposition leaders made on the floor of the Parliament. The official instruction issued by Chief Censor of the New Delhi is also being reproduced here.

Shri A. K. Gopalan—(C. P. I.-M.)

I rise to speak in an extraordinary and most distressing situation in which 34 members of Parliament are not here, not

on their own volition, but because they have been detained
without trial, and Parliament itself has been reduced to a farce
and an object of contempt by Smt. Gandhi & her party.........
On behalf of the Communist Party of India (Marxist), I totally
oppose the new declaration of Emergency and its ratification in
this house.........We cannot betray the interests of the people,
give our assent to the obliteration of all vestiges of democracy
in India—freedom of the person, freedom of speech, freedom to
form associations, freedom to approach the courts, freedom of
the press, freedom to criticise the Government and work for its
replacement by a Government of the people's choice.........

Take the Government's attitude to the RSS and the Anand
Marg which it has now banned. It seems that the Government's
attitude to these organisations changes from time to time to
suit its convenience. In 1965, during the Indo-Pak War, the
then Prime Minister, Lal Bahadur Shastri handed over Delhi to
RSS for civil guard duties. The present Prime Minister, Shrimati
Indira Gandhi, paid glowing tributes to the RSS Chief,
Golwalkar some time ago in the Parliament.........

Our party has clearly stated our difference with Shri J. P.
but at the same time, given our support to the democratic
demands which he has championed. Whatever our differences
with the movement, we have defended and will defend their
right to organise satyagraha, strikes, bandhs etc. which are
legitimate weapons in the hands of the people. The movement
led by Shri J. P. has accepted the challenge of Shrimati Gandhi
to face elections and was preparing for them. It is Shrimati
Gandhi who developed cold feet after the verdict in Gujarat.
Sections of the Ruling Congress were themselves in Gujarat and
Bihar movements ......

It is unfortunate that Communist Party of Soviet Union and
some other Communist Parties have allowed themselves to be
misled by the facade of attack against right action and do not
see that the real thrust of these measures is against the people
fighting for a better existence. They do not see that because of
the basic policies of the Govt. the contradictions between the
Govt. and the people are intensifying. The CPI, the wretched
traitors to the working class and the toiling people, continues to

function as Her Majesty's loyal opposition. Our party considers it as its foremost task to awaken and organise the people against the grave peril they are facing and throw them into the struggle for the withdrawal of the Emergency and restoration of whatever democratic rights they wrenched after innumerable struggles and untold sacrifices, for the resignation of Smt. Indira Gandhi from Prime Ministership and for the release of all political prisoners.

Shri Jagannath Rao Joshi (Jan Sangha)

Madam,

......I want to put only one question before you. What is the motive behind the actions you have taken during the last few days ? Did you do all these things for the sake of the Country or for saving your own skin ? Speak out the truth, we want to hear the truth, the unequivocal truth from you. It is said that Nehru family is known for their uncompromising truthfulness. So why hesitate to come out with the truth ? (pause) I know that you cannot say the truth. Everybody in the Country knows that you have promulgated Emergency only to save your throne. The bogey you have raised about lawlessness in the country is only a figment of your imagination. If you really believe that public opinion is overwhelmingly in favour of you then why not relinquish your post and seek for a fresh mandate. You will never dare to do that, never. You pretty well know that the moment you step down, you will be nowhere. There is no escape from public wrath, remember, your every misdeed will be accounted for.

Madam, no use looking at the members of the Treasury Bench. They back you not due to any ideological attachment, but out of sheer self-interest. They know that so long as you are in power their own existence is guaranteed. That is why they support your sinister game. But don't rely too much upon them. The moment you are out they will not recognize you even. They won't hesitate to leave you at lurch.

It is an open secret that not all the members of your own party support your nefarious acts. But they have been silenced by your illegal emergency. They cannot speak out the truth lest you put them behind bars. Already several M.Ps. of your party have been jailed.

I know in whose hands you are playing. But no power on earth can save a person who betrays the cause of his or her motherland for the sake of personal ends.

Shri N. G. Goray (S. P.)

......Why is it that elections are not held in Kerala ? Is the Kerala population in revolt ? What is happening in Kerala ? Because you know that this emergency is not accepted by the people of Kerala and it will be very difficult for Achutha Menon and his group to come back to power, you give them six months more......Both the sides must play the game. When you cannot answer the people, all the answer that you have is to put them in jail, throw them in jail and put them behind the bars. Is this the answer ? And even what we speak here, I know, will not be allowed to go out. When we come to attend Parliament session you arrest us.

......Sir, yesterday, I pointed out to you, the President calls us here for attending the Parliament and as soon as we come here we are arrested. You ask us to go to a meeting and when we go to the meeting, we are arrested. My friend Madhu Dandavate was arrested. Mr Advani was arrested, Mr Mishra was arrested, why ? Because they were attending a meeting which you yourself had called. What is this ? Is this democracy ?...

I am appealing to those people who still have theis heads on their shoulders. That is the point. What I am saying is, you take this 20-point programme. Let us come to the brass tacks. What is new in that ? You have been announcing this programme from the housetops ever since there was a rift in the Congress. There is nothing new. What prevented you from implementing this programme ? What are the main characteristics of this programme ? Give land to those who have no land. Who has prevented you from doing it ? Complete the land registers. Who has prevented you ? In Bihar there is no land register at all and in Bihar ever since Independence it is your Ministry which is functioning. Who has prevented you ?

The speech read out at both the houses before the opposition boycotted the session

It is after a great deal of deliberation that we in the opposition parties (excluding of course the C. P. I.) and some independent members decided to attend and participate in the present session of Parliament. Our reluctance arose from the fact (1) of the press censorship, but even more so from (2) the resolution standing in the name of Shri Raghuramaiah/Shri Om Metha, the Minister for Parliamentary Affairs, asking the House to suspend all rules relating to questions, Calling Attention and any other business to be initiated by private members. We could not but take note of the fact that apart from Government's business, Parliament has to perform other duties also, such as debate on Government policy, exercise effective supervision over executive action in various ways. Only by putting a question or giving a Calling Attention Notice or initiating a debate can a member focus the attention of the House and through it of the country, to matters of public importance. And that is why constitutional authorities have held that the right to put questions and Notice are among the most vital rights of an ordinary member. If all these were to be abandoned unceremoniously, we would really be acquiescing in something that cuts at the very root of the role of Parliament in its time-honoured functions. Nevertheless it was felt that perhaps the proceedings in this session of Parliament will be conducted in a normal manner and that speeches made on the floor of the House will be allowed to be reported freely and faithfully in spite of the pre-censorship.

To our dismay, we find that the reporting on the A. I. R. of yesterday's proceedings of the House is such that it can only mislead. It mentioned only the names of the participants whereas Shri Jagajivan Ram's speech was fairly and fully high-lighted. This morning's newspaper reporting of the proceedings is also on the same lines. We cannot but protest most emphatically against such unfair reporting of the proceedings which tells the country Government's point of view in regard to the emergency without indicating what the Opposition had to say on the floor.

It is clear that this has been done in accordance with the instructions issued to the Press and the A. I. R. by the Chief Censor on the 20th July under the heading "Guidance for the covering of Parliamentary proceedings." It is not indicated if these instructions that the speech or the speeches of members of Parliament participating in the debate shall not be published in any manner or form though their names and party affiliations may be mentioned, were issued with or without the approval of the Speaker/Chairman.

We have, therefore, been compelled to ask ourselves the question whether continued participation in the further business before Parliament on those terms would serve any useful public purpose. The decision to amend the Constitution to make the proclamation of this question more urgent and immediate. It is evident that Government, having already denied the entire people of the country the basic fundamental rights is now determined to ride roughshod over the rights of the members of Parliament.

Taking all relevant facts into consideration and bearing in mind in particular the fact that leading members of Parliament have been incarcerated, we are satisfied now that no useful purpose will be served by our taking part in further proceedings of this session of Parliament, for it is clearly in no position to discharge the function of a free and democratic Parliament.

Madam, with this, we all of us withdraw from the house.

(True Copy of Govt. Circular)

Message No. 31.   New Delhi, July 20, '75

SECRET/MOST IMMEDIATE :::

FROM : CHIEF CENSOR

To : ALL REGIONAL/BRANCH OFFICES

No. F. 2/1/75-CC,

OFFICE OF THE CHIEF CENSOR GOVERNMENT
OF INDIA SHASTRI BHAVAN

Revised guidelines for the coverage of Parliament Proceedings.

The following guidelines for the coverage of Parliament proceedings should be kept in view :—

(A) The statements of Ministers may be published either in full or in a condensed form but its contents should not infringe censorship.

(B) The speeches of members of Parliament participating in a debate will not be published in any manner or form but their names and party affiliation may be mentioned. When publishing names of members who participated in a debate, the fact that they supported or opposed a motion can be mentioned.

(C) The results of voting on a bill, motion, resolution etc. may be factually reported. In the event of voting, the number of votes cast for and against may be mentioned.

(D) The question of allowing references to walk-outs or other form of protests in the House will be decided by the Chief Censor on the merits of each case and instructions will be sent to censors accordingly.

NEW DELHI—1   Sd/- H. J. D'PENHA

Dated July 20, 1975.   CHIEF CENSOR

To,

ALL CENSORS.

S A N G R A M

Bulletin No. 1   Lok Sangharsha Samity 1.9.75

N. B. Sangram was published by R.S.S. men.

KHABAR

September 14, 1975.   Vol. 1. No. 1

On 26th June Mrs. Gandhi promulgated emergency and established dictatorship in Russian style and on Russia's advice.

Two reasons are, her defeat in the Allahabad High Court and as its result split in her party. Since that day censorship is on...

The news of arrests could not be known even. Some news can be collected through P. C. Sen or Abha Maity's bulletins and George Fernandes' or Nanaji Deshmukh's statements. On 22nd July at the Palam Airport three foreign Journalists were made naked to be searched. Yahaya Khan adopted the same technique in 1971. New Delhi is crowded with Russian Journalists and Russian Colonels, 300 of them are now staying incognito in Delhi Hotels.

On 26th night, India Government sealed the office of opposition weeklies, 'Pratipakshya', 'Motherland', 'Panchajanya' 'Organiser', Jayaprokash's 'Everyman's' and 'Lokniti' are also banned. In West Bengal, 'Juger Dak', 'Mayurakshi', Chowringhee Barta'have been closed.

West Bengal Jana Sangharsa Samity organised first protest meeting on 27th at Monument Maidan. Citizens committee organised protest on 1st August against the increase of Bus fare, 50 men were arrested. Citizens Committee was not given the permission to hold a meeting on Independence day. P.C. Sen launched a Padayatra on 8 August from Arambagh, he was arrested, released and sent back to Calcutta.

In West Bengal, among the leaders arrested after emergency and still in Jail are Khitish Roy Chowdhury, Prof. Haripada Bharati, Biman Mitra, Sushil Dhara, Swarajbandhu Bhattacharya, Ashoke Dasgupta, Sajal Basu, Chittagong armoury revolutionary Dinesh Daspupta, Jamuna Singh, Naresh Ganguly, Ajit Bose of Hooghly, 250 C.P.I. (M) Cadres, 300 Naxalites etc.

As a protest against Mrs. Gandhi's dictatorship, Mr. Appa Pant, Indian Ambassador in Italy, has resigned. Palkiwala has denied to stand counsel for Mrs. Gandhi in Supreme Court. Prof. Dantewala has resigned from Governorship of Reserve Bank. Bagaram Tulpule, Chairman of Sikh Security Board also resigned. In London, 2000 students demonstrated before the India House. Tamilnadu Chief Minister Karunanidi, in a public meeting, warned Mrs. Gandhi not to intervene in his state affairs. In Gujrat a public meeting of 50,000 condemned emergency. Corrupt Ashoke Sen took up the counsel for Mrs.

Gandhi in order to get rid of the charges against him concerning Basumati Newsprint case.

Editor's Note : KHABAR was published by independent Journalists and Intellectuals. Khabar, meaning news, used to collect and circulate news published in foriegn papers. It first reprinted the letter of Gour Kishore Ghosh to his son which was published in a journal and for which the noted litterateur was arrested. Niranjan Halder, Asst. Editor, Ananda Bazar Patrika, a leading daily in Bengali, was the spearhead of Khabar.

FACTS
NAIL INDIRA'S LIES

Here are some facts from Madhya Pradesh. They have been collected, printed and distributed facing constant threats of police zulam.

Madhya Pradesh Lok Sangharsh Samiti
BHOPAL

I. DANGER TO THE SECURITY AND UNITY OF INDIA !

World press is being repeatedly told that only such persons in small numbers have been detained whose activities are considered a danger to the security and unity of India. And their cases are reviewed periodically resulting in the release of nearly 30-40% detenues, whose detention was considered no more necessary.

(1) But, believe it or not, a 7 year girl Baby Arti Mishra whose both legs are crippled due to polio, is rotting under Maintenance of Internal Security Act (MISA) in Indira Gandhi's jail in Bhopal since July 6, 1975. Later her mother Mrs. Ram Kali Mishra was also hauled-up under MISA.

It is to be borne in mind here, that being a MISA detenue, baby Arti is neither supplied the grounds for detention nor she is permitted to go to a court of law for any remedy what-so-ever because Mrs. Indira Gandhi has suspended Fundamental Rights to save democracy in India—a country that is supposed to subscribe to the U. N. O. charter for protection of Human Rights.

It will not be out of place to mention here that Indira Government's counsel Mr. S. C. Chagla recently pleaded in Bombay High Court that even if the government chose to starve the detenues to death or shoot them, these actions could not be challenged in a court of law because of suspension of Fundamental Rights including one's right to exist.

(2) Mr. Subhash Banerjee and his wife Mrs. Jaya Shree Banerjee were both arrested in June 26, 1975 under MISA. The result is that NO-BODY is now left in the family to look after their four children—the eldest Ashish is 18 years and the youngest Deepanker is 7 yrs. To believe Indira government's cruelty, one has to see the condition of the 4 kids of Mr. Rajpal Chopra and his wife Mrs. Kanta Chopra both of whom have been detained under MISA again in Jabalpur. In Agar (District Shajapur) a labour family of ten members is left to starve with no earning member left after the arrest of Mr. Bansi Lal Parmar and his two sons Narendra and Ramesh under MISA since June 30, 1975. On August 15, a 5 year old son of Mr. Parmar died, but this heartless Indira regime did not grant Mr. Parmar any leave on parole to visit his mourning family. And it is a crime for the press to bring to public notice such inhuman acts of the government.

(3) Dr. Krishna Chandra Arora and his compounder Narendra were thrown behind the bars on June 30, 1975 under MISA leaving their patients due for long-term treatment to their own fate. Similar is the fate of the patients of distant villages in Tribal areas by forcing the closure of a hospital in Jashpur which was run on philanthropic basis by Dr. Rajendra Pathak who is again a prey of MISA.

(4) Dr. Deo Pujari of Sonsar (District Chhindwada) was not granted to parole to see his dying mother who herself had to go to the jail to meet her son. The critically ill mother could not bear the strain and died.

(5) Mr. Udhav Das Mehta, a highly respected citizen of

Bhopal, after a cancer operation in Bombay, was due in Bombay for periodical treatment on a pre-fixed date i. e. September 17 1975. But, again the notorious MISA was used to prevent him from going to Bombay for his cancer treatment.

(6) Arbitrarily any person becomes 'wanted' and when he is not available, his relatives are arrested or harassed. Mr. Deepak Kekre was hauled-up on July 26 under MISA from his College of Agriculture at Jabalpur when the police could not lay its hands on his 'wanted' father Madhukar Kekre of Siwani Malwa (District Hoshangabad). Similarly a technician of H. E. L. Bhopal, Mr. Narendra Paliwal was thrown behind the bars under MISA on July 20, because the police could not till then get his father Mr. Brijendra Paliwal whom they considered 'wanted'. The Indira regime felt no pangs of conscience in hauling the 17 yr. old son of Shri Rajendra Dharkar, an advocate of Indore and the 75 yr. old mother of Mr. Shri Ballabh—secretary of Indore Jana Sangh, to the Indore police station on June 29 and used all third degree methods on them during the whole night to know the whereabouts of their father and son respectively.

III. INTERFERENCE IN THE PROCESS OF JUSTICE

After the Legislatures have been crippled, the press gagged and the Executive reduced to a push button repressive apparatus to protect the office of Prime Ministership for a person, the last bastion of democracy, the Judiciary too is not left untouched. Censorship of Delhi High Court Judgement releasing the famous journalist Mr Kuldip Nayar is wellknown through the foreign press and radio.

(1) In Madhya Pradesh advocates have been arrested to interfere in the process of justice. Mr Sevakram Somani, an advocate of repute of Bhopal, was dealing with writ petitions relating MISA and was seeking interviews with his clients under detention. Thereupon he himself was haulded up at 12-30 A.M. (midnight) on July 3.

Mr Ram Krishna Vijayavargiya, an advocate of repute of Indore and engaged in an election petition against the Chief Minister Sethi ; received a phone call on August 12, that he

2

would be imprisoned under MISA if he prefered an appeal in Supreme Court against Mr Sethi. Mr Vijayavargiya ignored the threat and filed an appeal in the Supreme Court at 10-30 A. M. on August, 25. What was the result ? Mr Vijayavargiya was haulded-up under MISA by the police, right from the compound of the Indore High Court at 11-00 A. M. on the same day.

WEST BENGAL CITIZENS' COMMITTEE

PABANACO BULLETIN 22   Calcutta
                                                        15th Sept. 1975

The root of all Corruption in India is Indira Gandhi

The present Prime Minister of India, Mrs. Indira Gandhi is often speaking about her intention to restore democracy in India ; in reality, however, she has raped and murdered all the fundamental democratic rights of the Indian people which we had earned through the sacrifice of hundreds of martyrs.

Here is a letter written by Shri M. O. Mathai to Sm. Padmaja Naidu who had been a close friend of the Nehru family. Shri M. O. Mathai was the Private Secretary to Prime Minister Jawaharlal Nehru for long fifteen years. Shri Mathai had access to all documents including those dealing with the closest secrets of the Nehru family.

From the letter will be evident, to what extent Sm. Indira Gandhi, in her personal life, had been and still is a power-seeker, selfish and corrupt individual. Even a cursory reading of this letter will reveal the fact that it was written by Shri Mathai in his anguish and sorrow.

2 Willingdon Crescent
NEW DELHI-4.
7th January, 1967

Personal

My dear Padmasi,

Thank you for your New Year Card and for what you have scribbled in it. Yes, I too feel sorry that we could not meet while you were in Delhi for the Governors' Conference. I was out of Delhi then. On my return I learnt that you rang me up twice. I had several things to tell you. Since I may not see you for a long time, I am venturing to write this personal letters : and you told me once that letters marked 'personal' are opened by yourself.

Since a fortnight after Panditji's sad demise in May 1964 I had not met Indira. Suddenly on the evening of the 21st August, 1966 I received a frantic telephone message from her wishing to see me. Due to sentiments attached to the memory of Panditji, I went and met her for half an hour. Again on the evening of the 23rd August I met her for an hour at her own urgent request. During our two meetings, I found Indira pale and disturbed at rumours of impending personal attacks on her in Parliament. She had an inkling of the items of the attack. The obvious reason for her wanting to meet me was because I have been dealing with Panditji's personal and financial affairs till his death.

The dreaded attack came in the Rajya Sabha on the 31st August during which a Mink Coat, shares and the like were mentioned. You are aware of the manner in which the matter was dealt with subsequently.

During our two meetings I told Indira that there was little I could do help her out of her predicament and that she should deal with situation as best as she could. Who will believe that Panditji gave her Mink Coat ? He would have considered a Mink Coat an absurd and ostentatious vulgarity in the general context of wide-spread Indian poverty. Poor Panditji, when he went to Canada, a bitterly cold country during Christmas time, refused to have anything but a coarse and inexpensive overcoat from the Khadi Bhandar. Indira made matters infinitely worse by a subsequent public statement to the effect that she has not taken any expensive present from any one except her father and grand-father. She did not have the Mink Coat as long as I was with Panditji. And Panditji's accounts in subsequent years will not show any expenditure for acquiring an expensive Mink Coat or any other coat. Neither was it given to her by any foreign dignitary.

Anyway nobody is allowed to keep any gift from a foreign dignitary or a foreign Government costing more than Rs 200/- unless one is prepared to pay to the Government of India the entire market price of the gift.

It is a pity that Indira, without declaring and without paying to the Government of India its market price, retained a very expensive Sable Coat presented to her by the Soviet Government. I hope she is not pining for an exmine coat to be added to her ward-robe.

How will Indira explain away several other cases ? Here are out a few :—

(i) Rs 25,000/- for the purchase of land in her name near Qutab Minar.

(2) Rs 17,000/- for the purchase of a Dodge Station Wagon.

(3) The entire expenses covering the trip of herself and her two children abroad (travelling by the Polish Luxury ship S.S. Batory to Europe in 1953 and return by air plus the substantial foreign exchange expenses involved.) These and similar items can be verified from her two Bank Accounts.

(4) The Pearl Necklaces, ear-lobes and ring studded with pearls. Indira has not included these in the list of jewellery in her Wealth Tax Returns.

(5) A Silver Cutlery Set for Twelve.

(6) A German Cutlery Set for Twelve (modern design).

Indira cannot palm off any of these to her father and grand-father who died long years ago. Neither can she, for very obvious reasons, put any of these on her late husband.

When Finance Minister Sachindra Chaudhury advised Indira to use a small Government car in the interest of economy, she promptly had a new Hindustan car bought at Government expense exclusively for her trips to Parliament House (to impress

M.Ps,) and retained the newly imported provocative, air-conditioned American luxury car for her other travels. Such is her conception of economy and economics. No wonder the rupee was devalued by her. I am afraid Indira has for far too long a period of ever 20 years lived in luxury mostly at Government expense that she cannot adjust herself to modest living.

Political sharks are after Indira. I know you have her interest at heart. That being so, I would suggest that you might have a frank talk with her about the question of her continuance in perilous active politics.

I am sending you a spare copy of this letter in case you wish to give it to Indira. I have no objection to your doing so.

Love.

Yours affectionately,
Sd/-
M. O. Mathai

Miss Padmaja Naidu,
Raj Bhawan,
CALCUTTA.

FROM THE UNDERGROUND

There are three separate items mailed to you this time. The usual news-views sheet which follows, a note for discussion (on the elections), and the text of a document which I received from Japan (on the foreign money question). May I repeat the request which I have been constantly making ? Please share the information you get with as many people as possible. Make copies, translate, circulate. Above all, keep talking. If three people start, each speaking to three others, by the time the eighteenth round is reached, 38,65,00,000 of people – the entire adult population of the country—will have known what the first three had said. That is the power of the spoken word – or the whispered word, if you please.

Jayaprakash Narayan has been released on parole for a

month, and there is a general feeling that his release is a prelude to relaxation of the present situation and is the first move taken by the dictator to retrace her steps. Nothing is further from the truth. JP was released because the dictator was afraid that he might die in prison. JP's health had begun to rapidly deteriorate during the second half of October. In the first week of November, his brother saw him in the Chandigarh hospital and came back full of despair. He addressed a letter to the dictator on November 8, in which he emphatically declared that from all indications, JP was not expected to live for more than two months. While he did not request the dictator to release JP, he, nevertheless asked her whether it would be in the interests of her government to allow JP to die in prison. The dictator knows where her interests are. Two days after receipt of this letter, she ordered JP's release on parole. He is to report back to prison at the end of thirty days.

There is, of course, a possibility that the dictator will use JP's parole to create confusion in the ranks of the resistance movement. There are enough busybodies in the country who will now get to work—talking of normalisation, negotiations, and what have you. The dictator will use these busybodies in her own diabolical way. But what kind of a deal can one make with her ? How is anyone to trust her ? She believes that Indira is India. Where does anyone believing in democracy fit into that ? Her credibility is zero. Her strength lies in falsehood, repression and terror. To use her own words, it is only the Big Lie that sustains her. There is, only one way to deal with her. She has to go. And for that purpose, our movement has to be intensified.

Incidentally, the Chief Censor has issued the following "TOP SECRET" meassage to all State Censors on Nov. 15.

"In regard to further stories regarding Jayaprakash Narayan's health some Socialist leaders have been giving out statements to the effect that he is cheerful but some of his internal ailments remain. Similarly some prominent leaders have been calling on him. There is no objection to such stories being allowed provided there is no statement to the effect that his health is failing. Further reports about his movement from one hospital to another or from one place to another should not be published nor the place of the hospital where he is being treated. You should ensure that all reports about Jayaprakash Narayan by news agencies or news correspondents *must be submitted for per-censorship*. Please note that these instructions are for your guidance only and not to be conveyed to newspapers or correspondents."

*   *   *

Madam dictator and her courtiers have been celebrating her "Great Victory" in the Supreme Court. The dancing girls and the riff raff from Delhi and surrounding areas are herded daily outside the dictator's residence to hail the Hitler. The news of the Supreme Court decision were doctored to create the impression that the judgment of the Allahabad High Court convicting Mrs. Nehru Gandhi of corrupt practices had been set aside by the Supreme Court. Even an otherwise intelligent man like Sardar Khushwant Singh, editor of the Illustrated Weekly has been fooled into believing that "the Supreme Court has cleared Mrs. Gandhi of all charges of corrupt practices during her election to the Lok Sabha." (Illustrated Weekly, Nov. 23. page 31).

Let us get this straight. The Supreme Court has not cleared Mrs. Nehru Gandhi of any charges of corrupt practices held proved against her by the Allahabad High Court. Justice Sinha's judgment stands and the lady remains condemned as ever.

This is what has happened :

After the Allahabad High Court judgment, Mrs. Nehru Gandhi had her captive Parliament amend the electoral laws to the effect that all corrupt practices she had committed were no more eorrupt practices with retrospective effect from the day she committed them. The Supreme Court held that Parliament had the power to enact such patently perverse legislation. Ergo, the Supreme Court held that the judgment of the Allahabad High Court stood annuled.

One could illustrate this with the following example :

A man commits rape against a minor girl. The trial court convicts him to six years in prison. The man appeals to the

High Court against the conviction. Incidentally, the man happens to be the Prime Minister who has a captive Parliament under his thumb. He makes the parliament enact a law which says that rape of a minor girl is not a crime under the law of the land with effect from the date on which the Prime Minister committed the rape. The High Court holds that Parliament has the power to legislate that rape is not a crime from the date on which the Prime Minister raped a helpless minor girl. The High Court then proceeds to hold that the trial court's judgment convicting the man to six years of imprisonment is no longer valid. The man who is the Prime Minister then organises rallies to celebrate his "great victory" and the "vindication of his honour."

Do you get me Khushwant ? I thought you might understand it with such an illustration.

* * *

The nation-wide Satyagraha has started with a bang. In the first four days of the Satyagraha, over 10,000 people have been arrested all over the country. In Delhi, people have started writing anti-dictatorship slogans on the walls and on the streets. Posters, both printed and hand-written have also appeared in most parts of the city. (A detailed report on the satyagraha will be mailed in a few days).

* * *

The World Council of Churches which speaks for the entire Christian people of the world has, in a letter dated Oct. 9, 1975 addressed to the Indian dictator expressed its grave concern at the denial of human rights to the Indian people. The letter criticises the imposition of emergency, press censorship and the denial of legal remedies to those detained under the draconian MISA. It has also appealed for the immediate release of Jayaprakash Narayan and other detained leaders. The letter has also urged the restoration of democratic rights of the people for political expression, discussion and dissent.

* * *

The International Transport Workers Federation (to which

the All India Railwaymen's Federation is affiliated) has in a resolution condemned the imposition of dictatorship in India and said that "these developments as being totally undemocratic, unconstitutional and placing India under the equivalent of totalitarian rule." The resolution has called upon the President of India "to put an end to the state of emergency and its consequent repression of the Indian People, to release all trade union leaders and to restore full democratic and trade union rights which are guaranteed to Indian citizens by their constitution."

NOVEMBER 22, 1975   GEORGE FERNANDES

STOP PRESS : JP has been admitted to the Jaslok Hospital in Bombay. The Bombay Sarvodaya leader, Govindrao Deshpande called on him on November 22. He was arrested as he was leaving the hospital. So much for relaxation. Will all the remaining Gandhians now find their way into the prisons ?

KHABAR

20th Feb. 1976   R.N. No. B.S. 976

2nd year, 6th issue

LATEST NEWS

1. Inspite of the agrument of the Attorney General of India, Mr. Niren De that an Indian Citizen has no right of life and liberty during emergency, more than 1,30,000 peaceful satyagrahis all over India have courted arrest as a protest between 14th November 1975 and January 26, 1976. The number in West Bengal is 1400.

2. Arrested persons include Mr. Mohan Dharia, M. P., Mrs. Mrinal Gore, M. L. A., Miss Durgabai Bhagabat, Dr. G.

G. Parekh in Maharastra, Mr. Barun Sen Gupta, an eminent journalist, Mr. Ashim Mitra of Jugantar, Prof. Sandip Das, Mr. Sukumar Banerjee, Dr. Samanta Ghosh etc. in W. Bengal.

3. On 30th January, Congress goondas inside Presidency Jail assaulted unarmed political prisoners. Although the assault lasted 45 minutes in the presence of the Minister Mr. Gyan Singh Sohonpal no alram-bell was rung. Thirty satyagrahis have been hospitalised. Gour Kishore Ghese is now ill in a solitary cell in Presidency Jail. Naxalite boys and girls are still being tortured.

4. Four news agencies (P.T.I., U.N.I., Hindusthan Samachar and Samachar Bharati) were forcibly amalgamated into one namely Samachar by the Government by deliberate disconnection of Telex and Telephone lines.

5. There have been two thousand arrests so far in Tamil Nadu which include 25 DMK MLAs and 4 DMK MPs.

STOP PRESS

1. On 24th February, 1976, A Band of Naxalites (Charu Mazumder Group) broke open the Presidency Jail by bursting hand Grenades and released 45 Prisoners including Sri Azizul Hoque, Prof. Nisith Bhattacharya etc. 3 Prisoners were shot and 2 Sentries were killed.

2. Sri Gour Ghosh has had a stroke and been removed to Presidency Hospital.

3. Sri Robi Varma, acting general secretary, Lok Sangarsh Samity has been arrested and Sri Naran Desai has been installed as general secretary.

4. There have been another 10,000 arrested in Tamilnadu thus bringing the all India total to nearly 1,50,000

5. According to News Week U. S. Government has suspended aid negotiations with Government of India and there is increasing number of lockouts and more intense recession in India now.

6. Historians point out that only such countries as do not have common frontier with the USSR are eventually able to

throw off the shackles of totalitarianism DMK has joined Janata Front in the Parliament.

7. There have been attempts at Bankipur, Midnapur, Berhampore and Dum Dum.

N.B. False Registration No. was used to befool the Post office.

BULLETIN 4

JANA SANGHARSHA SAMITY

'So long Emergency continues and interference in writer's pen remains, Annada Sankar Roy won't write. This is his protest."

Somedays back, government tried to mobilise support of the writers in favour of censorship for which a writers' convention was held in the Great Eastern Hotel, Calcutta. But the writers present expressed strong remarks against the censorship. The summary of Sri Annada Sankar Roy's statement has already been published in one of our bulletin. Now we reproduce the lecture in detail which we have collected.

"In the name of censorship hands are now being laid upon literary works of art. Writers are being treated like infants by those who do the censoring although the extent of their, the censors' intelligence has not been tested. Censors are applying their pens to the work of accredited writers with much aplomb even though some of these writers are their seniors by many years, not only in age, but in reputation and qualifications.

How can a censor claim to have the literary judgement or insight required to qualify him to tamper with the work of an author who has been producing writing that is generally acknowledged to be of a high literary standard for over fifty years ?

The freedom, writers enjoyed under the British Raj, an alien regime, is in jeopardy today. Literary opinion and thought were untrammelled. Having been a high official in the Indian Civil Service and also a writer of repute under the British Raj, I am in a position to make a statement of this kind.

Side by side with what is today called creative writing is a verbal activity known as journalism. Journalistic work is topical and ephemeral. Creative writing aspires to a high literary standard and the quality of permanence. This has always been the case and will continue to be. It is also topical. Writers who are genuine creative artists do not open their mouths to speak on any and every occasion in the daily press. That does not mean their work is devoid of contemporaneity. Contemporaneity has its place in literature, an honorable place, but creative writing is not the routine writing of professional journalists. Newspaper editorials do not achieve the status of Tagore's famous *The Crisis in Civilisation*. This essay deals with a topical and contemporary situation.

On the pretence of exercising control over the writing of persons who are, in officialese, described as irresponsible journalists, censorship has been imposed upon all writers. Minor government officials who are both young and inexperienced have been given the responsibility of doing this task. These censors do not consider it necessary to inform themselves what writers of repute and conscience are actually saying nor have they considered it necessary to understand what is meant by literature. They use the scissors with lighthearted abandon, without inhibitions of any kind apparently. How are they going to explain what they are doing or excuse themselves to the public of the future ?

Shall writers not say what they think ? How can that be ? Writers cannot be blacked out like the moon by an eclipse.

For the special Puja issue of *Amrita* I wrote, at the editor's request, a humorous story. The point of the story was made in a pivotal line which ran as follows : "Aryuvedic medicine, to be effective, has to be taken with the proper accompaniment. Similarly, efficiency does not produce results unless accompanied by drinks. It is a method that formerly produced the best results. Is it not the best to use it at the present time also ? You know but you'll not admit it. The size of the dose of medicine has decreased nowadays. That is the only difference. The amount of the accompaniment has grown greater. The English may not be here but Scotch is everywhere."

The censor cut out the last lines. The sting was gone. The English may not be here but Scotch is everywhere. The prevalent notion that drinking is currently much in excess of the amount needed to maintain work efficiency therefore appears to be well-founded. Why else should the censor be so sensitive ? But what has all this got to do with politics ? Why should a statement of this kind come under the purview of any censorship ? Is it forbidden to cast an aspersion on the drinking of hard liquor ?

Perhaps the censor understood Scotch to mean a Scotsman. If I were to say the English have been replaced by the Scotch in this country patriotic feelings might be offended. Politics could be dragged into the picture. The censor deleted the passage however without stopping to consider whether the word 'Scotch' in this context means the people of a particular geographical area of the globe or a kind of liquor. He failed to distinguish between the possible uses of the word. He may not even be aware of the ways in which it can be used. And do people who are not writers themselves ever have the right to presume to tell reputed writers of conscience what their duty is, in any circumstances ? The quality of literature is bound to deteriorate if they are allowed or instructed to do so.

In the not distant future writers may find themselves being told what they ought or ought not to write. Specifications they may be expected to abide by may be stipulated. An apprehension that such a situation may develop is wholly justified in the present circumstances. Writers cannot remain silent. They have to protest. What form is their protest to take ? That is the question. I, as Annada Sankar Ray, cannot go down into the streets and throw stones. What then am I to do ? I can stop writing altogether in a fit of non-cooperative pique. Annada Sankar can refuse to put pen to paper as long as the state of Emergency continues, as long as writers' work is interfered with.

There are Government officials present in this meeting. It is apparent from the attitude they have taken that from now on only writing that is acceptable to women and children will be approved. I cannot agree to that. As long as the Emergency continues therefore this is the manner in which I, Annada Sankar, shall protest. I shall not write. My silence shall be my way of making known my refusal to be dictated to."

Speaker's Note: When this statement was made I thought the Emergency had served its purpose which had been declared to be the restoration of law and order. The law and order situation in the country had improved and I anticipated that the Emergency would be withdrawn within two or three months at the most. I hoped I would not have to remain silent for much longer. But the Emergency was extended for another year, indefinitely. I had been silent for four or five months. I waited a while longer before beginning to accede to requests for contributions from various journals. Most of the requests were for children's verse. Then I slowly resumed serious writing, contributing essays and stories to special Puja issues. It was not advisable to lose contact with my readers entirely. My relationship with them was too deep, too warm and too long. It is, of course, most uncomfortable to have to write with censorship always in mind. It creates a crippling uneasiness. The experience was without precedent for me. But I did not surrender my independence. Those who have read what I wrote during the unfortunate period of the Emergency will know that my freedom came through undiminished.

ANNADA SANKAR ROY

EDITOR'S NOTE :

The speech is taken from an underground bulletin. Afterwards, the speaker communicated that there was some mistakes in the version of the speech. Since the speech was not taped and collected through many sources, Sri Roy said in a letter that the Police showed him a photostat copy of the bulletin in which the speech was first published. I revised and edited it and handed it to the Police. They did not ask me anything about it after this even, he added.

*   *   *

In 25-26th April, an international conference for restoring democracy in India was held by the Friends of India at London. 380 delegates from 34 countries participated.

Makrand Desai, a former minister of Gujarat was present there, Mr Subramanium Swami, M.P. said that the conference was organised for the purpose of restoring democracy in India where abuse of MISA and DIR and torture on Political prisoners were abundant. Leaders of almost all the political parties of England were present in the conference.

In-group fightings amongst the Kourava Bahini of Bengal (meaning Congress youth) continue as ever. In Howrah 3 boys have been murdered. On 20th April at Konnagar (Dist. Hooghly) a congressman was beheaded by his own partymen in broad daylight. On 21st a bomb-fighting took place between the Laxmikanto Bose group and Subrata Muhkerjee group in the Hardinge hostel, Calcutta University, 10 have been injured, two were cut into pieces.

On 17th April Santi Sen and Debabrata Roy Chowdhury were arrested for publishing the translated version of 'Kolkata 75' which contains the letter of Sri Gour Kishore Ghosh.

From 14th April onwards the dwellers at Delhi's Turkman Gate were forcefully evicted by bulldozers, Sanjay Gandhi himself supervised the show. In course of action two mosques were vanquished. With this, one item of Sanjay's 4 point, viz. sterilisation was put into action by force. Johiruddin, a young bachelor living in Turkman area, died after forceful sterilisation, other 3 in the open colony where the turkmen refugees had to stay, also died. On 19th, 10,000 people resisted against the brutal tortures, police opened fire on the mass, 67 were killed and 300 got injured seriously. Now the Government version says that the mosques have been vanquished for reconstruction. The family planning centres now stand locked up. 10.5.76

N.B. Jana Sangharsah Samity formed in the pattern of Lok Sangharsh Samity. J.S.S. in W. Bengal was composed of the representatives of Congress (O), Socialist Party, Bharatiya Lok Dal, Jana Sangha andf Independents.

SATYA SAMACHAR

(OFFICIAL BULLETIN OF THE LOK SANGARSH SAMITI)

No. 1   June 12, 1976.

Why Satya Samachar

Ever since press censorship has been imposed in this country, news, except what the Government approves or invents has ceased to travel ; even false news cannot be contradicted. Sufferings of people in one mohalla or one village cannot be known in another. Arrests of friends get known only when they are continually missed Gandhiji's concept of a walking-newspaper has not succeeded.

The atmosphere of apprehension and mutual distrust and suspicion is so prevasive. Mouths remain sealed though hearts may be seared with anger and sorrow. Like Jawaharlal Nehru, we have watched the process of moral and intellectual decay settling in and have realised how autocratic power corrupts and degrades and vulgarises.

As a partial remedy for this situation, we are bringing out this fortnightly—Satyasamachar—giving news and such other matter as may help our readers to assess and understand the changing situation. In this venture the emphasis will always be on truth. Our self-imposed code will forbid incitement to violence, to communal passions and to anti-social behaviour ; we will scrupulously avoid character-assassination and tendentious writing, our constant endeavour will be to remind people that personal dictatorship is working to perpetuate itself and that they have to fight it. Today's fighters will command tomorrow—not for power but for justice ; not for politics but for ethics ; not for the domination of India but for her grandeur.

June 12 and June 26 have in the past twelve months assumed great significance. If events which took place on June 12, 1975 had been different and favourable to Indira Gandhi, June 26 could have come and gone like any other day in the calendar. But on that fateful June 12 the Allahabad High Court hold

Indira Gandhi guilty of corrupt electoral practices, the citizens of Gujrat rejected her and the rumblings within her own party became ominiously audible—all this within a span of twelve hours. Satyasamachar has chosen to appear on June 12 to commemorate the election of that day, however shortlived.

Gandhiji on Liberty of the press

Liberty of the press can be said to be truly respected when the press can comment in the severest' terms upon and even misrepresented matters.

The Government of India is now seeking to crush the powerful vehicle of expressing and cultivating public opinion and is proving its totally arbitrary and despotic character. Today all criticism is hushed. Let us use the printing machine and the type whilst we can to give unfettered expression to our thoughts. But let us not feel helpless when they are taken away by a paternal government.

Mahatma Gandhi.

Roll call of Martyrs

We salute the memory of over 100 martyrs who have laid down their lives for the sacred cause of restoration of democracy in our country since June 26, 1975. The following are some of the latest names added to the Roll call of Martyrs :—

Shri Bhairab Bharati : who died in Madhya Pradesh Jail. (A prominent trade union leader).

Shri Mohanlal Jadav, Vice-President of Delhi State BLD, MISA detenu was released on Parole on May 5 for ill health. But was harassed at home and called to the C.I.D. office on the 8th floor where he died on May 17.

Shri Tilak Raj Narule, a former Jana Sangh Councillor and Chairman of Delhi Transport Undertakings, died in Tihar Jail in the month of May. He was a MISA detenu.

Shri Vaid Baijnath Kapila, President Shahadara District Jana Sangha, a MISA detenu in Tihar Jail in the month of

January 1976. The police took a photograph of those attending his cremation at the creamation Ghat.

We also salute our brave brothers and sisters who have challenged the Dictator and are suffering behind the bars. We appeal to every citizen to contribute to the Fund for the needy families of those patriots.

Opposition leaders to the Nation

Bombay, May 23, 1976.

Having regard to the developments that have taken place since the proclamation of emergency on June 26, 1975, developments which showed only too clearly that the constitution itself was being utilised to transform our democracy into a totalitarian regime. At our last meeting in Bombay we came to the conclusion that the need for establishing a single democratic national alternative was urgent and imperative and appointed a Steering Committee, drawn up a policy and programme for such a party and to ascertain the reactions of the democratic opposition parties. After giving careful thought to the report of the Steering Committee we have decided to request Shri Jayaprakash Narayan to launch a new party whose basic objective will be the restoration of civil liberties, of the freedom of the press, of the independence and dignity of the judiciary, the establishment of a genuine egalitarian order, and the formulation and implementation of an economic policy designed to eliminate unemployment and maximise production, agricultural and industrial while safeguarding the just and fair claims of small and marginal farmers, of agricultural labour, of industrial workers and of the weaker section generally. We are glad to state that Shri Jayaprakash Narayan has acceded to our request and will take such steps as are necessary, consequent upon the decision to form a New Party.

Following are some of the persons who are party to this decision :—

Shri Charan Singh, Shri S. K. Patil, Shri N. G. Goray, Shri H. M. Patel, Shri O. P. Tyagi, Shri Santi Bhushan, Shri S. M.

Joshi, Shri Uttamrao Patil, Shri Erasmo de Sequeira, Shri Bhanupratap Singh and Shri Digvijaya Narain Singh.

Charan Singh to Smt. Indira Gandhi

The National Executive of the BLD has taken note of the Prime Minister's speech in which she have asked the Opposition to clarify

(i) That the need for clarification is as much—if not more —from the side of the ruling party, as from the.Opposition. If the Prime Minister is willing to restore the freedom of the people and the press, and the system of judicial review, there would be no difficulty in evolving a code of conduct applicable to all political parties.

(ii) That it would be more helpful in restoring normalcy in Indian Politics, if the Prime Minister, instead of talking about the Opposition parties, talked to them.

(iii) And that more the repression of healthy opposition, the greater the chances of extremist elements getting at the top both in the ruling party as well as in the Opposition.

Bharatiya Jana Sangha to Government of India

New Delhi, May 16 : The working committee demands that the Government should immediately (i) revoke the emergency, (ii) restore the fundamental rights and the fundamental free-doms; (iii) release all political prisoners who have been detained or sentenced under the pretext of emergency, (iv) accept that no organisation should be banned except through due process of law and the verdict of a court (v) withdraw the ban imposed on all organisations and appoint a judicial commission to scrutinise whatever evidence the Government may have to warrant the ban-ning of any organisation (vi) restore the dignity and jurisdiction of the judiciary and (vii) restore the freedom of the press.

Polit Bureau of CPI (M) to Prime Minister

Calcutta, April 9 : You have repeatedly stated that the Opposition should learn to behave as a condition for lifting emergency. We are unable to understand what this means. The role of the Opposition is very important in Parliamentary Democracy. The right of dissent is fundamantal. Even if Parliament has passed a measure by a majority the minority has the inherent and inviolable right to mobilise public opinion against the measure, get the majority converted into a minority and get the measure reversed or suitably changed.

We would urge the Government to immediately revoke the Emergency ; repeal the MISA ; remove pre-censorship ; repeal the 39th Amendment to the Constitution ; remove all those legislations that do not pertain to socio-economic changes from the 9th schedule ; release all leaders and workers of political parties and mass organisations who are under detention ; withdraw all pending warrants ; restore civil liberties and democratic and trade union rights existing before the imposition of Emergency.

The speakers resent a issue of ordinances

Simla, June 3 : Presiding Officers of State legislatures have expressed grave concern over the frequent use by the Government of the parallel powers of the issuance of ordinances and stressed that the Governments should use this power only under special and pressing circumstances. They also suggested that the right to property be deleted from the Fundamantal Rights and be, hereafter, regulated by statute.

—B. R. Bhagat, Speaker—Lok Sabha

Aftermath of Geeton-bhari-sham

New Delhi, May 2 : Kishore kumar, the wellknown playback singer has been punished by the All India Radio by his music being banned from its programme. Kishore Kumar had refused to participate in the Geeton-bhari-sham, a musical extravaganza organised by Sanjay Gandhi's youth Congress to collect funds ostensibly for the family planning campaign. He would not yield even to threats. Recently the All India Radio received instructions from high quarters to punish him, Pictures like Garam Hawa, made famous by his voice are no longer direction of being shown in Delhi ; 12 years old pictures have replaced them.

Naxalites kept in fetters

Patna, May 8 : Superintendents of Central and District Jails in Bihar have been putting all Naxalite prisoners in bar-fetters all the 24 hours since April. Under the Bihar Jail Code, Jail Superintendents have full and final discretion in ordering a recalcitrant prisoner into fetters ; such orders, however, are rarely issued. But in March last the State Government under the the Central Government instructed all Jail Superintendents to put all prisoners into bar-fetters.

Hostile Reception to Indira

Patna, May 1 (Delayed) : People of Patna gave Mrs. Gandhi a very unpleasant reception today, when she visited the city for the first time since the declaration of emergency. Thronging both sides of the streets she passed along, they shouted 'Indira Gandhi Murdabad' and also that she might soon have the same fate as Mujibur Rehman. The police looked helplessly on. An angry Mrs. Gandhi remarked that she was "pained to note that in spite of the emergency Bihar was beset with many evils". The administration, however, had done its best to make her journey through Patna safe. To detect mines grenades or bombs, they had even rolled with heavy rollers the all road along which she was to travel.

Naxalite Prisoners Butchered

Bhagalpur (*Bihar*) *May 12* : Six Naxalite prisoners who attempted to escape from the Bhagalpur special central Jail on May 4 were captured, beaten up and then brought to the Jail gate where they were barbarously shot down.

Rajghat Samadi case held false, fabricated

New Delhi, May 19 : All the seven accused—Sarvashri H. V. Kamath, Vishnu Dutt Sharma, A. B. Bhardwaj, Ravi Nayar, Narendra Nath Choudhury, Ishwar Chandra Patil and P. H. Mittal who had been arrested on October 2, 1975 at the prayer meeting in the Gandhi Samadi grounds on a charge of shouting objectionable, anti-government slogans were acquitted this afternoon by the Judicial Magistrate in the Tis Hazari Court. The Delhi Administration's permission being necessary even for holding a prayer meeting to pay homage to the Father of the Nation, such permission had been obtained. When after recitation from the scriptures, Acharya Kripalani began his pravachan, the police entered the grounds in force, stopped the Acharya from speaking, ordered the people to disperse and arrested nine persons on the spot ; the Acharya, however, was not arrested. Two of the arrested persons, Shri Rajmohan Gandhi and Shri Ram Chandra Gandhi were released later when the police discovered that they were grandsons of Mahatma Gandhi.

In acquitting the accused, the Magistrate observed, "Out of seven witnesses examined by the prosecution, two independent witnesses and even PW 4, police constable Malkiat Singh have been declared hostile by the prosecuting agency for not supporting the prosecution story. On a careful perusal of the statements of the official witnesses, I find them full of contradictions and none of these supports the FIR. Their subsequent statements to different effect in the court, therefore, seem to be an after-thought and give rise to suspicion in the mind of the court that the case has been fabricated...The defence version produced by the accused persons is wellfounded, well-reasoned and believable...For merely participating in the permitted prayer meeting at Rajghat and hearing the pravachan which is a part of the Gandhian prayer, the accused cannot be held to have committed a crime.

Prime Minister's donation returned

Bombay, May 20 : The Gujarat Sarvodaya Mandal has

decided to close the Jayaprakash Swasthya Sahaya Nidhi as the
collections have already exceeded two and a half lakh rupees. The
collection was mainly from small donations collected from all
over the country. Acharya Vinobha Bhave gave one rupee. It
is understood that he also sent an emissary to Mrs. Gandhi to
suggest that she also might make a contribution. Thereupon
she made inquiries about the cost of a dialyser and sanctioned
Rs. 90,000 from the Prime Minister's National Relief Fund. As
JP did not need any relief and the Nidhi had exceeded the
target, JP has instructed the Gujarat Sarvodaya Mandal to
retain only a token amount and return the balance to the Prime
Minister.

When Elections are not rigged

New Delhi, May 29 :

1. Shri Laksmi Sahai Saxena, A MISA detenu won the UP
Council election from the Graduates' Constituency, Allahabad,
securing 4595 votes against the 2594 votes secured by the sitting
member Shri J. P. Srivastava (Congress (R)).

Shri P. N. Lekhi, another MISA detenu was elected President
of the Delhi High Court Bar Association defeating the Congress
candidate by 50 votes.

Shri Lakhanpal, another MISA detenu was elected President
of the Punjab and Haryana High Court Bar Association
defeating his Congress rival.

Shri Kanwarlal Sharma, President Delhi Lawyers' Sangharsha
Samiti was elected President of the Delhi District Bar Association
defeating his Congress rival by 85 votes.

Shri O. P. Sharma, non-party man has been elected Chairman, Delhi. District Bar Council in place of Shri Lalit Bhasin
the erstwhile Chairman who had to resign as he failed to have
the support of his colleagues on the Council.

Service Chiefs protest

New Delhi, June 2 : Sanjay Gandhi recently barged into the
Defence Minister's room when Mr. Bansilal was having a

secret discussion with the three service chiefs fell silent and sat on in stony silence in spite of Bansilal's expressed desire to continue the discussion.

SATYA SAMACHAR

No. 2   June 26, 1976

Roll call of Martyrs

Here is the second list of martyrs who laid down their lives in challenging Smti. Gandhi's dictatorship :

1. Shri M. R. Gulavani, Vita, Dist. Sangli, Maharashtra, RSS worker, Dentist by profession, age : 53, released after an unsuccessful operation in Sassoon Hospital, Poona, expired within a week at Satara on May 31, 1976 ;

2. Shri Prabhakar Rajah of Katangi, Madhya Pradesh, a social worker ;

3. Shri Somnath Hadan, Seoni, Madhya Pradesh, student and social worker aged 19 ;

4. Shri Kullappa, Anakal taluq, Bangalore Dist...a Harijan worker aged 25 ;

5. Shri Harivadanbhai Bhatt, Jana Sangh worker of Surat (Gujarat) aged 60, arrested on March 13 and expired on April 14, 1976.

Letter from Rt. Hon. Philip Noel-Baker
to Mr. George Fernandes

16 South Eaton Place,
London S.W. 1
June 11, 1976

Mr. George Fernandes,
Dear George Fernandes,
     This is to send you the warm greetings of your many friends.

socialists, and people of all shades of liberal opinion in Britain, Social Democrats, Christian Democrats and many others in Europe and to tell you how deeply we sympathise with you in the grave trials through which you are passing, and in the difficult life which you and so many of your colleagues are obliged to lead.

We rejoice that JP was released from detention, but we find it sad that that only happened when the Indian Government were afraid that he might die while he was in captivity and we much regret that they gave the world so many assurances before he was released that he was "in good health." But we shall remain anxious for the safety and happiness of all of you while the so-called 'State of Emergency' is continued.

Experience in many countries has shown how relatively easy it is to establish a "state of emergency" where the Government is sustained by the armed forces of the police ; and how exceedingly difficult it is for the government which has set it up, to bring it to an end.

We know that Mrs. Gandhi pledged herself to end her 'state of emergency' at the earliest possible moment. But after many months there seems to be no signs that she is preparing to carry out this pledge, and there seems to be no development that make it easier for her to do so.

We remain convinced, however, that the strong support of the Indian people for democratic institutions and for the social and economic progress of India will, in some way we do not now foresee, bring about the restoration of representative parliamentary government. We pray that this may happen without and violent action, and that it may be accomplished by the principles which Mahatma Gandhi taught the world.

This is all the more necessary in a world where militarism and rule by force, instead of by law and justice, has become so widely prevalent. If mankind is to be spared from a Third world War which would obliterate our common civilisation, and perhaps the human race, it is vital that the Mahatma's teaching should triumph in the conduct of international affairs and we hope that India may soon be giving mankind an example in her internal affairs and leadership for the nations of the world.

Believe me, with warmest personal regards,

Yours sincerely,
sd/- Philip Noel-Baker
June 24, 1976

Amnesty International Appeals to India to mark Anniversary by Declaring General Amnesty for Political Prisoners

Amnesty International today (Thursday 24 June 1976) appealed to the Indian Government to mark the first anniversary of the declaration of a state of emergency on 26 June 1975 by declaring a general amnesty for all prisoners now held in detention without charge or trial. AI also urged the Government to restore constitutional safeguards and implement fully the provisions of the Universal Declaration of Human Rights.

In a letter to Shrimati Indira Gandhi, it is said that the curtailment of civil liberties in India had caused international concern. It said that the Indian Government had not replied to a letter suggesting that an Amnesty International delegation be allowed to visit India.

What the Nation has lost
—C.K. Daphtary's View

"The Supreme Court recently in perhaps the most important decision it has rendered in the course of its whole life, has finally given the guietus to any hope that a person wrongfully detained can pray and approach the court for any relief even though the ground be that there has been a case of mistaken identity or that the detention has been made not bonafide. This was pronounced by a majority of four judges out of the five. ...One learned Judge however differed in a forceful opinion which may rank with the great dissents in Olmstead Vs. United

States, Betts Vs. Brady, Minersville School District V. Gobitis, which dissenting opinions were justified, vindicated and approved in other subsequent judgements of the United States Supreme Court.

C.K. Daphtary Ex-Attorney General
President,
Bar Association of India
in 'Indian Advocate' Vol. XV

Solemn Pledge broken

Sixteen judges have been transferred from one High Court to another in recent months. The transfers have been made without the judges' consent. More transfers are under way. There is little doubt that these are punitive transfers ; for most of these judges had in the past few months decided a number of cases rejecting the Government's contention.

Jayaprakash Narayan

Camp : Bombay-5,
June 11, 1976.

Dear Indiraji :

I am writing about the ninety thousand rupees which you have so kindly contributed from your relief Fund for the purchase of a Dialyser machine for my treatment. Some weeks back when Shri Radhakrishna, on Professor P.N. Dhar's advice, had sent a friend here to enquire if I would accept a contribution from you, I had given my consent without knowing that the money would be from the Prime Minister's Relief Fund. I took it for granted that it would be from your personal account, though a little thought on my part should have shown that it was not possible for you to contribute personally such a large amount. Be that as it may, the position is that before the contribution from your Fund was received, more than three lakhs of rupees had already been collected from the Public in response to the appeal made by Shri Ravishankar Maharaj, Swami Anand (Since deceased), Shri Kedarnathji and Dada Dharmadhikari. Out of that money a dialysis machine and accessories and supplies for a year had already been purchased ; and enough money is left to pay for monthly expenses for a year or two.

There are two other relevant points that I should mention here. One, the Committee had announced that only can small contributions would be acceptable. Some friends had offered donations, but they were not accepted and only small amounts were taken from them. Two, before the contribution from your Fund was received by Shri Radhakrishna, the Jayaprakash Health Fund Committee had closed the Fund through a public announcement on the ground that the Fund had already been oversubscribed.

In these circumstances it is not right that I should accept such a large donation from your Relief Fund. There is so much of relief to be rendered that every pice of a relief fund should be used where it is needed most. Therefore, I am advising Shri Radhakrishna to return the draft received by him. I do fervently hope that you will not misunderstand me and think me ungrateful and discourteous. There is no discourtesy meant at all and I am grateful for the concern shown by you for my health.

With my best wishes,

Yours Sincerely,
Sd/-
(JAYAPRAKASH NARAYAN)

Smt. Indira Gandhi,
Prime Minister of India,
New Delhi.

Arrested

New Delhi, April 29—Shri S.D. Paliwal of the Socialist Party and his colleague Shri Kamlesh were arrested here on

April 9, Shri Paliwal was detained in police custody for ten days ; was interrogated non-stop without being allowed to sleep. It is understood that though arrested under the MISA, Shri Paliwal is going to be tried as an accused in the Baroda dynamite case.

Bangalore ; May 2 : On April 24, Shrimati Saraswati Bai Hegde, the 80 year old mother of the Former Minister, Shri Ramakrishna Hegde who is at present a MISA detenu accompanied by Shri Kshetrapal of the Sarvodaya Mandal went on a protest fast in the Mysore Bank Square. They were arrested and detained in Police custody but were released at night.

On the same, day, four women, all relatives of MISA detenues and one male worker of the Lok Sangharsha Samiti observed a fast near the bus stand and also displayed placards and distributed pamphlets demanding the withdrawal of Emergency and release of political prisoners. They weres all arrested and detained in police custody till April 30 when the women were released and the male member was sent to jail custody.

Bombay : June 1. Dr Datta Samant MLA (Congress R) an INTUC leader has been detained under the MISA since May 28 for serving strike notices on three factories. Shri P.J. Mehta, President Engineering Mazdoor Sabha was arrested on May 28 (on) for demanding a public enquiry aganist Rajni Patel for accumulating black money.

Worker's Participation—Point 15 of the 20 Point Programme.

Calcutta : June 2 ; Shri. An anda Bharati, Congress Party member of the West Bengal Legislative Assembly disclosed yesterday that last week another worker of the Bengal Potteries committed suicied. This, Mr. Bharati said, brought the number of such deaths to 32. He explained that the workers had little choice. The two factories of the company had been closed for the last ten months and about 5,000 of their workers are out of job. Mr. Bharati is the President of the INTUC union of the Bengal Potteries Union.

Indira Gandhi's Statement 'not true'

New Delhi, June 3 : On May 30, Mrs. Gandhi told the AICC (R) that the Catholic community had stated that it was not aganist the sterilisation programme, "from the point of religion'. When contacted, the spokesman of the Catholic Bishops' Conference of India said that no such assurance had been or could have been given by any of the Bishops, Archbishops or Cardinals of the Church in India. On the contrary, the Bishops' Conference had issued a statement on April 29, disapproving of sterilisation as it does 'violence to the conscience" and calling for a day of fasting on May 14 and for a crusade of prayer during the entire month of May. When asked if Mrs. Gandhi's statement was false, he said 'It is not true'.

Political prisoners on Indefinite fast :

Calcutta, June 4 :—About 300 political prisoners in the Calcutta Presidency Jail went on a week-long hunger strike from May 18 in protest aganist the denial of certain rights, refusal of permission (i) to meet their relatives ; (ii) to cook their own meals ; (iii) to go out in the open yard for a breath of fresh air or for normal exercise. Six of them Proft. Sandip Das, Prof. Amal Basu, Shri. Sukumar Banerji, Shri. Himangsu Haldar, Sri. Sant Basu-Mullick and Shri. Gour Hari Dutta detained under the MISA are on a indefinite fast since then. Others are on relay fast with them in batches of 250. On June 9 there was a sympathetic mass fast.

Indira Honours Vinoba

Waraha June 10 : Indira Gandhi's police raided the Paunar Ashram and carried away 4200 copies of Vinoba's Hindi Journal "Maitri" which had printed news of Vinoba's proposed fast. Mrs. Gandhi had been Informed of Vinoba's decision before she left for Moscow and she had ordered her Home Minister to do the needful only after her departure.

Gentle and civilised pressure

Lucknow, June 12 :—The Government of U. P. has issued orders for withholding the pay for the month of June of those employees of the Family-Planning and Health departments who do not fulfil their first quarter quota of bringing 6 and 3 cases respectively for sterilisation by the end of this month.

Patna, June 12 : It is reliably understood that the Bihar Cabinet has decided that in future no ration card will be issued for more than three children in a family.

New Delhi, June 15 :—According to a Delhi Administration Press release :

(i)   No person with three or more children will be treated free in a hospital without producing a certificate of sterilisation of either spouse ;

(ii)   Patients will have to show their ration cards to prove that they have less than three Children.

(iii)   Only Children up to five years of age and eligible persons and eligible couples will, hereafter, be treated free. Others will have to pay Rs. 5/-per visit to out-patient ward and Rs. 10/-per day for indoor treatment.

(iv)   Even emergency cases will be required to give before attended to as undertaking to be sterilised. It is presumed that a pauper involved in a serious accident and brought to the emergency ward in an unconscious condition will be kept unattended till he regains consciousness and signs such a declaration.

Price Index moves up

New Delhi, June 19 : The general index of whole-sale moved by 3.9 points from 288.5 for April to 292.4 for May 1976. The rise was of the same order in May, 1975, before the declaration of emergency. During the month under review food articles and manufactured items advanced.

SATYA SAMACHAR

PUBLISHED BY LOK SANGHARSHA SAMITI

[We could not bring out our issue of 12th September because of the reasons beyond our control]

Vol. No. 7-8   September 26, 1976.

NEWS FLASHES

1.   Wave of resistance against the Family Planning drive :

While the Government is bent upon putting cart before the horse by putting family planning before economic development, there is a wave of unrest all over India against high handed and vulgar encroachment into their private lives without involving them emotionally in the campaign.

Quite a few family pllanning camps have been put to fire in Delhi itself during the last few weeks. As a result, the Municipal Corporation has ordered that no unauthorised camps be put up in the Union territory. Such 'unauthorised' camps were being put up in almost every street by the Youth Congress Workers, in a bid to extort money by hauling up the people of weaker sections like rickshaw-wallahs and daily wage earners.

In Shahdara (a suburbs of Delhi) there was an open clash between the shopkeepers who were coerced into getting themselves sterilised and the Corporation staff. The police watched the scene without trying to intervene. As a result, the Corporation staff got a good beating.

Subsequently, there was a hartal when the authorities tried to arrest one of the shopkeepers. The Union Minister for Housing, Shri H. K. L. Bhagat, who hails from this constituency, had to intervene to persuade the shopkeepers to open their shops.

Shri Bhagat had also to intervene in the same area when the weekly market at more than one place was disrupted because of the insistence of the Corporation staff that the stallholders produce certificates of Sterilisation before being allowed to set their wares in the market. This led to a clash as a result of which, there was brick-batting on the Corporation staff.

(a) VIOLENT CLASHES OVER F. P. IN U. P. TOWNS :

Violent clashes have occurred in number of towns in U. P. including Sultanpur, Kanpur, Shamli, Bareilly, Allahabad, Almorha, etc. over the government insistence in performing F. P. operations on unwilling people.

Dozens of persons were killed in Sultanpur when groups of people belonging to all communities offered determined resistance to the Police and the doctors of the F. P. Department. Policemen and doctors were among the casualties.

(b) TEACHERS BLAST FAMILY PLANNING TACTICS OF THE GOVERNMENT :

Great resentment prevails among teachers in North India including Delhi against the government fait to them to bring a required number of cases of family planning, failing which their salaries will not be released.

This order has resulted in great harassment to teachers especially the ladies who have to hear cutting and vulgar remarks when they go knocking from door to door in search of F. P. cases. They have to pay something like Rs 50 to Rs 100 to each case to motivate them.

Such a situation reached boiling point in Mathura in the last week of August when teachers of all categories—from Primary to post-graduate ones—started courting arrest as a protest against the withholding of salaries for failure to fulfil the quota of family planning cases.

3. AKALI MORCHA AGAINST EMERGENCY GOING STRONG :
REPORT BY SATYA SAMACHAR REPRESENTATIVES
RECENTLY ON TOUR TO PUNJAB :

More than 30,000 leaders and 17 of its 20 male MLAs have courted arrest so far against the imposition of a fake emergency

4

by Smt. Indira Gandhi. The Satyagraha has been stepped up since July 16, 1976, after a decision to carry on the struggle till the lifting of Emergency was taken at a big conference held at Amritsar.

At present daily Satyagrahis offered in front of the historic Akali Takht at Amritsar and on all festivals including the Amavas (New Moon Day) and Sankranti (First of every month) at a dozen other places in Punjab.

5. TRUCK CARRYING CAPTIVE AUDIENCE OVERTURNS : TEN DEAD

At least ten persons died and many including school children had their limbs fractured when an overloaded truck carrying about 100 men, women and children to Haryana Chief Minister's meeting, struck against a tree and overturned near Jind in the second week of September.

The meeting was held at Uchana and in keeping with the practices of Mrs. Gandhi herself, and all the Chief Ministers and Congress party bosses, people were being dumped into the venue from places within a 15-20 miles radius and even from further off.

The place presented a horrible scene after the accident. However, the worst part of the tragedy was that no responsible doctor was available in the nearest hospital at Jind as they had also gone to the C. M.'s meeting. There was no proper supplies of medicines even. Some local philanthropists came forward to help purchase medicines for the victims.

As expected, the Censor killed the news of the accident at the request of the Haryana Government.

10. MRS GANDHI ASKS V. C. SHUKLA TO APOLOGISE TO S. S. RAY :

Not content with running down the democratic opposition, V. C. Shukla's Press Information Bureau has started meddling in the internal politics of the ruling party also.

One the eye (on the eve) of the meeting in Delhi of West BengalCongressmen the Bureau released an article against S. S. Ray.

It was published with minor differences in content, in two papers of the capital Indian Express and Hindustan Times. Both these papers are now presided over by Mr. K. K. Birla.

It is clear that Sanjay asked Shukla to release such an article and Shukla ordered the Birla papers to carry them. Birla's consent was there of course, though not of the editors one of whom hails from West Bengal went on leave for fear of offending Ray.

The article accused Ray of blaming the Centre for the ills of West Bengal and "trying to run the Centre from Calcutta".

On seeing the articles, Ray complained to Mrs. Gandhi who, it is said, phoned to Shukla asking him to apologise to Ray for the publication of the Article. Shukla rang up Ray six times without success. It was only at the seventh call that Ray condescended to respond to Shukla's call and heard his apology in silence.

13. MISS DURGABAI BHAGWAT, a renowned critic in Marathi literature and President, Marathi Literary Conference, Karhad, detained under MISA on 19th September 1976.

Mrs. Mrinal Gore, M.L.A., is transferred to Bombay Central Jail, and the order is served to transfer her to Dhulia District Jail.

14. The latest issue of 'HIMMAT' weekly is ordered for censorship.

15. SINCE JULY 1975, 1,108 STRIKES IN THE COUNTRY :

In reply to Shri Saroj Mukherjee's question as to how many strikes took place and how many workers were involved in the last one year, the Deputy Minister of Labour gave the required details in Lok Sabha on August 26, which have been summarised below.

In the year between July 1975 to June 1976, the number of strikes in India was 1,108. The number of workers involved was 4,50,152 and the mandays lost were 31,891 (Samachar)

Separate figures for States with higher incidence are also shown here :

States	No. of Strikes	Workers involved	Mandays lost.
Tamilandu	190	1,70,748	11,25,886
West Bengal	135	88,984	10,94,945
Maharashtra	326	52,788	3,14,501
U. P.	77	1,05,233	1,41,795
Kerala	39	8,497	71,910
A. P.	27	14,322	69,012
Bihar	77	17,832	61,196
India (including All States)	1,108	4,50,152	32,68,891

16. BIG LIE OF MRS. GANDHI : In an interview to an independent T.V.Centre of U. K., Mrs. Gandhi has said that only half a dozen or so opposition leaders are detained. The statement is preposterous as it flies in the face of facts. Here is a list of some of the prominent leaders of the democratic opposition parties in detention in addition to 33 members of Parliament who were detained and whose list we gave in our 6th issue.

Jana Sangh : Yagya Datt Sharma, Madho Prasad Tripathy, Nanaji Deshmukh, V. K. Malhotra, Krishnalal Manni.

Socialist Party : George Fernandez, Madhu Limaye, Ramananand Tiwari, Mrinal Gore, S. D. Paliwal.

Congress (O) : Babubhai Patel, former Chief Minister of Gujarat, Sikander Bakht, Dev Gowda, M. L. A., Manubhai Patel, K. S. Hedge.

CPI (M) : All members of the Tripura Legislative Assembly numbering 40.

Akali: Prakash Singh Badal, former Chief Minister of Punjab, G. S. Taura, Mohan Singh Tur.

Bharatiya Lok Dal : Jaswant Kumar Chaudhury, Bihar, Chand Ram, Devi Dayal, MLA.

17. AN OFFICER TO THE SOVIET EMBASSY was caught by the Indian Military Intelligence with some classified documents. This was reported to the Government. Foreign ministry instead of

declaring him personal non-grata complained to the Soviet Embassy and that too on the reported insistance of the Defence Ministry. As a result of that, he has been sent back by the Embassy to the Soviet Union. He is popularly known as Yuri.

18. In Allahabad High Court Bar Association, a resolution was moved by Government Counsel to accord a reception to the Chief Justice of India Shri A. N. Ray. Only eight people voted for the resolution and the rest voted against.

FROM NEWS ITEM PUBLISHED IN *Tribune* :

JOURNAL OF THE COMMUNIST PARTY OF AUSTRALIA (PRO-MOSCOW) DATED THE 8TH SEPTEMBER, 1976 :

On August 26, the M. S. W. State Council of the Australian Railways Union (ARU) protested strongly at the jailing of thousands of Indian Workers under the Emergency regulations introduced by the Gandhi Government a year ago.

PART OF THE ARU's RESOLUTION STATES :

Among those workers and union officials is George Fernandez, President of the All India Railwaymen's Federation, who because of his leadership......has been the object of detailed prosecution by the Indian Government. At present he is in jail and his wife, who is also a leader in Woman's organisation and activities, has been forced to leave India.

The State council has called on the national ARU Executive to lead a protest deputation to the Indian Ambassador about the matter.

SATYA SAMACHAR

Published by Lok Sangharsha Samity

Vol No. 90   Dt : 10th November, 1976

Roll Call of Martyrs :

Given hereunder are the latest additions to the list of martyrs who died fighting Mrs Gandhi's dictatorship :

Shri Pandurang Kshirsagar, Akhila Bharatiya Vyavasthe Pramukh, RSS (Secretary, Central Office, Nagpur) ; aged 55, detained since emergency in Nagpur and later Thana Jail ; died of heart attack in Thana Jail on September 23, 1976.

Shri Baidyanath Prasad Choudhary, veteran Sarvodaya leader ; aged 80, detained in Purnea jail since proclamation of emergency ; released from jail when his condition worsened, died in Banaras soon after in September, 1976.

160 Respectable Citizens Detained Illegally & Harassed :

One hundred and sixty innocent persons were detained in a Police-lock-up in Mangalore since September 6, 1976 for alleged murder of one Ismail of Santwal Taluk. The detenus include popular doctors, lawyers, political leaders, social leaders, progressive farmers, businessmen, etc. among those arrested is a lady doctor also.

The detenus have been harassed in every possible way including denial of clothes and a number of them tortured in the notorious police methods including making an "aeroplane" of the victim by hoisting him through a pulley. Those suffering from police torture have been denied medical aid.

It is well-known all over the area that the arrests have been made as an act of political vendetta and that all those arrested cannot have been the remotest connection with the murder which has been used by the government for political purposes.

A memorandum submitted to the State Government on 20-9-1976 highlighted the illegal nature of detentions in police-lock-up and the alarming condition of the detenus and demanded their release. It also demanded full enquiry into the shameful episode, and punishment of the guilty officials. It deplored the statement of ministers accusing RSS of complicity in the murder even before any enquiry.

Ministers Fear of Overseas Indians

Here are a few examples of how some trusted lieutenants of Mrs Gandhi behaved during their tours abroad to explain Emergency.

(1) *Dharam Vir Sinha :* He went to Washington in April,

1976. He refused to speak on Emergency, but agreed to speak on "Gandhiji and his Relevance." The gathering was small, but questions were plenty. Members of the audience quoted Gandhiji on civil rights, press freedom and democracy, and asked Shri Sinha whether he agreed with it. He fumbled then lost his temper and left the hall. Later on, he cancelled a press conference due to "lack of time."

(2) *H.R. Gokhale :* He came in late April to USA. He appeared in one TV interview, refused to enter into a debate and declined to address overseas Indians. After dinner at the Indian Ambassador's residence, he disappeared.

(3) *Om Mehta :* He proved to be the greatest joker of all. He came to New York in early May, 1976. He refused to address overseas Indians or appear on the TV. Later in New York, he called twelve persons to dinner at Tandoor Restaurant. The apt Samachar news-agency pass it off as a Public Meeting.

(4) *Hitendra Desai :* He came in June, 1976 to London as "Prime Minister's Special Emissary." He refused to talk about the Emergency. He addressed a small invited group at the Bharatiya Vidya Bhavan on "Hindu Culture." Later he spoke at a Hindu Temple on "Moral Values", to 25 persons. When one of them asked him how he could reconcile his silence over Morarji Desai's arrest with moral values, he said he would answer the question later on. But he never did.

Intellectuals Reject Ruling Congress

Elections were held last month to the posts of four Vice-Presidents and eight executive members of the Indian Council of World Affairs in New Delhi. The ruling party's official candidates could get just one seat—that of an executive member.

Cinema Advertisement for Mrs Gandhi's paper only

The Delhi Administration, now functioning directly under Mr Sanjay Gandhi, has ordered that, of the eight English dailies in the capital, only Nehru family's National Herald will carry cinema advertisements.

New Advertisement Policy of DAVP

The Directorate of Audio-Visual Publicity has run out of its annual budget in just six months and is awaiting supplementary grants. An idea of the DAVP's costly partisan activities can be formed from the fact that during first six months of Emergency it produced 180 (one hundred and eighty) documentaries in support of Mrs Gandhi's 20 Point Programme. And it has been inserting full page advertisements in Newspapers to boost Mrs Gandhi's sagging morale and image, like hell.

Determined aid to ruin Indian Express

The Government has withdrawn its earlier notice to close down the press of the *Statesman* after its purpose of closing down the *Seminar* (a prestigious journal devoted to debating public affairs) has been achieved. The notice was withdrawn when the paper challenged the Government order in the High Court. However, three other cases against the Statesman are still pending.

In case of Indian Express, the Government managed to appoint Shri Suman Dubey (35), a Special Correspondent of the paper and class fellow of Mrs Gandhi's son Rajeev at the Doon School, as the Chief Editor of the paper in place of the Veteran Mr V.K. Narasimhan. This has done with the help of K.K. Birla who has been installed as the Chairman of the Board Directors and also of the newly appointed three-man committee to control editorial policy.

But the former Chairman and the present Managing Director R.N. Goenka, M.P. refused to implement the decision. At this the power connection to the press of the paper was cut. This was resorted after two days when Shri Goenka approached the High Cour t.

But two days later, the Press of the paper was sealed by the Delhi Corporation on the excuse that the Company had not paid the house tax. This was a wrong plea as out of an assessment of Rs 5 lakhs, the concern had already paid Rs 4 lakhs and the Rs one lakh was subject of dispute in the local Court. Shri Goenka again approached the High Court and got the stay order and the press was opened.

Meanwhile, it is learnt that Shri Suman Dubey has refused the appointment as Chief Editor of the paper. However, the

Government is bent upon changing at least six senior editorial hands to have complete control of the paper.

Shri K.K. Birla is working zealously as the trojan horse in this respect.

Successful Hunger Strike in Hassan Jail

Sixteen workers of the Lok Sangharsh Samiti lodged in Hassan Jail in Karnataka for the last 9 months resorted to hunger strike when the Police Officers concerned stopped producing them in Court to punish them for shouting the slogan Bharat Mata Ki Jai in the Court premises.

The Satyagrahis started the fast from 8-9-1976. By 10-9-76 the health of five of them deteriorated and they were admitted to the hospital. The news spread like wild fire and their relatives and well-wishers rushed to the hospital in hundreds, but they were not allowed to see ailing Satyagrahis.

At this the District LSS wrote to the District Collector cautioning him against such illegal behaviour of the Police. They expressed their resolve to take up the matter at the higher level.

This had the desired effect. The District Collector, the Police Officers and the medical officer met the Satyagrahis in Jail on 19-9-1976 and assured them that they would be produced before the Court. As a result of this assurance, the hunger strike was called off.

Firing and Lock-out in Indian Telephones Industries, Bangalore : Workers denied Bonus :

In callous disregard of the fine service record of the workers and interests of the company, the management of the I.T.I. Bangalore declared a lock-out on 20-9-1976 to dodge the workers' just demand for 20% bonus.

Even last year the management paid 10% bonus, though the amount of profit-sharing with workers worked out to 15.7%. This was done by arbitrarily classifying the I.T.I. as non-competitive industry under the new ill-advised bonus ordinance of 1975. The dispute over it is under conciliation still.

This year again, the management resorted to dilatory tactics. It failed to announce the bonus on 18-9-1976, as promised. The workers of the end shift recorded their protest the same day by foregoing their meals. On 20-9-1976, almost all the 8000 squatted in front of the Chairman's office and demanded 20% bonus, notwithstanding the ordinance.

When the Union Leaders met the management, they were informed that the bonus worked to 8.8%. After vehement protest from the employees, the management was prepared to grant 10% bonus. At this workers launched a peaceful sit-in protest joined by even the watchmen. The management summoned the Police and workers were treated to teargas shells and brutal beat inside the factory premises. Even lady workers were not spared.

Factory was declared close for the day and workers ordered to clear out. But when they were coming out of the factory gates at about 3.45 P.M., they were trapped in a pincer and brutally lathicharged, leading to serious injuries to workers as well as to policemen.

In the resulting incidents, much damage was caused to the machinery. The loss is estimated at amny (many) crores. It is said that workers were chased into departments and lathicharged. The factory is locked out since Sept. 20. More than 100 arrests have been made, and 1000 are on the street.

Thus the "jewel among public undertakings", as the ITI was once called and which had never seen any ugly incident in the earlier strikes and whose workers had been complimented even by the Police Officers for "exemplary and disciplined behaviour during the sit-in eleven day strike of 1966, lies in a shambles now.

SELF IMMOLATION AS A PROTEST AGAINST DICTATORSHIP.

30th October, 1976.

On October 11, Prabhakar Sharma, a 65 year-old Sarvodaya worker immolated himself at Surgaon, two miles from Vinobha Bhave's Ashram at Paunar, Wardha.

His intention of "atmadan" (Self-immolation) as a protest

against the prevailing dictatorship in the country was conveyed
by him to Mrs. Indira Gandhi before he died.

In a statement sent to the Prime Minister, he said : "If
during the Moghul rule cruelty such as this had been perpetra-
ted, people would not have been too surprised. But it is being
inclicted (inflicted) by a Congress Government which was
trained in nonviolence by none other than Gandhiji.

"If someone by sweet talking manages to enter my house, at
gun point ties me up, robs me of my wealth, and assaults the
women in my house, then with what words am I to describe
such an act ?

"The fact is that her (Mrs. Gandhi's) command is considered
a sacred word, her whim has become statecraft, her wishes are
culture, her power-drunkeness has become law and what she
ordains justice.

"Taking away the freedom of the press does not lead to true
democracy. Nor does it make possible any non-violent mass
movement against tyranny of the Government. I call this the
murder of the country's soul."

Sharma referred to the issue of "Young India" of 5th
January 1922 in which Gandhiji had written, "We must be
content to die if we cannot live as free men and women."

As an artist, Sharma had responded to Gandhiji's call in
1945 for young men and women to devote themselves to
"Gram-seva" (service of villages). For 31 years, till his death,
he remained devoted to that cause. "He had hoped that India
would translate into reality the aspirations of her great leaders,
thereby helping herself and the world. Now that is not only a
distant aim but I feel I cannot even continue to exist in today's
India as a human being."

Prabhakar Sharma sent copies of his statement to Acharya
Vinobha Bhave, the Chief Minister of Maharashtra and some of
of his friends. Thousands attended his funeral at Surgaon
inspite of police terror.

N. B. The telegraph message and news of self-immolation was typed
and circulated underground.

CHAPTER II

NEWS ITEMS AND EDITORIAL COMMENTS

SWARAJ

For democratic self government in India.　　　No. 7
Published by Free J.P. Campaign　　　Price 7p

---

12 Watermead Lane, Carshalton, Surey, England,

Mahatma Gandhi :

> Democracy is not a state in which people act like sheep, Under democracy individual liberty of opinion and action is jealously guarded."
>
> —Young India. March 2, 1922.

> "The democracy of my conception is wholly inconsistend (t) with the use of physical force for enforcing its will."
>
> "The Epic Fast" P. 102

THE SPIRIT OF RESISTANCE IS NOT YET PARALYSED

KARUNANIDHI, CHIEF MINISTER OF TAMILNADU ADDRESSING A MASS PROTEST MEETING. 7TH JULY

"If Rajaji were here, he would call upon us all to pray. If Periyar were here, he would urge us to start a revolution, and if Qaide-i-Milat were here, he would say : There is no necessity for a state of emergency. If Annadurai were still alive, he would have said : Under no circumstances shall we allow democracy to die.

"...Today we are not concerned with whether Mrs. Gandhi remains Prime Minister or not. Our main concern is with democracy. Tamilnadu has known democracy for ever (over) a thousand years, to which a stone inscription in Chingleput bear witness."...Friends, this afternoon, as on every Sunday from 3-4, I listened to the radio-play broadcast by All India Radio. In the play an exceptionally beautiful girl called Santhana was being held up for auction by a merchant for £5,000. After endless bargaining a rich man bought the girl for £2,500 and took her home, presenting her to his wife with the words, "Dearest, I've brought you back a slave girl. Look after her ; I've still got some business to attend to but will return soon." His wife bade the girl welcome and asked her to remove her veil. Now when she saw the girl's face, she was taken aback by her beauty and immediately became fearful lest her husband should fall in love with her. There-upon she cut off all her hair and disfigured the girl's face. When she was asked why she had done this she answered : "My husband could have fallen in love with her." Likewise fearful lest something may happen Mrs. Gandhi is in the process of disfiguring democracy.

"...Yesterday I received a three page letter from a former MP and educationalist. Its contents moved me to tears. The minister wrote about the Press censorhip and about these eminent politicians, who during India's independence struggle suffered imprisonment and who, now once again, are under house arrest or even in prison. Only Indira Gandhi is able to dry these tears by freeing those men immediately.

"I urge you all to rise and swear an oath of allegiance that we shall defend our democracy."

THE STORY OF THE TIMES AD

(A report from the Press Officer of the FREE JP CAMPAIGN).

Bishop Trevor Huddleston signing the first coupon during a concert interval on Wednesday July 23 and one of our volunteers dashing across London on August 13 to pick up Dame Peggy Ashcroft's signature from the Old Vic Theatre, marked the beginning and the end of the whirlwind campaign to get a 6-column advertisement into THE TIMES on August 15 : India's Independence Day. (A copy of the ad. appeared in the sixth issue of SWARAJ).

The Free JP Campaign (Chairman : Philip Noel-Baker) had just three weeks to find the 400 people to sign the appeal to Mrs. Gandhi : "Don't Let the Light Go Out On Indian Democracy—Free JP—Free All The Political Prisoners Held Without Trial."

Starting with just £58 in the bank, the first problem was to raise the nearly £3,000 necessary for the ad. Not an easy task at any time, but during an economic crisis and with many people on holiday, some thought we had set ourselves an impossible task.

Money trickled in painfully slowly at first. On July 24 we banked £50. ; July 25, £190 and on July 28, £238. Despite frantic phone calls to friends of committee members by July 30 the total stood at just £801—good by any other standards than the formidable task in front of us. Then the mailing we had sent out to supporters of various groups such the London School of Nonviolence, *Resurgence* Magazine readers, supporters of the 1971 Bangladesh campaign, the Peace Pledge Union, other Peace Groups, Amnesty International supporters, Christian Action and other social action and civil rights groups, began to take effect. As well as an escalating supply of small contributions, the campaign received a great boost when a long time supporter of the Peace Movement sent a cheque for £200. Having passed the £1000 figure we could take stock of the names that had begun to come through.

A hasty mailing to all the M.P.'s before the House of Commons went into Summer recess on August 7, produced a magnificent response which came from all parts of the House. Ian Mikado, Sir Geoffrey de Freitas, and former Minister Douglas Jay were among some 50 Labour M.P.'s who signed ; the Rt. Hon Geoffrey Rippon, Q.C. headed a list of 12 Conservatives—a good cross section of the party ; Jeremy Thorpe, the Liberal Party leader was joined by three others from his party and Winifred Ewing (Leader of the Scottish Nationalist Party) and Gwynfor Evans (Welsh Nationalist) made the total up to 68 M.P.'s whose names reached us before the deadline (7 more M.P.'s have reached us since).

Two International telephone calls to the committee within the space of an hour—the first from America and the second from Zambia, signalled that the campaign was going to get more than just British support. The first call came from Daniel Ellsberg (of Pentagon Papers fame) and the second came from John Papworth (former Editor of *Resurgence* and a close friend of JP)—both wanted their name on the ad.

Then names began to come in from several other countries :
5 came on one telegram from Sweden ; Prof George Woodcock
(a biographer of Mahatma Ghandi) wrote from Canada ;
Mirabehn (Madaleine Slade—the former personal secretary of
Mahatma Gandhi) wrote from Australia ; Milovan Djilas (for-
merVice-President of Yugoslavia) wrote from Yugoslavia—the
country which was first to congratulate Mrs. Gandhi on her
'progressive' actions ! ; Fritz Prechtl (President of the International Transport Federation) wrote from Austria where he is an
M.P. ; Werner Meier (President of the Swiss Railwaymen's
Federation) phoned through to have his name on—he had not
forgotten the brutal suppression of the Indian Railway strike
which had preceeded Mrs. Gandhi's June 26 crackdown ;
Michael Harrington (an American writer and Socialist) tele-
gramed from the States and Robert Lowell (another American,
and probably the most important poet writing in English today)
also signed.

I have mentioned only well known names so far. But it
cannot be emphasised strongly enough that the ad. wouldn't
have been possible without the support of hundreds af
individuals who are not so wellknown. Everyone whose name
appeared on the ad. sent a contribution towards its cost. About
88% of those that signed, contributed £5 and under. A further
£409 came from supporters who did not want their names to be
published.

By August 13 we had our 400 names and the money to pay
for the ad. which thus allowed our committee members to join
PPU in the organising of a candlelight vigil outside India House
on the eve of India's Independence Day...

On August 14, two telephone calls produced two more names
for the ad. Could we put them on ? A phone call to the Times
found that we could and so Ron Hoywood CBE, secretary of
the British Labour Party and Ray Buckton, General Secretary
of the British Railwaymen's Union (ASLEF) joined the list...

Back to the vigil (this was the one that Mrs. Gandhi ridicu-
led by saying that only 28 people attended : actually 28 people
was just over 3 times the number that were required). There
were nine placards which had to be carried from the feet of the

Gandhi Statue in Tavistock Square to India House and those placards bore one work each, to make the message : "DONT LET THE LIGHT GO OUT ON INDIAN DEMOCRACY." By the time the vigil ended at one minute past midnight. THE TIMES, with the assistance of over 400 friends of India, was carrying this same message to all parts of the world.

Paul Connett.

POSTSCRIPT : *Names that arrived too late to appear on the ad. included : Heinrich Boll (German Nobel Laureate in Literature) ; Pierre Emmanuel (Member of the French Academy and former President of PEN—the writers' union) ; J. H. Plumb (Professor of Modern History at Cambridge) ; Rt. Hon. Hugh Jenkins, M.P. (Member of the British Government) ; 6 other British M.P.'s (Alan Clark, Bob Edwards, Brian Walden, Hugh McCartney, Bob Cryer, Neil Kinnock) and a Member of the German Parliament, Philipp Seibert (President of the German Railwaymen's Union).*

The Times advertisement has proved to be a burning issue in London. The pro-Moscow Indian Workers' Association in South-all placed a counter ad. in the Guardian asking : 'Has the light gone out on Indian democracy ?' ; and at a demonstration held in Hyde Park on August 7, they ceremoniously set fire to The Times advertisement.

SWARAJ

For democratic self government in India.
Published by Free J.P. Campaign   No. 10
12 Watermead Lane, Carshalton, Surrey, England   Price 7p

HUMOUR IS DEAD
SO IS SANKER'S WEEKLY

We have been shocked to hear, an unbelievable story, that Shanker's Weekly has folded...not because of any financial difficulties but because HUMOUR IS DEAD says Mr. S. K. Pillai, the founder of this great publication.

In a farewell editorial Mr. Pillai makes a sharp reference to the conditions in India and we wonder whether he has preferred to close down rather than be gagged by the censorship in India. Here is what the final editorial says :

"This is what brings us to the nub of the matter. In our first editorial we made the point that our function was to make our readers laugh—at the world, at pompous leaders, at humbug, at foibles, at ourselves. But, what are the people who have a developed sense of humour ? It is a people with a certain civilised norms of behaviour, where there is tolerance and a dash of compassion. Dictatorships cannot afford laughter because people may laugh at the dictator and that wouldn't do. In all the years of Hitler, there never was a good comedy, not a good cartoon, not a parody, or a spoof."

FREE J.P. CAMPAIGN APPEAL

In this issue we are printing the names of many more world leaders appealing to the Indian Government to return to the spirit of Gandhiji.

MAHATMA IN EXILE

When the assassin's bullet felled Mahatma Gandhi on January 30 1948, it stopped his heart but it did not stop his message circling the world. Where it has been heard there has been hope, where it has been ignored there has been pain.

When, on June 26 1975, Mrs. Gandhi arrested Jayaprakash Narayan—who had been leading a non-violent movement along Gandhian lines and who had attracted massive popular support in the fight against corruption and the struggle for social justice —she set in motion actions which have not only deprived the Indian people of their fundamental rights, but also put the spirit of Mahatma Gandhi into exile.

We, the undersigned, appeal to Mrs. Gandhi to summon all her courage and let Mahatma Gandhi come home.

To this end, we call on her to take the following steps :

(1) End the state of emergency ;

5

(2) Release all the political prisoners or bring them to trial;
(3) Lift the censorship of the press ;
(4) Lift the ban on free speech and association, and
(5) Return the fundamental human rights to the Indian people.

AUSTRIA

Dr. D. Gisel, M.P. Doz. Dr. Eberhard Gwinner, Dr. Helga Gwinner, Dr. Johann Hauf, Heidi Hauf, Hans Janitschek (Sec. Gen. of the Socialist International) Harald Prinzhorn, Fritz Prechtl, M.P. (President of the International Transport Federation)

BELGIUM

P. Ballenghien,* Charles Deletrain,* M. Engel,* Jean Fabre,* Irene Petry (President of International Council of Social Democratic Women), Geoffrey Pope,* Kathleen Sheehan,* Ulli Reisberg,* Marc Wagener*

BRAZIL

Archbishop Dom Helder Cemara

CANADA

Dr. George Woodcock (University of British Columbia)

DENMARK

Frode Jakobsen

FRANCE

Michele Bose, Helene St. Jacques

GERMANY

Gesellschaft fur bedrohte Volker (Society for Endangered Peoples), Alfred Knaus Dr. phil. Ines Kohler, Jens Wulff, Dr. med. Paul-Fritz Pinath, Wolfgang Weyrauch, Tilman Zulch

ISRAEL

Yoram Peri (London Representative of the Israel Labour Party)

NORWAY

Dan Borge Akero, Arne Bjonviken, Vegard Bye, Elizabeth Christensen, Asbjorn Eide, Atle Forbord, Nils Petter Gleditch, Aase Helseth, Ole Kristian Holthe, Erik Ivas, Aslak Leesland, Sverre Lodgaard, Helge Stange Nilsen, Arve Ofstad, Dag Poleszynski, Per Olav Reinton, Kristen Ringdal, Kjell Skjelsbaek

SANTO DOMINGO

Jose Feo, Pena Gomez (Gen. Sec. Partido Revolucionario Dominicano)

SWEDEN

Tord Wallstorm

SWITZERLAND

Friedrich Durrenmatt, Gole Mann, Vera Matthiras (Secretary of International Council of Social Democratic Women)

U. K.

Barbara Acquah (Hon. Sec. of SERVAS), Stanley Alderson, Michael Allaby, Frank Allaun, M.P., Godric E.S. Bader, Hannah Baneth, Alan Beith, M.P., Humphry Berkeley, Lindia M. Best, Peter Bonnici, Shirley Du Boulay, Dr. Jeremy Bray, M.P., Heather Bremer, Huglt Brock, Carol Burns, Jane Buxton, Rev. T.J. Carter, Liz Chapple, Margaret Cheney, Dr. Jagjit Singh Chohan, George Clarke, Alasdaire Clayre, Paul and Ellen Connett, Adrian Corcoran, Prof Adam Curie (Prof. of Peace Studies at Bradford University) Arthur Darlington, Guy Dauncey,

Charles Davey, C.H. Davies, D. Davis, Geo. H. Dixon, E.M.
Engleman, Rev. Adrian Esdaile, Fred Evans, M.P., Gwynfor
Evans, M.P., Eva Figes, Angela Fraser, Arnold Glickman,
Raymond Grimwade, Rev. David Goodacre, Kati Granville,
Peter Hain, Jennifer Harriott, Trevor Hazelgrove, M.A. Heard,
M.S. Hoda, R.H. Hodgson, David Hoggett, Antony Hopkins,
Eve Howes, Heidi Humphrey, Anthony Hyman, Timothy
Hyman. Prof. Ghita Ionescu (Manchester University), Harriet
Isaacs, Mrs. P. Jackson, R. Hon. Hugh Jay, M.P., Rt. Hon.
Hugh Jenkins, M.P., Russell Johnston, M.P., Bedwyr Lewis Jones,
Mervyn Jones, Prof. Lord Nicholas Kaldor, Krishan Kapoor,
Mgr. Bruce Kent, Douglas A. Kepper, Ursula King, Arthur
Koestler, Bernard Kops, Madk William Kramracsh, Satish
Kumar, P.M. Lightbody, John Lipetz, Evan Luare, M.P., R.R.
Lucas, John Lyle, Francis Mackeith, Lesley S. Mair, Lesley
Marrioott, Stuart Marriott, Maurreen Mathews, Hugh McCart-
ney, M.P., Jan Melichar, Verna Metcalfe, Spike Milligan, June
Mitchell, Eric Moonman, M.P., Prof. Robert Neild (Cambridge
University), Barbara Nicholls, Walter Padley, M.P., Sister
Pavitra, Mike Phillips, Rex Philips, F.M. Prideaux, Walter Rich,
Rex Richards, Rt. Hon. Geoffrey Rippon, Q.C., M.P. Bernard
Rivers, Patrick Rivers, Alan Roberton, Dr. Saul Rose, S.K.
Saxena, Rosalind Schama, Hester Scott, Fr. Brocard Sewell,
John Seymour, David Steel, M.P., Josef Szware, Margot Tenny-
son, Millie R. Thomas, Merfyn Turner, D. Walford, Robert
and Helen Waller David Weitzman, Q.C., M.P., Arnold Wesker,
Rev. Austen Williams, Prof. Peter Winch, Michael Wolf

U.S.A.

Roger Baldwin, Fr. Daniel Berrigan, Prof. Noam Chomsky,
Daniel Ellsberg, Prof. Earry Gara, Homer A. Jack, Prof. Thomas
A. Rusch, Gene Sharp, Studs Teokel, Unny Sommerfelt, Kjell
Vesje

YUGOSLAVIA

Milovan Djilas.

*Those names marked with an asterisk signed an appeal which
called for the immediate release of all the political prisoners.

MAKING OF AN AUTOCRAT

As Kashmiri Brahmins, they inherited an attitude common among members of their privileged class : that the responsibility for ruling India was theirs virtually as a birthright. But whereas Jawaharlal Nehru managed to curb his autocratic instincts during the turbulent years he led India's struggle for independence, his daughter, Indira, did not grow up to share her father's acquired taste for the principles of liberal democracy. She did not achieve prominence by an ability to rally followers, reason with doubters and compromise with challengers. She rose to power in the shadow of her famous father, and the lessons she learned were essentially those of political manipulation. Aloof, independent and blunt, she grew accustomed to getting her own way—even, as she demonstrated last week, by main force.

Vain, with an easily wounded ego, Nehru's daughter had a lonely childhood filled with politics. In those days, she said years later, "my favorite occupation was to deliver thunderous speeches to the servants while standing on a high table. All my games were political games ; I was like Joan of Arc perpetually being burned at the stake." She also had an unsuccesful marriage ; she bore two sons to Feroze Gandhi (no relation to Mahatma Gandhi), but their life together crumbled as she spent more and more time as ceremonial hostess to her father the Prime Minister.

Miscalculation : Once she became Prime Minister herself, however, Indira showed just how tough she could be. In 1966, two years after the death of her father, Congress Party wheelhorses picked her because they apparently thought that she would be easier to manipulate than a man. That proved to be a capital miscalculation. Three years later, with a ruthlessness and cunning that might have made her father blanch, Mrs. Gandhi turned on the Congress Party kingmakers, remade the party in her own image and forced her would-be manipulators into virtually impotent opposition. Since then, she has ruled like an autocrat.

Her direction, during most of her nine years in office, has been toward increased personal power. "She feels she is crucial to the future of India," one diplomat in New Delhi said recently. "That is probably why she fights so hard for political survival." She has also been winning that fight consistently. In March 1971, she called a general election a year ahead of schedule and campaigned tirelessly on the slogan *Garibi hatao*— Hindi for "abolish poverty." In response both to that populist promise and to her vast national prestige, Indian voters returned her to office with a majority almost as lopsided as her father once won. In December of that year, in the wake of India's decisive victory over Pakistan in the war that led to the birth of Bangladesh, Mrs. Gandhi stood so high in the eyes of her countrymen that she seemed indeed to be the Joan of Arc of her girlhood fantasies.

Muscle : Mrs. Gandhi's political successes have not rendered her immune from challenge. Last year, India's Railway workers went on strike in demand for higher wages, plunging the country into a severe economic crisis. With a show of muscle that awed and stunned her supporters and opponents alike, Mrs. Gandhi decided to arrest dozens of key union leaders on the eve of the walk out. When by a coincidence of timing, her government was able to announce that India had exploded a nuclear device, thereby becoming the world's sixth atomic power, the railway strike disappeared from the headlines. The explosion also triggered widespread criticism of India, which seemed to have turned its back for good on the principles of nonviolence to which Gandhi and Nehru had been so devoted.

Her extreme sensitivity to any criticism—and vehement response to it – partially explains her overreaction to her opponents last week. By a revealing irony, the law under which Mrs. Gandhi ordered the mass arrests was based on similar laws that the British had used three decades ago to crack down on the Congress movement of which she is now the leader. In the declining days of the British Raj, many of India's colonial rulers were convinced of their natural right to power and were intolerant of the popular movements that challenged them. It was hard to see, last week, that Indira Gandhi was acting much differently.

Newsweek, July 7, 1975   —Angus Deming with Loren Jenkins in New Delhi

JANATA

Vol. XXX No. 24.   August 3 1975

Editorial

Chandu and the Tiger

In the village of Gangapur, there lived a young man named Chandra or Chandu. He did not know any particular trade but he was certainly very clever and knew how to play on the sentiments of the simple villagers. He would sometimes play the role of an astrologer and tell Govinda in which direction his missing buffalo must have gone and what must be the colour of the man who had stolen it. At other time he assumed the role of a "Vaid" and brought for the ailing grand-mother of Laxmi some concoction prepared from rare herbs which according to Chandu were to be found only on the far off Nil Parvat. Chandu had hardly any formal education and people suspected that he had left his home, his school and even his village because he was incapable of any serious effort in any field. But when after ten years' absence Chandu returned to Gangapur, the villagers were astonished to hear from him that he had made a name for himself in the university, he had travelled even up to and beyond Delhi and he had met the high ups in the establishment. He had told them that he had in fact discarded a bright career and only his burning desire to serve the poor and the ignorant in his village had brought him back. Thereupon the villagers stopped suspecting Chandu and began to feel proud that such an educated and handsome man should have chosen to live amongst them.

Chandu had a real break when Gangapur was given a Panchayat. The villagers never had heard of democracy, the ballot box and the right of franchise. So they felt relieved when Chandu offered himself as a candidate for the post of Sarpanch. But Chandu condescended to this only after the villagers had taken a solemn oath in the temple of Bahiroba (which literally translated means the deaf-god) that they would abide by his ruling for the next five years and accept him as their leader. As a token of his gratitude Chandu promised to increase the yield of their lands threefold and make hunger a thing of the past. "I shall make milk and honey flow down the streets of Gangapur or else..." Chandu left unsaid the rest of the sentence.

Chandu or Chandasaheb as he now came to be known decided to make hay as fast as he could while the sun shone. First he established a cabal of like-minded youth who swore to cling to him through thick and thin. Gangapur was situated in the midst of a luxuriant forest of teak and other valuable trees. Taking advantage of the fact that quality wood was in great demand the trashing firm of "Chandasaheb and Associates" started leasing coups to unscrupulous forest contractors who promised them a share of profit. Then the villagers discovered to their dismay not only the teak trees but one after another their valuable bullocks and milch cows started disappearing. Chandasaheb and Associates were clandestinely selling them to the butchers. When the villagers started complaining bitterly Chandasaheb and his henchmen assembled all the villagers in a meeting in which he declared that he and his trusted friends had seen at least half a dozen ferocious tigers roaming the nearby forest and unless they were killed the cattle drain could not be stopped. Six jeeps and a dozen double-barreled guns will have to be provided for, that was the minimum. Give us the weapons and leave the rest to us. Then we shall raise a batch of forest guards who would take care of the cattle. But if you are not agreeable to purchasing the equipment, then let us cut down the forest so that the tigers will no longer remain in their hide outs.

"But neither is necessary, neither the purchase of equipment nor cutting down the forest," said Ramji, the village veteran, in his soft voice. "Because there are no tigers in our jungle." "Are you in your senses, Dadaji ?" growled Chandasaheb, "or have you made a secret deal with tigers ?" He quipped and loudly laughed at the joke he had made.

The villagers did not know whom to believe, Chandasaheb and his friends or old Ramji. That the cattle were disappearing was a fact. So they decided to raise the necessary funds by subscription.

Chandasaheb and his friends, once they had the jeeps and the arms, became very arrogant. The change in their attitude was astonishing. However they could not produce a single tiger before the villagers dead or alive. After six months the villagers started whispering that after all old Ramprakash might have spoken the truth. None of them had seen even the tail of a tiger. How could it happen?

This made Chandasaheb furious. "This wretched Ramprakash," he said, "was demoralising the villagers. He must be stopped from doing that. No, we have tolerated him long enough. I cannot allow him to go on like this." Curiously one day Ramji got knocked down by a jeep in the jungle. The forest guard said he had seen Ramji actually talking with a tiger. This, of course, was plain nonsense. But was it not safer to keep quiet? Wise men know when to lie low.

Old Ramji was never seen again nor were the tigers. What one could see every day however was Chandasaheb and his forest guards lording it over the village of Gangapur!

S W A R A J

Number 19   Price 15p

"A government that...suppresses the press and literature, that bans hundreds of organisations, that keeps people in prison without trial and that does many other thing that are happening in India today is a government that has ceased to have even a shadow of justification for its existence."—Jawaharlal Nehru, 1936 (Mrs Gandhi's father!)

Indians on India

1. Journalist Romest Thapar :

"What we have experienced up till now is a carefully coordinated suppression of the opposition, a drastic restriction of freedoms of the press, the use of state machinery against politi-

cal opponents, blatant interference in normal administrative
procedures, the spread of fear and uncertainty ; the submission
and silence of the ruling party, a complete strangulation of
parliamentary debate and finally the indefinite postponement of
elections, as is possible under the state of emergency. All this,
it is argued, is aimed at bringing an end to corruption, protecting the country from anarchy and chaos, and guaranteeing the
working population a fair deal. However such rosy statements
fade away when we investigate thoroughly actions which have
taken place until now under the state of emergency. Now safe
from any electoral confrontation, the ruling party remains untouched by the demands to fulfill at least a minimum of tasks.
Also the opposition is not concerned with providing sensible
alternative programmes, but only with how to reappear politically without losing face. The bureaucracy blunders on and is
directed by people more concerned with themselves than with
the country. The old passions have been extinguished. Self-
preservation has become the key-world. Only the ragged sail
against the wind. They have nothing to lose !"

2. Political Scientist Rajni Kothari :

"Naturally", writes Kothari, "there are large numbers of
people who believe that the state of emergency has shown a
row of good results—that because of the 20 point economic
programme social and economic changes have been set into
motion ; that the ending of the political agitation has made it
possible for the government, industry and the universities to
work in peace again ; that because of severe action against
hoarders, smugglers and blackmarketeers prices have successfully
been brought under control, social welfare has been improved,
exports have risen, and the foreign exchange reserve increased ;
that the government finally has the opportunity to set about the
long overdue tasks in such important areas as family planning
and the elimination of slums. Such assumptions can of course
be refuted with four counter arguments :

(a) most things have not even the slightest connection with
the state of emergency, and are rather the results of independent
or purely coincidental factors ; (b) a state of emergency should

not have been necessary to undertake any of the steps which have so far been taken ; (c) many of the changes considered to have taken place under the 20 point programme exist simply on paper and are more rhetorical than real ; (d) many of the steps taken up until now have led to repression and intimidation and have affected the weaker part of the population—like the actions in connection with forced sterilisation and the forceful eviction of poor people from the cities—and on the other hand caused repercussions and violence. The real beneficiaries are once again the rich who also support the state of emergency without reservation, the middle and lower officials and the police who, now that they see the danger of exposure largely removed, demand extortionate prices by using any conceivable method either to guarantee someone advantages or spare them disadvantages."

3. The following statement was issued by the National Committee for Review of the Constitution, a group of members of the various opposition parties in India :

"It is well known that the emergency provisions of the Wiemar Constitution were misused in Germany by Hitler to establish his personal dictatorship. When the Constitution of India was drafted, it was perhaps never, envisaged that emergency would become a constant feature of the national life and the safeguard against the abuse of emergency powers would be nullified by a systematic erosion of checks and balances provided in the Constitution such as a free press, judicial review and fundamental rights. Exercise of emergency powers particularly during the last one year has demonstrated the need for a thorough review of the emergency provisions so as to provide effective safeguards to protect the interests of the people against arbitrary and oppressive actions of the executive.

"The constitutional changes proposed by the Swaran Singh Committee—(That is the Committee that made the recommendations regarding the constitutional amendments—)

"are calculated to emasculate the concepts of checks and balances in respect of the exercise of executive authority by seriously diminishing the scope of judicial review. It is not difficult to envisage that once the powers of independent courts are eliminated from such a vital field as elections, the very concept of free and fair elections would disappear and peoples' right to govern themselves would be seriously compromised."

JOURNALISTS PROTEST

Malta News, October 25 ;

Sixty-seven Indian journalists in a letter of protest to Prime Minister Indira Gandhi, have said they are "gravely disturbed" by Government actions against some of the country's leading newspapers.

The sending of the letter to Mrs. Gandhi marked one of the rare occasions since a national emergency was proclaimed 16 months ago and censorship imposed that journalists have come together to criticize Government policies.

The letter whose signatories include editorial executives, columnists, senior reporters, photographers and cartoonists, expressed concern about actions taken against The Indian Express, the country's largest newspapers chain—the right-of center Statesman, and the pro-Moscow Patriot.

The 400-word letter dealt primarily with the case of The Indian Express, which had to go to court earlier the month to have its electricity restored and its presses freed from a Government-ordered padlock.

"The manner in which various authorities appear to be acting (against the Express) suggest an orchestrated effort on the part of the Government to cripple and silence an independent journal and to inflict on it a series of officially imposed lockouts hurtful to its many employees and larger readership," the letter stated.

"As professional journalists committed to a free Press we are gravely disturbed by all that has happended......to the Statesman, Patriot and other journals in Delhi and elsewhere, and by what is even now happening to the Indian Express.

"Our anxiety and bewilderment are all the more since the Government and official media tirelessly exhort the citizen of the country to up-hold and conform to the highest norms of democracy, responsible behaviour, discipline and right conduct, all of these values that we sincerely cherish."

The signatories include Chanchal Sarkar, Director of the Press Institute of India—B.G. Verghese, former Information Adviser to Mrs. Gandhi, Former Editor of the Hindustan Times and now an editorial adviser to a weekly commerce magazine—G.G. Mirchandani, former general manager of United News of India news agency—D.R. Mankekar, a leading Indian author and former executive of the Times of India—Sri Mulgaokar, former editor of the Indian Express—S.P. Chopra, Editor of the Eastern Economist, and P.D. Sharma, a retired senior journalist now president of the Press Club of India.

USA : WALK FOR HUMAN RIGHTS

The culmination of the 120 mile walk organised by members of the Indians for Democracy group was the mailing of a memorandum to various public personalities in India. In the memorandum, addressed to Mrs. Gandhi, they question her reasons for declaring the state of emergency, the imprisonment of thousands without trial, the assault on the press and judiciary, the unconstitutional amendment of the Indian Constitution, the dissolution of the Tamilnadu and Gujarat assemblies, and the postponment of national elections.

The memorandum was endorsed by Nobel Laureates Linus Pauling and Owen Chamberlain, Reps. Donald Fraser and Millicent Fenwick, former Sen. McCarthy, writers Noam Chomsky, Ved Mehta and Nayantara Sahgal, and the Mayor and City Council of Berkely, Calf., among others.

Newsweek, February 16, 1976

INDIRA'S HEIR APPARENT

Until recently, Sanjay Gandhi, the Prime Minister's 29-year-old son, was known to the Indian public chiefly for his youthful pranks, his stunning ex-model wife and his attempts to mass-produce a "people's car." But now he is being groomed as his mother's heir apparent and creating front-page news as he barnstorms India espousing her post-emergency policies. "After

Indira," says one senior government official, "Sanjay is the second most important figure in India today."

Though his only official post is membership in the Youth Congress, Sanjay now has immense power within the government—and he is not reluctant to use it. Cabinet ministers and top civil servants have grown accustomed to his peremptory instructions. The tales circulate endlessly : former Defence Minister Swaran Singh resigned because he could not tolerate Sanjay's interference in his domain ; U.S. Dikshit, a veteran Congress Party leader, was demoted from Cabinet rank to a governorship supposedly at young Gandhi's insistence ; and in a more sinister vein, at least one leading official who rejected Sanjay's orders went home to find that plain-clothes policemen had ransacked his belongings, ostensibly in search of illegally held foreign currency.

Turbulent : Sanjay's youth was turbulent. As a child, he was sent home from one of India's top boarding schools for being "uncontrollable." His adolescence was marked by a series of escapades, such as joy-riding in Delhi in borrowed cars. "He has had two passions from the age of 15 on : cars and politics, in that order," says one Indian who knew him as a child. In the late sixties his first love drew him to the Rollce-Royce factory in Derby, England, for a course in auto mechanics. He flunked the course.

The setback failed to dampen his enthusiasm for the auto industry. Returning home, he designed a two-cylinder minicar, named the Maruti after the Hindu wind god, and with considerable backing from his mother built a factory to produce them on a mass scale. The project, however, has proved to be both a business fiasco and a political embarrassment for Mrs. Gandhi. Prior to government censorship, the Indian press had a field day with the story—reporting that Sanjay had funded the project by obtaining bank loans at abnormally low interest rates, that land 20 miles from New Delhi had been made available for his factory despite a negative court ruling, and that villagers evicted from the site had been poorly compensated. Originally, Sanjay proposed to produce 10,000 Marutis a year by 1973. His target date has been postponed for several consectutive years and, to date, only a few prototypes have been built.

In his public appearances, Sanjay has downplayed his role in the emergency government, insisting that he is only interested in furthering Youth Congress activities in education and hygiene in rural villages. He also claims to doubt that he has a future in Indian politics. He has acted as a forthright—if somewhat arrogant—defender of his mother's programs. Consistently, he has contended in speeches that "democracy is fully preserved and protected" in today's India, blaming the "false propaganda" and "ulterior motives', of the foreign press for contrary reports.

Rhetoric : That brand of rhetoric clearly conforms to his mother's current anti-Western stance. In private, however, Sanjay reportedly likes to discuss the achievements of the free-enterprise system, an outlook decidedly foreign to Indira. A clue to Sanjay's apostasy on this and other matters came last July, when he gave an interview to Surge magazine. "I think that nationalized industries should function only in competition with the private," he said. "When they cannot function, they should be allowed to die a natural death." The system of free competition in Europe and the U.S., he added, was instrumental in keeping prices down. "Why don't people in the U.S. hoard ?" he asked. "It is because of the competition in the supply of goods."

In the interview, Sanjay also took potshots at excessive taxation ("one method of removing the black market is to lessen the taxation, it's forcing the people to cheat"), at India's Communist Party ("If you take the party's bigwigs, I don't think you'll find richer or more corrupt people anywhere"), and at his own Congress Party ("Congress has a lot of leaders and not enough people who would go down to the grass roots to do some work"). His comments, which were prematurely released by the Indian wire services, touched off a furor and the interview was suppressed by the government. Later, Sanjay, who lives with his wife in Indira's house, issued an explanation : "I am not used to interviews and did not know what meaning would be given to my remarks."

Though his words had an independent ring, most observers dismiss the possibility of a mother-son doctrinal clash—especially since the pragmatic Indira could well endorse any of Sanjay's views that became popular out of political expedience. His professed anti-Communism and support for the free-enterprise system clearly pleased India's business community, a group that could provide valuable aid if and when he seeks to build his own constituency. He would also be assisted in that task by ground-work being done for him right now in remote villages around the country. Hindu teachings include belief in the transmigration of souls and it is being whispered that the soul of Motilal Nehru, Sanjay's revered grandfather, entered his body at birth.

—Kenneth Labich with Edward Behr and bureau reports.

THE VOICE

KAHO NAKHUDA SE KI LANGAR UTHADE
MEIN TUFAN KI ZID DEKHNA CHAHATA HUN

23 February, 1976

Tamilnadu Govt. Sacked

Tamilnadu Government, which commanded absolute majority in the assembly, has been sacked all of a sudden. The term of the assembly was already due to expire on the 21st of this March, hence to sack the government one and a half month earlier is unusual. This arbitrary act of the Central government is another example of its arrogance and thoughtless arbitrary functioning. Though opposition parties had levelled some charges against Karunanidhi Government and also submitted a memorandum before Central Government, these could not become a ground for removal of a government in democracy; of course it is a different matter if the charges are proved already. At present there was no public resentment or people's movement against the Tamilnadu government either. The sacking of the government in the given circumstances, seems to be a part of political game of Mrs Indira Gandhi. We would like to recall that Mrs Gandhi refused to concede the demand of the great people's movement of Bihar to remove the corrupt Bihar Ministry on the plea that the government having majority support must be allowed to function throughout the term of five years. The partisan attitude of the Central Govt. towards Kerala, in this respect,—by extending the term of assembly and consequently more life to Keral Government is another example of politics of convenience. It is now clear—Governments which shall function according to whims of Centre shall be awarded, otherwise...

Orders from High Ups

Mr Inder Mohan, a 52 year old gentleman of Delhi having good connection with some trade unionists and C.P.I. leaders, was approached by few street traders of Jama Masjid Area, whose shops and stalls were demolished by the local administration. These traders, who had been there for decades, were asked to erect their stalls outside the town, but there would be no customers. Inder Mohan discussed the problem with his C.P.I & Trade Union comrades. They thought that in this case only one person can help, and he is Sanjay Gandhi. Inder Mohan then went to see Mr Sanjay Gandhi and asked for help for those traders. Sanjay did not want to support them. In course of discussion, the arguments gradually became hotter and noisier, and at the end Inder Mohan was thrown out of the room. The same evening Inder Mohan was beaten severely and hit at the head and genital part at his home, and dragged to Daryaganj Police Station 7 Kilometers away. When Mohan asked for the reason for his arrest he was told that the order for it came from very high up. The next day he was brought to another Police Station near the Jama Masjid, kept in a latrine and beaten up again. After three days, a lawyer could trace Inder Mohan and was able to obtain the release of a physically and psychologically broken person.

6

Sanjay Gandhi's Emergence—
A Conspiracy to Establish Dynasty

The person who is benefited most due to emergency is dictator's heir Sanjay Gandhi. He was involved in the corruption of Maruti before emergency, and now he is polluting politics. Ignoring all democratic norms and values, a conspiracy is going on to establish the rule of one dynasty in our nation. Not even a single word of criticism could be published in newspapers regarding this conspiracy since they are in full control of the government. This happens in dictatorship : papers could not publish even those news, which we know for certain. The way papers are praising Prime Minister and her son is a sign of dictatorship. Newspapers of Patna and Calcutta published special numbers on the eve of dictator's heir's visit to Patna and Calcutta and even described him as messiah of the poor and depressed. Could it be possible for Prime Minister's son to establish himself in this manner, had there been no emergency in the country ?

Flouting all democratic norms, the chief minister of Bihar and speaker of Bihar Legislative Assembly went to aerodromes of Patna and Calcutta on 20th and 21st February to receive Sanjay Gandhi. Sanjay Gandhi toured on Bihar government's plane and a running commentary was relayed on radios and television. They consider Sanjay Gandhi a messiah who shall give them relaxation in taxes and fully help them to crush workers. Industrialists and communists are in the same camp —Stalin and Hitler were also together at the same time.

Even if we ignore Sanjay Gandhi's past deeds, his public image that forms now is humorous. People were heard laughing and saying during his public meetings that he is made of wax. When in a meeting he tried to hide his lack of knowledge and incapability to orate and said that he believed in deeds, not in words, someone commented, "you have talked so much about Maruti and have been talking for the last four years that it would come on roads very soon. But we have not yet got the opportunity to see it." At this even C.I.D. officers, standing nearby, laughed.

Who will believe that Sri Jai Prakash Narain was leading a movement for some personal interest and Sanjay Gandhi has come in politics with a spirit of selfless service and sacrifice to serve the nation ?

Smt. Gore Ill-treated

Smt. Mrinal Gore was arrested on 29th of December in Bombay. Government's behaviour with her has been very disgraceful. Setting aside all rules, she was kept at Akola District jail, where she was the only MISA detenue. No class I female prisoner had been kept at Akola jail ever before, nor is there any arrangement for it there. She was kept alone in a barrack of size $10' \times 40'$ with a door only having no window or other door. The rats and mongooses scrambled over the place day and night. Adjoining her barrack, a leper in advanced stage was confined in a small cell, and used the same latrine which was used by Mrs Gore. Opposite her barrack a dangerous unatic prisoner was kept in a barrack. The lunatic wore no clothes and kept shrieking in shrill voice day and night. The Government had, thus, deliberately lodged Smt. Gore at Akola ail to cause inconvenience, hardship and disease.

Smt. Gore has not been produced before court even after repeated orders from court, for some excuse or other. It is reported that she was then transfered to Dhulia central jail.

She was brought to Bombay on orders from the court, howsoever she was not produced before the court. She was taken back to Dulia again. Throughout this journey from Dhulia to Bombay and back to Dhulia, she was given nothing for her meals and refreshments. Presently she is lodged at Bombay Central jail.

Grandma's Spirit

Bhau Padhye, editor of famous film weekly 'Jhoom', and Abhay Padhye son of a socialist worker Sri Shoshanna Padhye, offered Satyagraha in an interesting way. They distributed pamphlets of 'Jan Sangharsh' in a local train of Bombay, and for this 'offence' they were sentenced for one month's imprisonment. The mother of Bhau Padhye Smt. Sulochana Bai surpassed even her grandson. This old lady of seventy offered satyagraha at Dadar, Bombay. When police took her to her residence before sending her to jail, one of her grandsons asked, "Dadijee, perhaps you had gone to visit temple, then how all this ?" At this Sulochana Bai replied, "Till there is repression and injustice in our nation, jails are like temples for every patriot." Hearing this conversation, tears came in the eyes of police officer who had arrested her.

N.B.   From The Voice 15 March, 1976

"KEEP THE FLAG FLYING"

Following is the text of JP's interview to Geoffery Ostergaard on 30th of December and published in the Swarajya, *England :*

"I have been released", said JP, "but the rest of the things remain as they were before. The Prime Minister does not want to lift the emergency yet. She thinks the time has not yet come, the dangers have not disappeared. I dont see what dangers there are—internal as well as external. I see neither of them to be of such proportions as to justify this kind of situation. I had been warning the country for months, before the 26th June last, of the dangers of a dictatorship developing." And he added, soberly and with no trace of self-glorification : "I feel I have been justified by history." "I do not know," he continued, "if the people of this country, the youth particularly, will accept the situation as it is today. But I do hope that, whatever happens, happens peacefully and that the reconquest of civil liberties and civil freedoms is all peacefully done."

Commenting on Vinoba's statement (of December 25th when he ended his yearlong silence), JP said : "I don't want to say this in any spirit of criticism, but I had hoped that Vinobaji, when he broke his year's silence, would give a lead to the Sarvodaya workers and the Sarvodaya world. But he hasn't done so, and this has been a great disappointment to me, and to many others."

"I was among those who were disappointed," he said. "It seemed to me a highly diplomatic statement." "I may be unfair in saying this," commented JP, "but Vinobaji himself seems to have given up this task of bringing about a revolution by peaceful means. I don't know what he is about now, what his main objective is. Throughout the programmes he has taken up at this last Conference—the one at which he broke his silence—there is very little talk of Gram Swarajya (village self-government). And that used to be the foundation on which he wanted to build up an alternative kind of policy, economy and society. I really don't know if he has his aims defined at all. Personally, I don't think he will be able to do much now."

I then asked JP whether he agreed that his own contribution to the development of the concept of nonviolent revolution was his injection into it of the component of struggle as a basic element.

"I think so," replied JP. "Previously, when Vinobaji was asked, he never denied that there was a place for struggle, but he never showed any way to it. And I felt that whenever a situation arose (calling for struggle), he would try to somhow evade it. So if I have made any contribution, it is probably this : not only in the field of thought—Sarvodaya thought— but also in action, I have actually done something in a small way."

Finally, I asked JP whether he had advice for his friends and supporter in Britain. What could they do to help him and his movement in India ?

JP showed a natural reluctance to advise people thousand of miles away, working in a situation about which he himself had no personal knowledge. But he was quite definite on one point : "The British people should be kept well informed of what was happening in India". And they should be told "the real groundwork of facts, even if they are discouraging.".

"The Indian Government has partly retrieved the situation by its own propaganda offensive in the West, and, may be, many people have been taken in by the notion that the Indian Government was really faced with a serious situation (last

June). I have a vague impression that this has happened in the West already. The difficulty is the Indian Press : the Indian Press has been completely emasculated. ...It would be very difficult for correspondents of the Western Press to go round and find the truth."

Concluding our conversation, JP said—looking at the tape recorder—"Through this machine I send back my best of wishes and my greetings to all my friends in Britain, both British and Indian. My message to my friends there is : Keep the flag flying !"

INTELLECTUALS IN INDIA FEEL FEAR AND CONCERN

NEW YORKS TIMES SPECIAL, MAY 26

New Delhi, May 25 Seminar, a highly literate Indian Journal of opinion, brought out its 200th issue last month, after 17 years of publication. To mark the anniversary, the magazine had scheduled a retrospective and comprehensive look at the directions that India was taking "the assertion of the harshest truths," as the editors put it.

But in today's Intellectual climate here, they could not find contributors willing to write the bold things they wanted to publish, and, so the anniversary issue was devoted instead to such tame fare as an article on Hindu Holy men, and yet another analysis of what was wrong with Calcutta.

"That we are unable to gather material despite considerable trying is a sad and demoralizing fact which no censor or Government edict can obliterate," the seminar editors said, in a statement published in the Magazine.

"Fear has taken hold. Silence is the rule. We are witnessing the slow death of the social sciences in India."

The unsuccessful anniversary issue, and the gloom that it brought to Seminar's editorial offices in New Delhi, is a reflection of what the magazine called "the deteriorating condition of intellectual inquiry in our Land" following the Indian Government's suspension of civil liberties 11 months ago.

And there are other signs on the change all over India, a

vast, diverse country where the exciting clash of ideas used to mark countless conversations every day.

In Calcutta, Satyajit Ray, the famous film maker, has decided that his next picure will steer clear of the biting social realism that characterized his last one because "This is not the time to be making sharp comments on political subjects".

At the universities, the mood has grown cautious, the talk more subdued. A very prominent historian shakes his head and says with anguish :

We'll become semiliterate, insensitive, brutalized.

Section Two

"We're fighting a short of rear-guard action," the Professor explained. "They'd love to have us signing petitions for them, writing letters to the guardian or the economist saying things are just fine here in India. But inground and keeping quiet : It's all we can do."

Government intellectuals on India feel "somewhat lonely. In our position, now that the journalists have knuckled under, the politicans have caved in or gone to Jail, and the lawyers have been over-whelmed by the rulings of pliant judges."

"We're still holding firm, but I'm afraid the time will come pretty soon when the Government will no longer be satisfied to have us merely silent. They'll want active support, and what will happen then, I don't know."

This professor and others reported that there was increasing talk of Professorial "codes of conduct," which would guard against political dissent. And in the classroom, when the subject is politics, caution has become the rule.

"If you're teaching about the Indian Independence movement in the 1940's, for example, you bend over backward to stress that it was domination by a foreign power—Britain—that the freedom fighters were fighting against, and not just the imposition of laws they considered unjust," one lecturer explained.

"But there are still ways around the new Strictures," another Professor said. "You make a lecture saying what was awful about Senator Mccarthy or President Nixon, when you're really talking about India 1976 and everyone knows it "

In what is viewed as a pressure tactic, the Government is said to have spepped up its examinations of past income-tax returns of dissident Professors, and Prime Minister Gandhi, in a number of speeches, has adopted a position that some of them perceive as anti-intellectual.

"The young and the intellectuals are usually anti-establishment," the Prime Minister said a few weeks ago, "This is all good, until it becomes destructive. But the minority must realize that is has no right to bulldoze the majority."

She also chastized the intellectuals for their dependence on ideas they had learned from the West, particularly Britain and the United States, instead of seeking "Indian solutions" to Indian problems.

PEOPLE

9 August 1976

Vanquished ? Never !

N. G. Goray

It was but proper that the Prime Minister should have given to the people her own evaluation of the national scene after a full year of emergency. After all she alone had master minded this distortion in the history of India's democracy and she alone could be held responsible for the good as well as the bad that has happened in this country since emergency was promulgated. After the sweeping poll victory of her Congress Party in 1971, it was she and none else who had the last word on every-thing. Very quickly the concept of the Prime Minister being the first among equals had got eroded and she was looked upon as the leader, unparalled and uncomparable. Then came emergency and she became Amba, Durga and the Delphic Oracle all rolled into one. She was considered wiser than the wisest in the land, she had the Parliament at her command, neither any law nor the courts could touch her. Never in the long long history of our country had any monarch or hero enjoyed such total authority. Therefore when such a potentate with unlimited authority condencends to speak all of us should listen with utmost respect and then come to our own conclusion, of course without forgetting even for a moment that reactions of ordinary citizens like us have ceased to have any significance.

Evidently the Prime Minister's whole effort had only two objectives, one primary and the other secondary. Let us take these objectives in the reverse order. The secondary objective was to convince the people in other countries as well as people here that India has come out of the jungle of economic crisis, the acute economic situation of 1975 being now a thing of the past. It will be interesting to recall in this connection that when a couple of years back commodity prices in India were running amok, atleast one of the arguments from the government side used to be that it was a world phenomenon and unavoidably we were affected by it. But now no spokesman of the establishment has the candidness to mention countries like Japan who have also staged remarkably recovery from the near fatal blow they had received from the OPEC block without resorting to emergency. The attempt here is to create an impression that India alone has succeeded while in other countries the crisis continues unabated. This is not to suggest that in 1975-76 India has not registered significant progress. Remarkable production targets have been achieved particularly in the field of public sector undertakings like steel, coal, electricity,cement and railways. On the food-front an all time high productivity has been reached. However it is necessary to think separately of the industrial production and production in the agricultural sector. The disquiet on the industrial front was not the cause but the result of inflation, which again was brought about inter-alia by deliberate under-production, hoarding, profiteering and last but not the least by unchecked smuggling. A paralell economy had become part of our life. Will it be possible for the Prime Minister herself to deny that opposition parties with-out exception were urging her and her government to adopt stringent measures against this economic anarchy and forr ea-sons best known to them it was her own partymen who were dragging their feet ? Had she or her establishment the will, the vicious circle of discontent, inflation and blackmoney could have been smashed long before the emergency.

As regards the food production, though the government will not accept it, the fact remains that the break-through in our production was mainly due to the exceptionally model behavi-our of the monsoon in the Kharif as well as in the rabi season. In a poor and ever-hungry country like India, to have good monsoon is like winning not half but three fourths of the battle against inflation. Whether this observation of ours is an inst-ance of carping criticism or otherwise will be proved beyond doubt if this year's monsoon becomes erratic, which God for-bid. Therefore it is too early to celebrate our victory over the economic crisis. Problems of population growth, unemployment and mass poverty continue to haunt our economy and taking advantage of our complacency they may pounce upon us any moment.

But the Prime Minister's whole essay was really aimed at what was described a little before as her primary objective : which was to hold the opposition parties responsible for the economic debacle and exploit the crisis with a view to concen-trating all power in her hands. The Prime Minister knows better than any one else that her accusations against the opposi-tion of resorting to or preparing for violent mass action, of hav-ing foreign money and connections, of distorting the press, are nothing but figments of imagination. But all this baseless pro-paganda was necessary to justify the unleashing the hounds of emergency against thousands of patriotic men and women. This art of the white lie has been now perfected to such an extent that repeated assertions by the opposition leaders to the effect that they stand for democracy and peaceful means are uncere-moniously killed by the censor. Is it any wonder that the censor dares to act in such a manner when the Prime Minister in an important statement such as this observes "The opposition has been subdued but not vanquished." Has any Prime Minister of any democratic country in the World talked in terms so hostile and so ruthless ? But our Prime Minister has left us in no doubt as to what her objective is : it is to vanquish the opposition.

May we say to her equally clearly : "Madam, vanquished we shall never be."

N. B. After *Janata* being banned and its printing press also ordered not to print *Janata*, "People" came into being. Socialists in Bombay mainly organised this fortnightly publication.

A DICTATOR'S PRISONER
by George Fernandes

My arrest took place at about 3.45 p. m. on June 10, 1976 at Calcutta. At 4.30 p. m. I was taken to the office of the Deputy Commissioner of Police (CID), where till 6 a. m. the following day I had to sit on a hard wooden chair while Police and intelligence officials took turns to keep me awake throughout the night.

An order of Detention under MISA issued by the Delhi Administration was served on me at 3. a. m. on June 11, at 7 a. m. I was at Dum Dum Airport and was flown to Delhi in an India Air Force Transporter, AII 12—which had earlier flown into Calcutta with my detention order.

Guards and pistol-totting Police officials maintained an intimidating watch on me all through the period I was in Police custody.

The plane touched down at Delhi Airport at 10. 05 a. m. and was brought to a halt on one of the runways where carloads and vanloads of Policemen had already arrived.

I was driven in one of the cars to Delhi's ancient Red Fort where I was to stay locked up in a dark, ill-ventillated dungeon till the 14th, except when I was taken out for interrogation by batches of the officers of the Central Intelligence Bureau (RAW) and the Central Bureau of Investigation (CBI).

NOT ALLOWED TO HAVE A BATH

From June 10 to June 14, I was not allowed to have even a bath although the Police officials kept on telling me that I would be a allowed to have one. I was not allowed even to keep my handkerchief with which to wipe the sweat off in this hot oven of a lock-up, not an old newspaper with which to fan myself. My bed consisted of a dirty blanket spread over the cement floor.

ABUSES HURLED, VIOLENCE THREATENED

On June 14, I was moved to CBI offices where I was housed in a hall with intimidatory guards placed inside and outside the room. Insipid and stale food from some wayside restaurant was served to me throughout this period under Police custody.

Immediately after my arrest I told the Police that I would make no statement whatsoever in regard to my movements and activities during the period of June 25, 1975 to June 10, 1976. I made the same statement before the Metropolitan Magistrate, Delhi before whom I was produced on June 11. That may have provoked the Police to convert their interrogation sessions into demonstration of their capacity to indulge in obscene language and hurl abuse. While the more sophisticated among the interrogators held out veiled threats of violence against my person, the uncultured among them had the nerve to threaten me with it then and there. It was another matter that they soon realised that they were barking up on the wrong tree.

NOT ALLOWED SLEEP

While again the Police could never summon enough courage to have me handcuffed when I was being shifted from one place to another they kept heavy chains and handcuffs in the vain hope of intimidating me. All through this period of interrogation I was hardly allowed to sleep.

At 5 p. m. on June 23, I was driven to Delhi's Tihar Jail where after being confined to the ante-room of the office of the jail Superintendent till 8.30 p. m., I was driven in a closed vehicle to the jail yard where I was kept in solitary confinement.

HUMILIATING SEARCH AT HISSAR

Around noon on June 25, a Police van drew alonside the gate of my yard and I was driven to Hissar, some 100 miles North

West of Delhi. On Admission in the Hissar District Jail I was subjected to an humiliating search of my person and my belongings with the Jail staff trying to discover if I was not carrying something dangerous or clandestine, hidden in the private parts of my body.

EXPOSED TO HEAT AND RAIN

I was marched off to a barrack with Iron gratings allaround and no protection whatsoever against heat or rain. Hot summer winds piercing through the open grill almost made my brain melt allowing me no rest during day or night. The early Westerly monsoon turned my yard into a swimming pool. The Jail officials refused to provide a covering on ground of security. Powerful electric bulbs burnt in my barrack throughout the night while the entire yard was flood-lit giving it the appearance of a flood-lit sports ground. My cot stood chained to the grating, perhaps to symbolise my status in a dictator's prison.

SOLZHENITSYN'S BOOKS WITHHELD

A 24 hour guard was mounted at the terrace of the adjoining office block. A set of six books by Alexander Solzhentisyn which I had earlier carried with me were withheld and my appeals to the State Govt to release them were not even acknowledged.

INTERVIEWS REFUSED, LETTERS WITHHELD

My letters to my parents, wife and child, mother-in-law and brothers were not sent to them nor were theirs delivered to me with the exception of letters from my mother-in-law and, from my wife (two only), and in September two from my brother. Although rules permit interviews once every fortnight with relations and friends, my mother-in-law's request for interviews was not considered untill August 19, when she was allowed to interview me for an hour. My mother and brother were allowed to meet me only on August 31. A second interview with me was allowed to my mother-in-law on September 16.

A few books brought by my mother-in-law concerning economics and politics on her second visit were also withheld and my repeated applications for interviews with my lawyers were not even acknowledged.

A daily allowance of Rs 6-00 (35 pence) was allowed to me to manage my kitchen and all my dietary needs.

(The above is the text of a letter from Mr George Fernandes received by one of his friends in London—Editor Evening view, Oct 26, 76).

Labour's Concern

London—Grave concern on denials of basic human rights to 600 million citizens of India has been conveyed to the Indian High Commission here on behalf of the British Labour Party.

The concern was conveyed by a delegation of the Labour Party which met the Indian High Commissioner here a few days ago.

At its annual Conference at Blackpool, the British Labour Party approved of a statement made in the Programme presented to it on India in the following terms :

"The establishment of the state of emergency in India has been a matter of deep concern to the Labour party which has long admired and supported Indian democrats and socialists.

"We hope that these moves away from democracy are only temporary and that soon there will be return to full democratic rights in India."

Circles close to Labour Party National Executive make no secret of their dismay at the continued denial of basic human rights in India and the proposed changes in Indian Constitution which in the view of many among them would institutionalise the dicatorial measures undertaken under the current emergency.

Indian High Commissioner had before the Blackpool Conference made his best efforts to have these two mild paras on India deleted from the party programme, but in vain.

THE NEW YORK TIMES, THURSDAY, OCTOBER 28, 1976

Mrs. Gandhi Confirms Some Died In Protests Over Sterilization Drive

By William Borders

Special to the New York Times

New Delhi, Oct 27—Prime Minister Indira Gandhi disclosed today that some people had been killed in clashes with the police growing out of India's campaign of mass sterilization.

In a speech in Parliament, the Prime Minister confirmed reccurring rumors of rioting by people protesting the sterilization program, which many say is the most vigorous in the country's history. But she gave no details.

"Some deaths have taken place, due to firing," she said, in the course of a speech defending a set of far-reaching constitutional amendments that her Government has proposed. "On the other hand, several policemen and other citizens were killed by violent groups even though they were not connected with the family planning compaign."

The Prime Minister called the riot deaths "tragic," and again emphasized that "we do not approve of compulsory sterilization."

"But we do believe," she continued, "that the program of sterilization and the adoption of all other known effective measures for the control of population are important and most urgent."

Prime Minister Gandhi's discussion of the family-planning program, which occupied only a few minutes in a 25-minute speech, was apparently prompted by oppositions' statements earlier in the debate that 40 persons had been killed in clashes with the police in a heavily Moslem area of Uttar Pradesh, north of New Delhi.

Ebrahim Sulaiman Sait, a Moslem League member, had declared that "people have been butchered and are being murdered in this country" by zealots of the family-planning program. "I am very happy that the Prime Minister has said that there would be no compulsion of sterilization," Mr. Sait said. "But the officers are going against it and they are not abiding by the directions of the Prime Minister."

Today Mr. Sait and six other opposition Members of Parliament drove to Muzaffaranagar, 50 miles north of here, and came back with an estimate that several dozen people had been killed and 150 wounded in incidents earlier this month.

The group of lawmakers reported that after talking to some local residents they had been turned away by local police there, with the official warning that further investigation "would not be conducive to law and order under the present circumstances."

Because some members of India's Moslem minority consider birth control inimical to their religion, the New Delhi Government has been at great pains, in its family-planning promotion, to avoid which parties have sought to create an atmosphere of misunderstanding and fear," Mrs. Gandhi said. "As we know, fear leads to irrational action. Therefore, when a situation of confrontation is deliberately created, there are tragic consequences."

Members of the small parliamentary opposition have been staging a boycott to protest censorship and the continued imprisonment of two dozen of their colleagues. Referring to the boycotting members, in her defense of the proposed constitutional changes, the Prime Minister said :

"They demanded full discussion of the amendment, yet they kept away from Parliament, which is the supreme forum of discussion. To noncooperate with Parliament is to noncooperate with the people."

MOSLEMS REPORT AT LEAST 50 DEAD

Muzaffarnagar, India, Oct. 27 (AP)—Several Moslem leaders said today that at least 50 persons and as many as 150 were killed when the police opened fire last week on villagers protesting the Government's sterilization policy.

The district magistrate for this predominantly Moslem region acknowledged in an interview that "a minor problem, a small scuffle" had taken place, but he denied any shots had been fired and denied anyone had been wounded or killed.

SWARAJ

No. 17   Price 15 P.

For democratic self government in India.
"Democracy is not a state in which people act like sheep. Under democracy, individual liberty of opinion and action is jealously guarded." — Mahatma Gandhi.

Political Detainee

People in India, more so those of us who are political detenues in jail, have been denied access to the "hostile" western press or opinion. But any favourable comment on, or expressed support to the dictatorship of Mrs. Gandhi is extensively reported in the managed and controlled Indian Press.

One such report that has been publicised extensively is the speech of Jennie Lee at an Indian Independence Day meeting in London. She is reported to have reiterated her favourable views of Mrs. Gandhi and her regime, and how she was justified in denying the basic freedoms to the Indian people for their own sake. Such statements coming from Jennie, who with Aneurin Bevan, was source of admiration and pride to young Indian democrats and socialists, are no longer a surprise as she has singing this refrain during and after her visit to India last year. But her statement that she has personal knowledge of the treatment of political prisoners and that they are treated very well, is a gratuitous insult.

We do not know how Jennie acquired her personal knowledge. Most certainly not by meeting political prisoners or visiting jails where they are lodged. We wish she had visited us in Tihar Central Jail in the capital of the country which is administered and controlled directly by the Central Government and seen for herself the state of affairs.

No rules govern our detention, advisedly, we presume, because then it would be officially known the precise nature of the conditions of our detention, and the facilities given to us. We bathe under a tap in the open rain, summer, or winter. Lavatories are filthy and inadequate. Prisoners are packed three to a cell and have no facilities for reading or writing. Drains stagnate for months breeding mosquitoes and emiting foul smells. The municipal authorities would not certify the wards we live as fit for human habitation. Food is unbalanced, inadequate and cooked and served in unhygenic conditions. After assuming responsibility for maintenance we are given one pair of clothes once in a while at the discretion of the administration. Medical facilities exist in name only. The Jail hospital centre often has no thermometers. The doctors do not use a stethoscope or B. P. instruments to examine patients. and dole out an all purpose analgesic for all aches and pains. Serious cases have deteriorated because of neglect. Resultant deaths have not been uncommon. What relief we have received is through courts who have fortunaheld that no punitive condition can be introduced into what is said to be preventive detention. As a result, however, we have had to suffer vengeful penalties.

Senility and surrender have and do bring relief. As we do not propose to submit to arbitrary treatment despite repeated representation, we propose to go on relay :hunger strike from 1st September.

This then is the general treatment meted out to us in detention. Individuals have in addition been singled out for beatings and punishment. Recently, a member of the ruling congress and a sitting member of the Metropolitan Council was assaulted by convicts at the request of and in the presence of the Superintendant of the Jail. Police brutality on the streets and in lock-ups is so common that we have to accept it as a risk that political dissentees have to run. A recent instance is of a brother of George Fernandez who was recently given the full treatment for three weeks, càusing fractures and permanent damage to his vital organs. Students of Delhi University were picked up a couple of days before 26th June and were given a severe and continous beating for ten days in police lock-ups and otherwise tortured. One of them was brought in here bleeding internally and is still unwell.

And yet, Jennie Lee claims to have knowledge of humane treatment. We suggest that she visits India again, not at the inviation of the Government of India whose hospitality she enjoyed last year, but on behalf of Amnesty International. Amnesty, we are sure would finance her trip. Because of her often proclaimed support of Mrs. Gandhi, she should have no difficulty in obtaining the permisson to visit us, a permission that has so far been refused to others who have tried to ascertain the truth. She would then see for herself the truth or otherwise of Mrs. Gandhi's claims, reinforced by her certificate, that we are treated as human beings.

Tihar Jail, New Delhi.

August 8th 1976.   Political Detenue.

Passport Seizure Rouses Unions

Affiliates will be well aware of the conditions of repression which exist in India as a direct result of the seizure by Mrs Gandhi of dictatorial powers of government.

Much of her attention has been concentrated on the Trade Union movement as she can see, in the existence of organisations devoted to the advancement of social justice and the eradication of governmental abuse and corruption, a threat to her power. Where and when it has been possible for her to imprison those opposed to her malpractices she has done so.

Fortunately, not all of her critics are within the grasp of her police and this includes the ITF, which has been one of her strongest critics, particularly following the arrests of J. P. Narayan and George Fernandes, the President of the All India Railwaymen's Federation. Nevertheless, the Indian Government appears to be under the impression that it can silence ITF criticism by attacking one of the officers of the ITF, who happens to be a citizen of India.

Mohammad Hoda has wørked for the ITF since 1965 (since 1968 as the Secretary for the Civil Aviation Section) and that appears in thc eyes of Mrs Gandhi, to be a crime which warrants the seizure by the Indian High Commission in London of Mr Hoda's passport which was impounded on 2 August on instructions from Delhi. In return he was offered a document which would enable him to return to India to undoubted imprisonment without specific charges being made against him and without the right of appeal to any court.

Despite several telephone calls to the Indian High Commission the only reason given for impounding Hoda's passport was "in the interest of the general public".

We would like Mrs Gandhi to know that, so far as the work of the ITF is concerned, this particular example of dictatorial venom is only a minor irritant, but for Mohammad Hoda this puts him in the position of being an exile from his homeland. This should serve to strengthen the resolve of affiliated unions to assist the Indian people and trade unions to achieve a society in which social justice prevails, in which abuse and corruption have no place and in which freedom of speech and democratic action are not denied.

Affiliates are requested to give publicity to this Circular in their trade union publications and the Press of their countries.

DURING THE LONG DARK NIGHT

Reproduced below is a partial list of oral censorship orders (compiled and released by Janata Party.) It reveals the sort of doublespeak and illegality indulged in by the Government during the months of emergency. It exposes the claims repeated day in and day out by Government spokesman that censorship had been withdrawn and that only a set of guidelines "voluntarily" framed and "freely" accepted by the Press was at work. These orders were never given in writing, but delivered over the telephone, and non-compliance was visited with punishment. The nature of these fiats reveals how little they had to do with any pretence for the security of the country aud its integrity. Contrary to the law, the Press was forbidden from publishing even certain court judgements and orders, including several instances in which the newspapers themselves were a party.

Censorship and doublespeak

The Censor's almost daily "precensorship guidelines" were given orally—over the telephone. Infringement is visited with punishment. Precensorship has been used to suppress or 'moderate' Court proceedings and judgements, black out parliamentary proceedings, prevent the public from knowing the Opposition's point of view on major issues, cover up official embarrassments of various kinds, favour select individuals and 'expose' others. Comment or sometimes 'adverse comment' was banned. News and comment on the transfer of High Court judges were blacked out. The proceedings in the case of Mr Tul Mohan Ram, the Congress MP facing trial on forgery charges in the Pondicherry 'licence scandal' case, were also subject to precensorship.

Sometimes, only the Samachar report is permitted to be used. Samachar is now a Government agency despite Mr Shulka's pained denials. It was a forced merger 'voluntarily' obtained at pistol point through blatant Government pressure. The initial idea of outright nationalisation of the four private news agencies was abandoned, but official control remains. Even the registration of the Samachar Society in January 1976 was formally witnessed (signed) by a Deputy Secretary of the I & B Ministry. Samachar's association with the Non-Aligned News Poll has been arranged and is being operated by/through the Government. So Samachar too has become part of the censorship/news management apparatus, notionally independent but in fact a tool.

The following is a partial compilation of oral censorship orders.

Oral Censor Orders

Code : P for Precensorship ; B for Ban ; NM for News
Management

Serial No. & Date		Subject or Item	Code
September 1975			
1	9	All reports, features, photos & captions about demolitions of JHUGGIS in Delhi.	P
2	9	No reports, comments, articles or edits on bonus until further notice.	B
3	10	Reports and comments on Bangladesh.	P
4	24	No ads from either North or South Korea.	B
5	24	Token strikes on bonus	B
6	24	Afzal Beg's speeches on J & K's links with Centre	B
October 1975			
7	8	No reports on today's disturbances in Tihar Jail, Delhi	B
8	20	No adverse comment or report on Godavari waters accord between the CMs of Maharashtra and Andhra	NM
9	20	No comment on Presidential order on 6-point formula	B
10	29	Delhi High Court judgement striking down Administration order restricting interview with MISA detenus	B
11	30	Justice Khanna's judgement on the Bombay appeal case	B
November 1975			
12	4	No edits on Bangladesh for the present	B
13	7	Edits on Bangladesh now subject to precensorship	P
14	22	JP's visit to Bombay is subject to precensorship. No photographs to be used.	P&B

Serial No. & Date	Subject or Item	Code

December 1975

15	3	No report or pictures of DDA demolition around Jama Masjid are allowed except those issued or authorised by DDA. Edits must be cleared	P&NM
16	10	Details of the Congress Working Committee draft resolution not to be published	B
17	7	No report about Badr Abdul Aziz of the Saudi royal family, now in Amritsar, to appear	B

January 1976

18	mid-Jan	All stories from Madras especially statements by Karunanidhi or statements in Assembly to be cleared	P
19	„	News about JP, his health and comments thereon	P
20	22	Today's walk-out in Rajya Sabha on Bonus Bill	B
21	31	The question at Wild Life Board meeting as to why a certain Maharaja's brother was given a hunting licence.	B

February 1976

22	2	Bangladesh news bearing on India must be cleared	P
23	3	Tulmahan Ram case copy to be precesored	P
24	13	Reports on questions in J&K Assembly on MISA arrests	P
25	29	NUJ resolution on working journalist's interim relief and formulation of wage board	P
26	26	Karunanidhi's petition challenging imposition of President's rule in Tamilnadu in Madras and Delhi High Court is not to be published	B
27	27	Morarji's examination today on commission in the Gandhi murder case	P

Serial No. & Date		Subject or Item	Code
		March 1976	
28	5	All reports on Tulmohan Ram case	P
29	8	No edits on Indo-Canadian (nuclear) talks at this stage	B
30	9	Rajya Sabha starred Question 60 on Philips Petroleum International Corporation	B
31	15	Reports & comments on imposition of President's rule in Gujarat	P
32	15	The Finance Minister rested for a while in the course of his budget speech ; not to be mentioned	B
33	17	Answers on parliamentary question on censorship, court case on censorship, and Prevention of Publication of objectionable Matter Act	B
34	17	Supplementaries to Lok Sabha question 133 on generation of nuclear power not to be used; main reply may be used	B
35	17	All reports on Tihar jail	P
36	23	Gujarat judgement on Bhoomiputra case	B
37	23	Maharashtra opposition leader's comment on Emergency	B
38	29	Reference if any, to censorship at AINEC meeting at Patna. No edit, comment on censorship	B
39	29	Junior lawyers march to Delhi High Court	B
40	30	Reports on ONGC oil exploration contract with Iran (or Iraq ?) to be cleared	P
41	31	Samachar report on Lok Sabha Question on Cola Cola Export Corporation may be used. Otherwise precensorship	NM
		April 1976	
42	1	Rajeswara Rao's press conference at Bhopal today	B
43	1	No criticism of family planning programme ; this includes letters to the Editor	NM

Serial No. & Date		Subject or Item	Code
44	2	No report on Indian Press Counsellor in Dacca being expelled	B
45	7	Various Congress leaders are issuing statements supporting the FP programme ; must be cleared	P
46	8	Nothing to be published on release of Farakka waters	B
47	8	The authorised version of Acharya Bhave's statements at the Acharya's conference at Paunar in Jan. 1976 issued by Sriman Narayan to be cleared	P
48	8	Resignation of B. K. Karanjia from the Film Corporation and appointment of a new chairman	B
49	14	Reports on FP/vasectomy follow-up centre set up by Lok Kalyan Samiti (in Delhi)	B
50	19	DDA demolition activity around Turkman Gate	P
51	21	Censor is issuing the official version of the Turkman Gate incident. This is not to be cleared played up and should be used with the suggested heading. Any other heading must be cleared.	
52	22	Play down or abstain from criticism of the current negotiations between Pakistan and Egypt	NM
53	23	Nothing to appear about Hardinge Hostel incident in Calcutta even if it comes up in Court	B
54	23	Bangladesh Mission (Delhi) statement on border incident today	B
55	25	Reports including speeches & resolutions at National Conference meeting at Jammu today	
56	26	No report is to be published on Monday about the arrival of a Pakistani delegation in Delhi. An official statement is due on Tuesday	NM
57	28	Sanjay Gandhi today walked out of a function	

Serial No. & Date		Subject or Item	Code
		held in his honour. No report or pictures to be published	B
58	28	No report of a small fire that broke out at TV Centre (Delhi) to be published	B
	May 1976		
59	1	No edit or comment on Nepal King's visit to Tibet	B
60	1	Any news of a reported air crash near Srinagar	P
61	5	Only Samachar to be used on PM's statement in Lok Sabha on law and order situation in Bihar in reply to Misra's question.	NM
62	5	Incidents about Bhagalpur Jail, Bihar	B
63	6	No criticism of Sadat	NM
64	6	No criticism of Bhutto nor any anti-Pak propaganda in view of the proposed Indo-Pakistan talks	NM
65	7	Nothing should be published for three days until May 9 about the demolition of the Threatre Communication Building, Connaught Place, New Delhi	B
66	8	News and comments on US Nuclear Regulatory Commission's hearing on India's application for enriched uranium fuel replacement for Tarapur	P
67	12	Report on interception of a car on Tilak Marg, New Delhi	B
68	14	Use only Samchar on Sarkaria inquiry Commission ; own copy must be cleared.	P&NM
69	18	Press conference by O.P. Tyagi of Jana Sangh on party working commitee resolution	P
70	20	May use the Canadian External Affairs Minister's statement (made in Ottawa yesterday) on abrogation of nuclear agreement with Iudia. But it should be preceded by Chavan's statement in Parliament	NM

Serial No. & Date		Subject or Item	Code
71	22	News of Begum Vilayat Mahal squatting at New Delhi railway station	B
72	22	Rajya Sabha starred question 304 on searches at the office and residence of Vinay K Shah of Bombay	B
73	27	Use only Samachar story on V.C. Shukla's statement in Rajya Sabha today on code of ethics for Journalists in reply to Bhupesh Gupta	NM
74	28	No publication of London report of arrest of actress Verghese—later corrected to Nargis—for shoplifting	B
75	30	Indian diplomat's walk-out from Bhutto's banquet in Peking not to be played up	NM
	June 1976		
76	1	Bhutto's press conference in Peking and Sino-Pak joint communique not to be played up	NM
77	1	Pictures of the dacoit surrender	P
78	2	News/comment on the transfer of High Court judges	B
79	2	No news about Acharya Vinoba Bhave's proposed indefinite fast from Sept 11 on cow-slaughter ban nor any reference to this to be lifted from the Sarvodaya journal (Maitri), nor any statement by the Acharya or his secretary	B
80	2	Nothing about B.D. Goenka (corrected on June 4 to D.P. Goenka) the industrialist to be used	B
81	3	Parliament Street, New Delhi, fire not to be played up and no picture to be used	NM&B
82	4	Use only Samachar on Arab student's demonstration in Delhi in bid to occupy Syrian Embassy (in protest against Syrian intervention in Lebanon). No pictures to be shown	MN&B

Serial No. & Date		Subject or Item	Code
83	8	Transfer of an Andhra Pradesh High Court judge	B
84	5	No news/comment on jute export or the jute industry until middle of next week	B
85	9	In any report on Bansi Lal's speech in Rohtak today, delete any reference to future relations or conflict with Pakistan	NM
86	10	No comment on measures taken by Govt to regulate production of jute goods	B
87	16	Articles and comments on forthcoming meeting of non-aligned nations to discuss the creation of the NA News Pool	B
88	16	JP's letter to PM about her contribution from PM's Relief Fund for the purchase of dialyser for JP	B
		Revised order on above : Only use Samachar	NM
89	22	Reports on Boeing payoffs	P
90	23	No anti-Pakistan references permitted	NM
91	24	No comment on Parathasarathi's goodwill visit to Bangladesh	B

July 1976

92	1	No critical comment on Mizo accord with Centre	NM
93	2	Precensorship on any statement by Laldenga, the MNF leader	P
94	2	News on national symposium on films and TV	B
95	8	Until July 14 no news, comments, pictures on Isreali raid on Entebbe Airport, Uganda. In particular no justification of or eulogising the raid	B & NM
96	10	Security Council debate on Entebbe raid	P
97	10	Samachar (UPI) story on Sadat's interview comments on Gaddafi's role in attempted Sudan coup not to be published from any source	B

Serial No. & Date		Subject or Item	Code
98	12	The exchanges on bilateral issues at the NA News Pool conference and walk-out from the conference are subject to censorship. Samachar copy cleared	P&NM
99	15	Cancellation of passport of Kumar Poddar wealthy Hindenberg (?) businessman & permenent US resident	B
100	16	JP's movements not to be published in interest of law and order	B
101	17	All news comments and edits on the price situation	P
102	17	Gujarat Govt's action in countermanding earlier order confiscating the Navjeevan Press, Ahmedabad	B
103	19	Reports of members of the J&K Assembly crossing the floor or forming a separate bloc	P
104	28	No adverse news, comments or edits on FP programme of education cess in UP.	NM
105	29	No news or comment on J&K Assembly debate on Thursday on Ordinances issued by the State Governor	B
106	29	No news or comment on Delhi High Court order on Statesman petition with regard to a censor order	B
August 1976			
107	1	Statement of National Review Committee on constitutional amendments	B(?)
108	1	K.S. Hegde's reference to constitutional amendments in 2nd Narasu Memorial Lecture at Hyderabad	B(?)
109	10	A statement by Radhakrishna Bajaj on behalf of Acharya Vinoba Bhave being circulated by Samachar should be published prominently	NM
110	10	Items about Acharya Bhave subject to censorship	P

Serial No. & Date		Subject or Item	Code
111	10	No news or comment about Subramaniam Swamy, Rajya Sabha member, having raised a point of order today in Parliament should be used	B
112	12	Lok Sabha question and answers on uniform jail reforms and supplementaries, especially those relating to hunger strike by detenus in Presidency Jail, Calcutta, not to be used	B
113	20	News and articles about likely revelation of President's rule in Gujarat & speculation about ministry-making in the State	P
114	24	Jamiat-ul-Ulem-i-Hind resolution on Syriam intervention in Lebanon	P
115	24	Correspondence between West Bengal Chief Minister and Jyoti Basu, CPI (M) leader	B
116	26	No ref. to CIA activities by PM in Parliament. Revised order : PM's intervention in Parliament on foreign intelligence and any reference to CIA activities in that question not to be used	B
117	27	No speculative stories or any report or comment likely to create a scare regarding foodgrains or price situation should be published	B
118	27	Report of today's trial of Kanailal Sarkar before SDM, Alipore	B
119	28	J&K Ministers' statements on affairs in the State (political controversy between National Conference & Congress.)	B

September 1976

120	1	Precensorship on today's proceedings in Parliament (44th Constitutional Amendmend Bill introduced and Opposition leaders allowed to state reasons for their abstaining from sessions)	P
121	2	PAC Report on purchase of furnaces from US for use in Ordnance factories	B

Serial No. & Date	Subject or Item	Code
123 6	Gazette order circulated by Censor's office regarding notification dated Sept. 2 imposing precensorship on all news and comments on family planning	P
124 6	News and comments of Jethmalani, President, Bar Council of India, now in the US.	P
125 8	Reports on today's incidents at Sealdah and Ultadanga	B
126 9	Demand for a corridor between Ambala and Chandigarh in the Punjab Transport Minister's statement on the Punjab-Haryana bus dispute must be deleted	B
127 11	No story based on so-called eye-witness accounts of hijaking or any reference to the identity, nationality or intentions of the hijackers should be published. All stories to be precensored.	B&P
128 16	All news reports or comments on Philips Petroleum Company should be referred to Censor.	P
129 21 :	NYT's William Border's interview with Kewal Singh shouldn't be published.	B

September 1976

130 20	DMK walkout of Sarkaria Commission should not be mantioned.	B
131 20 :	Supreme Court proceedings on a writ petition of Nagi Reddi (late) against CM of AP regarding contempt of court should not be published	B&NM
132 22 :	Story of Jaigarh treasure hunt should be precensored	P
133 29 :	Do not publish speculative or sensational stories about Sundar dacoit, as these may hamper investigation. Only what is given out officially should be published	NM
134	No report of the release of two members of Ananda Bazar staff is to be published	B&NM

Serial No. & Dale	Subject or Item	Code

October 1976

135 5 :	Fernandes statement in court in dynamite case not to be used	B
136 5 :	Kindly do not publish any news about the strike in Dhariwal mills	B
137 7 :	Only official version of Indo-Pak talks. No editorial comment on the same.	NM
139 13 :	(Cal) KK Maitra, MLA, made a disparaging statement on FP programme. should not use it.	B
138 12 :	Any special report on Sheikh Abdullah's press conference subject to precensorship.	P
140 14 :	Story on reported bomb scare where the Defence Minister was staying should not be published	B
141 16 :	All news reports and comments on US arms sale to Iran is subject to precensorship	P
142 20 :	Nepal PM's statement or speeches on restrictions in border areas of India on Nepalese citizens subject to censorship	P
143 21 :	Naga Peace Council delegation's visit to UK to meet Phizo may not please be published.	B
144 25 :	Swearing in of new Ministers of Kashmir which did not take place as scheduled. Only J & K press note can be published. No commentative report.	B&NM
145 29 :	Nothing contemptuous about Arab tourists should be published.	B&NM

November 1976

146 4 :	Any story on Gujarat High Court proceedings on transfer of judges should be submitted to precensorship	P&NM
147 15 :	Nothing on the trouble in Jalpaiguri should be published	B
148 19 :	Nityananda De, Sanat Roy and Nurul Islam	

Serial No. & Date	Subject or Item	Code
	issued a statement against CM. This should not be published (Calcutta).	**B**
149 22 :	Speech of Mrs Ambika Soni and Mahesh Joshi at AICC session should not be used. For PM's speech please take Samachar copy as model	**P&NM**
150 30 :	In reports on the supplementary budget 1976-77 in the State Assembly in Bhopal, any reference to the provision of subscription for National Herald should be deleted.	**B&NM**

December 1976

151 Dec. 1 :	No report or comment on Indo-UK air services talks now in progress should be published at this stage.	**NM**
152 15 :	Orissa stories are not to be cleared by censors in Delhi, but in Bhubaneswar, if needed.	**P**
153 17 :	No statement or speech on apartheid by Mr A. N. Mulla, Chairman of South African Indian Council, should be allowed to appear in your esteemed paper.	**B**
154 19 :	With immediate effect, all stories, comments, reports relating to intra-party rivalries within the Congress and between the Youth Congress and the All India Congress should not be used. This applies particularly to West Bengal, Orissa and Kerala. In case of doubt, please refer the stories to the censors.	**P&NM**
155 9 :	Any statement by Chief Ministers or Congress leaders regarding the celebration of Mr Sanjay Gandhi's birthday on Dec 14 should not be published.	**NM**
156 10 :	Kindly do not publish any report on the supply of US jet fighters (Skyhawks) to India. Only official announcement must be used.	**P**
157 23 :	Statement of (Miss) Hulgol in the dynamite case magistrate's Court should not be publishd	**B**

8

Serial No. & Date	Subject or Item	Code
158 23 :	Pak Embassy's functions, one at the India International Centre, another the presentation of Jinnah medals at Rashtrapati Bhavan on Dec.25. There might be other functions also. Stories on these functions have to be given in low key.	NM
159 23 :	Stories and articles on insurgency in the North-Eastern region should not be published without clearance from the censor.	B & NM
160 28 :	Nothing may kindly be carried about the collapse of the TV tower under construction at Raipur. (12-55 hrs)	B & NM
161 28 :	(1607 hrs) Samachar report on Raipur TV tower can be used.	NM

January 1977

162 4 :	Statement by Mulla of African National Congress who represents the aspirations of the African people may be fully published. He made a statement at Bhopal and is likely to make another at Indore shortly. The earlier advice on A.N Mulla, Chairman of South African Indian Council, a stooge organisation of the SA Government stands. His statement should not be published.	NM&B
163 8 :	All stories on intra-party affairs in the Congress, including meetings of leaders, may be kindly sent for precensorship.	P
164 10 :	News report regarding the judgment in the case of Dalmia-Jain Airways should not be published.	B

CHAPTER III

STATEMENTS, RESOLUTIONS AND SPEECHES

TAMILNAD CONGRESS COMMITTEE

Working Committee Resolution

The Working Committee views with grave concern the new Proclamation of Emergency issued on the 26th June 1975 on the alleged ground that the security of India is threatened by internal disturbances, though as a matter of fact, there were no internal disturbances of any kind at the time of the proclamation. The Prime Minister's broadcast in justification of the emergency relies on incidents long past and on circumstances which are neither grave nor such as cannot be handled under the normal legal and administrative procedures of the country. The Working commitee therefore considers that the proclamation of emergency suppressing fundamental human rights is neither warranted nor justified in the prevailing circumstances in the Country.

The Working Committee condemns the wholesale arrest and detention without trial of all the leaders who have sacrified their lives for the liberation of the country from foreign yoke. The Working Commitee recalls that similar repression was let loose by the British in August 1942 by mass arrest and detention of National Leaders like Mahatma Gandhi, Jawarharlal Nehru, Sardar Patel etc and thus plunged the country into violent disturbances and the Working Commitee apprehends that by the suppression of fundamental rights and human liberties, similar consequences may follow.

The Working Commitee is deeply disturbed by the suppression of freedom of information through rigorous press censorship leading to complete black-out of news and information about the conditions in the country and the fate of its leaders.

The Working Committee recalls that during the two earlier occasions when emergency proclaimed in the wake of Chinese Aggression in 1962 and Pakistani aggression in 1965, it was not considered necessary to control the press and the public information and therefore deplores that a press censorship should have been enforced for the first time in the history of free India.

The Working Commitee also criticises the abuse of mass media of information like the All India Radio for the suppression of truths and for the propaganda of patent untruths.

The Working Commitee therefore urges the Government to revoke the proclamation of emergency forthwith, release all the leaders and restore to the people their cherished democratic rights.

The Working Commitee appeals to the Party Units, Congress workers and the people to be vigilant and be prepared for any sacrifice to preserve Democracy.

N.B. This type of resolutions of Political Parties or professonal Organisations, were cyclostyled and sent to local sources for undergrouud circulation.

Speech at Rajya Sabha
Krishna Kant

I rise to speak in great agony. The kind of fog descended upon our country was naturally affected all of us. Many of our dear colleagues are missing from these benches on both side of of this august House. J. P.—one of the tallest living patriots and verily one of the last representative of Gandhian ethos is now suffering solitary incarceration in independent India. This produces a vaccuum in our hearts and feelings of loss and anguish.

We know that the arrests were made under MISA in the morning of 26th June even before the Emergency was proclaimed. In other words Govt. had all the powers to deal with any kind of conspiracy.

It has been stated that they are only a handful of people. If only a handful of people were responsible, why the whole nation is being punished ? If only a handful of people were involved, as the Govt. claims, then there is only one logical conclusion that Govt. has taken this action in panic and out of fear. No wonder the methods used by the Govt. are also those of panic and fear.

In the light of the new euphoria for 20 point programme, I would like to ask — who amongst the Congress leaders have been punished for sabotaging the Congress programme during the last few years ? Only Krishna Kant, Chandra Shekhar, Mohan Dharia, Ram Dhan. Their only crime known to the people in the country was their total commitment to an continuous insistance upon implementing party programmes and policies both in letter and spirit.

Today, who are the supporters and enthusiasts of the 20 point programme ? Read the censored newspapers. The daily retinue to PMs house will show that the saboteurs of the Congress economic programmes are now the enthusiastic supporters of the Emergency. Those who have profited by inflation and sabotage of the Govt. policies have turned overnight into loud mouthed supporters of the 20 point programme.

I shall not be surprised if the idea of the emergency is traced to the brain of the CIA because CIA likes non-ideological dictatorships. No privileges of the privileged classes are being touched. They have been reassured. There is going to be no nationalisation of textile and sugar industries accepted by the Congress long ago. On the other hand the emergency will come down on the workers, on students, the intelligentsia and the fixed income groups.

In one of the interviews to a foreign journal, the Prime Minister very correctly assessed that in this country no dictatorship can be imposed because dictatorship in this vast and multi-ethnic nation will break the country rather than keep it united. Another statement attributed to her says that nation is greater than democracy. These two are mutually contradictory. Another statement attributed to the Prime Minister says that the number of persons arrested is a very small proportion to the Indian population.

July 22, 1975

Shri Uma Sankar Joshi (Nominated)   July 22, 1975

Mr Deputy Chairman, Sir, this is the most agonising moment in five years of my association with this august House. I came here as a poet and a Vice-Chancellor with what fond hopes and dreams !

However yesterday our Home Minister came forward with a plea in favour of emergency, giving up all hopes for democracy in this great land.

He was pleased to lay the blame at the doors of opposition parties and certain happenings in our country. I belong to no party and I would take this opportunity to refer to one detail about Gujarat. He was not holding this charge when the Nav Nirman movement started in Gujarat. I would like to point out to him that in the beginning it was the Congress Party people themselves who saw the rebirth of Mahatma Gandhi in in the Nav Nirman Youth. The Communist Party also, as far as I remember, was with the Nav Nirman youth. It was a different story after the ouster of the Ministry. Why did this happen ? My plea is for a little self-searching rather than laying the whole blame at the door of the opposition. I have been crying hoarse that the ruling party like the musk-deer runs in vain all around for the opposition, for it is within its own self.

A clamp down of pre-censorship has never happened in India, not even under a foreign regime. We are afraid of truth. Where does this fear emanate from, fear—which has engulfed the length and breadth of this vast land ? Wherefrom has this dark cynical shadow of fear—I mean, terror—which shows its ugly face all around ? How many walls have been created after the 26th June ? You want to see that the country is not disintegrated. With one stroke you have disintegrated the country, by switching off all information. Rumours run amuck and truth is stifled. This is the fear of truth in a country which has a reputation of being a seeker after truth. This has damaged the image of India all over the world more than anything else.

I should like to refer to a harrowing description given in the book of polity, in the Raja Dharma Parva, of the Mahabharata. Rishi Vyas describes in very agonising terms :

—'Then was destroyed the vast truth of life.' Perhaps in this country in its long history we have arrived at a point where the vast truth of life is being destroyed.

I appeal to the Members of the ruling Party because now there is only one party. Already there are signs of their heading towards one party rule, towards Presidential type of Government, towards the destruction of the federal structure replacing it by the unitary structure. Already there are signs that the Gujarat and the Tamil Nadu Governments may find themselves in trouble sooner than later.

Not being a politician I do not want to enter into a discussion with the Home Minister, but how many Governments have been toppled by the ruling party? How many people have migrated from the Opposition parties even here in this House to the ruling party? We are nominated Members, Independent members, not belonging to any party. The ruling party on that side sucks from this side and whatever is left of the Opposition is perhaps the best of them. So put them in the jail. Have a unitary type of Government. This allergy for non-Congress type of Governments has gone a long way in the ruining of the Indian polity.

Re : **RAJYA SABHA SPEECH**   6.1.76

Shri N. G. Goray (Maharashrtra) : Sir, I wanted to draw your attention to an order issued by the Chief Censor, Government of India. Sir, I want to refer to this notorious Mr. Penha, Chief Censor...

Sir, his order is as follows :

"The attention of the accredited correspondents, including foreign correspondents and Editors is drawn to Statutory Order 278 dated 26th June, 1975, and as amended on the 12th August, 1975, made under Rule 48 (1) of the Defence and Internal Security of India Rules, to state that all news, comments, including editorial comments, rumours or other reports relating to the proceedings of the 15th session of the Fifth Lok Sabha 1976, and of the 94th session of Rajya Sabha, falling within the provisions of the Statutory Order 75-K, shall be submitted for scrutiny and shall not be published without permission in writing."

Sir, I think this is a serious encroachment on the privileges of this House. I would like to know from you, Sir, whether you have been consulted before issuing this Order...

Sir, if you will pardon me for saying so, the Address of the President is a drab and colourless document and, therefore, there is hardly anything that I need say about it. Perhaps it only reflects the reality that Rashtrapathi Bhavan has become only a subsidiary of the South Block. It has neither its own face nor soul of its own. But what President's Address lacked in colour and thrust was supplied by my two friends, one from the Congress side and the other from the Communist Party. I suppose that the two speeches taken together, one by my friend Prof. Dutt and the other by my friend Z.A. Ahmad, sum up the argument from the Congress side as to why this emergency had to be declared and how beneficial this emergency has proved to the nation as a whole. I must say that when I was listening to Shri Ahmad, I found that, unless you were a master of the Marxian dialaches (dialectics), it was not possible to reconcile what he said in the beginning with what he said in the end. He supported the Emergency. He said that the Congress forces on the one hand and the Communist forces on the other, one representing the patriotic urge and the other representing the masses would stand together and achieve the socialist revolution. Then, in the end, he had his doubts. What did he say in the end ? He said that somehow it has happened that the Congress is not following the right policies. Which were the policies that he criticised ? One was the bonus issue and he lamented the fact that in spite of the great Communist Party of India supporting the Congress in all its deeds and misdeeds, the Congress did not have even the courtesy to consult the Communist Party of India when it took the decision on bonus in spite of the fact that a man like Mr. Reddy was sitting there as a Minister in charge of labour. That was his first charge. Number two was, he said that the Congress was encouraging the bureaucracy, giving it a free scope. The third was that the land reforms were not being speedily implemented. And the fourth was that the capitalists were getting whatever they wanted. Sir, I was reminded of a story of Birbal and Akbar which tells us that Akbar had a pet parrot of his own. One day it died. But knowing that this was a pet bird of the King nobody would tell Akbar that it had died. But when Akbar asked them to bring that bird to the *durbar*, nobody dared to do so. Then he sent for Birbal and asked him to report on the state of affairs. Birbal came back and the King asked him, "what happened to the bird ?" Birbal said, "Sir, its beak is open, and it has stretched out its legs. It has collapsed. It does not fly or flutter". Then the King said that most probably the bird is dead. Birbal said, "Yes, Sire, that is the truth". So, because of the close collaboration of the Communist Party with the Congress, Dr. Z. A. Ahmad does not say that the Congress is a reactionary party. But he describes by implication that it is pro-capitalist, it is pro-bureaucracy, it is pro-landlord and it is anti-worker. And still it is a progressive party. Why ? Because the Communists are in league with the Congress.

Sir, Prof. Dutt was equally emphatic in saying that there must be democracy here. I would like to know from Mr. Dutt —professor that he is—whether he will be able to point out a single instance of democracy anywhere in the world where Members of Parliament have been lifted and put in the prison without any charge for the last six months. Not only that. They cannot approach any court even. The press is gagged...

It is not only the Parliamentarians but I would like to say that there are thousands of people against whom you cannot bring any charges who have been thrown into prisons. I will give you an instance. One MLC from Karnatak came here to attend the Commonwealth Parliamentary Association Conference and because Shri Tridib Chaudhary was not allowed to speak he straightaway walked out. What happened to him ? As soon as he returned to Mysore, he was arrested under the M.I.S.A. Is that the way you treat people ? Remember that he did not belong to any party. He is an Independent Member of the Karnataka Legislative Council. He was elected from the

Teachers' Constituency and simply because he did something which you do not approve of, you put that man into prison...

Niren De told a very ghastly truth in the Supreme Court. When the Judges asked him the question again and again that supposing a Police Inspector were to shoot a man, does it mean that he has no redress, Niren De said—I must say that Niren De is a very honest man—"My Lord, it may shock your conscience but that is the law". Is that the law in a democracy ?...

Jayaprakash has never said that the people should take to violence. I thought that when you speak, a distinguished professor of a university, you will be more charitable. You levelled certain very serious charges against Morarjibhai and very rhetorically you asked, once or twice, "He was once our Deputy Prime Minister and should he talk like that ?" Should he create some ill feeling towards Kashmiris because of..."

Dr. V.P. Dutt : Have I misquoted him ? Are you saying...

Shri N.G. Goray : Let me have my say also.

Dr. V.P. Dutt : I would like your answer. I won't interrupt you after that. In India two cases of political liquidation took place. Mahatma Gandhi. Who Killed him ? After him, L.N. Mishra. Who killed him ? I would like to know which are the forces indulging in political liquidation.

Sri. N.G. Goray. I would like to answer this question here. Mahatma Gandhi was killed by some fanatic Hindu.

Dr. V.P. Dutt : R.S.S.

Shri N.G. Goray : I won't say that. Because.........

(Interruptions)

Dr. V.P. Dutt : How can Goray say that ?

Shri N.G. Goray : Let us be very clear about this. When you say that Morarjibhai was......

(Interruptions)

When you said that Morarji Desai said something about somebody killing Indira Gandhi and all that, I thought that as a professor you will have the fairness to say that the man is not here.

Dr. Z.A. Ahmad : No. No. But he said that.

Shri N.G. Goray : If he said that I condemn it and I say

that even the most condign punishment should be given. I am not saying that......

Dr. Z.A. Ahmad : It was before

Shri N.G. Goray : At that time Morarji Desai was in jail and I would like to ask why don't you give a chance to the man whom you have put in jail to say something in self-explanation ? About Jayaprakash Narayan you have again and again said that he tried to create disaffection in the Army. What did he say ? He told the soldiers not to obey an order which was against their conscience.

An Hon. Member : Who will decide ?

(Interruptions)

Shri N.G. Goray : Please listen to me. Now I would like to ask you : In Bangladesh Mujib was liquidated because Major Dalim asked his soldiers to liquidate him. Was that right ? Would it not have been much better if the soldiers who liquidated his family had appealed to their own conscience ? (Interruptions) Why ? An order is an order. You cannot have it both ways, once you say that the order must be obeyed. I say that it would have been much better if a spirit like Jayaprakash Narayan were there to tell them not to obey simply because it was the officer's order and in this way Mujib would not have been liquidated. So my appeal to you is.........

Shri M.R. Krishna : You can talk many more things but not this silly sort of things.

Shri N.G. Goray : This is very necessary because this is the argument that is always levelled against us. Therefore, what I am saying is, if you want to have a democratic India, if you want to have a parliamentary system in India, you must first of all agree that we must not challenge each other's bonafides. You must not challenge my bona fides and I must not challenge your bona fides. Unless that is there, it will not possible for us to come and talk together...

Now I would like to say something about the progress that the country has made during the period of this emergency. I would like to ask you, in Gujarat they are not following all the emergency rules which you have proclaimed, in Tamilnadu they are not doing it...

An. Hon. Member : They are opposing it.

Shri N.G. Goray : Very good, you have said it. When I went to Tamilnadu, when I went to Gujarat, I could move freely. Not only I could talk, Hitendra Bhai could talk. When Subramaniam goes to Tamilnadu, he freely tells the people that this is the Government that we do not want......

Shri N.G. Goray : I was there in Ahmedabad during the elections. I have seen it. Do you mean to say...(Interruptions)

Shri Harisinh Bhagubava Mahida : And they did not allow us to hold the meetings.

Shri N.G. Goray : Do you mean to say that without holding meetings you got all those votes ? What are you talking ?

N.B. : Parliament proceedings could not be published, the censored portions were typed and circulated by M.P'.s. and their close circles, first to state sources, then again recirculated to lower levels.

Left Front Parties Resolution

Resolution adopted by the CPI (M), R.S.P.,
F.B., W.P., S.P., R.C.P.I., M.F.B. and B.B.C.
for placing the same before a public meeting at
Calcutta scheduled to be held on 9.1.76 which
was prohibited by the Commissioner of Police.

This meeting of people of West Bengal expresses its deep concern and sense of alarm about changes on the Constitution of India that are being proposed and canvassed in the top circle of the ruling party and the Government.

These changes aim at virtual elimination of all fundamental rights of citizens ; they seek to close all avenues of legal remedy and redress against arbitrary, unreasonable, autocratic and injurious Executive action and to impose a personal dictatorship of the Head of the Executive.

With their talk of anti-fascism and supremacy of Parliament the leaders of the ruling party are trying to put up a smokescreen through the pre-censored Press, the Radio and other media to cover up these attempts to destroy the last vestiges of Parliamentary Democracy. In fact they are aiming at a fascist Constitution, and they are seeking to reduce the Parliament into an instrument of mere recording of their will. Instead of ending the State of Emergency, they are now seeking to perpetuate it in the Constitution itself.

The present Constitution of India was framed by a so-called Constituent Assembly formed under the aegis of the British Government on the basis of an indirect election and a franchise limited to not more than 13 per cent of the population. It was not a Constitution for the people, and it could never be an instrument of social progress ; the great slogans of Liberty, Equality, Fraternity and Social Justice mentioned in the Preamble were soon discovered to be empty words.

Progressive public opinion in the country was never satisfied with the present Constitution. Left and Democratic Parties, and toiling people in general always demanded that among other things the Right to Work must become a justicable fundamental right, Right to Recall must be embodied in the Constitution to ensure effective democratic control, free and fair elections must be guaranteed, there should be greater and real autonomy of the States, justice must be made impartial fair and accessible to the toiling people, democratic rights and liberties should be inviolable and detention without trial shall not be permissable.

The current proposals are, however, exactly in the opposite direction. The aim of these proposals is not to broaden, extend and secure people's rights and liberties, but to further curb, restrict and eliminate them. The aim is not to ensure employment for all, living wages, and social security ; the aim is to suppress all legal avenues of raising such demands. The aim is not to enable the masses to participate in the administration of the country, but to end even the nominal and insignificant mass-participation in political life. The aim is not to make justice impartial and accessible to the poorer sections of the people, but to prevent the courts from judging the acts of rulers.

This meeting strongly and unequivocally condemns all such proposals.

This meeting is of the opinion that the present Parliament has no moral right to bring about such drastic changes in the Constitution. Whatever was the nature of the mandate for the present Parliament, it never included such powers, and no such proposal was presented to the people at the time of the last General Election. To rush through such alteration of the whole basic structure of the Constitution without a fresh mandate from the people would amount to gross betrayal. The life of the present Parliament is also being extended beyond its term ; it would be shameless violation of all norms of Parliamentary Democracy to alter the Constitution during such extension. Morever all this is being proposed to be done during a State of Emergency while all civil rights remain suspended. If the ruling party were at all inclined towards decent and civilized political conduct, they would bring forward their proposals in clear and concrete terms before the people, end the State of Emergency, release all political prisoners, end the rule of terror, create a climate for free expression of opinion, and await the verdict of the people.

This meeting demands :

1. Immediate end of the State of Emergency ;
2. Release of all political prisoners ;
3. Repeal of MISA, DIR ;
4. Repeal of Pre-censorship Order ;
5. Repeal of the Prevention of Publication of Objectionable Matters Ordinance and Prevention of Circulation and Distribution of Objectionable Matters Ordinance.

P E O P L E

15 September 1976

India Will Emerge From This Darkness

In an interview with the British Broadcasting Corporation on February 12, 1976, Mr. Jayaprakash Narayan said, "The people should not lose their courage and keep steadfast. The youth should remain at their post. The future appears dark at the moment but it is really bright. The country will emerge from this darkness."

The following reproduction of the interview gives an insight into J.P.'s thoughts on the constitutional dictatorship of Mrs. Indira Gandhi.

Health

Q. : Babuji (respectful address to Mr. Narayan), how is your health now ?

J.P. : My health is not good at the moment (since then J.P. has recovered to a large extent). It seems as if the present illness (kidney malfunctioning) will remain with me for the rest of my life. I might get better over the next few months, but I shall never be as well as I was earlier. I'll have to change not only the way I work but my entire way of life. It appears that I'll have to work mainly staying at one place.

Q. : Does it mean that you will have to use the dialysis for the rest of your life ?

J.P. : Yes, that's true. Doctors have advised me to keep a machine with me and in India at least it isn't possible to cart a machine around wherever one goes. It will have to be kept at my place in Patna.

Q. : Would you like to say something about the events that led to this sudden deterioration in health ? It seems as if your health deteriorated rather suddenly after two or three months in jail, after 26th June last year, when you were arrested. You yourself wrote in your diary that your health was alright until 27th September 1975. On that day you developed a sudden stomach pain.

J.P. : This is a question for which I have no clear and definite answer. Whatever I may say may be interpreted by different people in different ways.

I talked about this to Dr. Chatani, the Director of the Post-Graduate Institute for Medical Education and Research in Chandigarh, where I was kept then. Even he could not say why I suffered from this pain.

I always had stomach trouble, namely constipation, but there was never any specific pain like the one I developed on

September 27. It was sudden, severe and unimaginable. There must have been some cause, but it is still unknown. I didn't notice having eaten anything which could have brought it about.

That is all I can say. However, I shall have to live with its consequences for the rest of my life.

Both the kidneys have failed and they are not going to get any better.

Q. : Is there a doubt in your mind that your condition did not change for the bad because of unnatural causes ? Perhaps it was engineered from outside.

J.P. : With full responsibility I must say that there is some doubt in my mind.

I would like to add however, that I do not have any suspicion of the doctors of the Institute, or of any particular person. But the occurrence of sudden affliction, resulting in the failure of both my kidneys is naturally very odd.

Q. : Were you under solitary confinement and not treated well otherwise when you were detained ?

J.P. : My food and living arrangements were satisfactory. Everyone was courteous in the hospital where I was given a good room. Everyone from the Director of the hospital to the Commissioner treated me well.

But of course I was alone. I was given newspapers but had no one to discuss with. This was deep mental suffocation and life continued like that.

Q. : You mean you got newspapers to read ?

J.P. The newspapers came after few days of total non-communication. But then after a time I stopped reading them. There was so much falsehood in them.

But then someone told me it was a mistake. I should keep myself informed of events.

Anyway partly as a result of pressure from others and as a result of cooling down of my anger, after a while I began reading the papers again.

Q. : Were you allowed to listen to a radio ?

J.P. : They were willing but I refused because other political prisoners were not allowed. I did not want this extra facility which was not allowed to others.

The Emergency

Q. :   What have you to say about the emergency ? You had written to the Prime Minister. Your letter of July 21, 1975 seems to be a significantly important one. Is there any response ?

J.P. :   I felt very angry at the time of the declaration of the emergency. I do feel even so now. The reason is that the declaration of the emergency was on totally false grounds. There was no such crisis in the country, no such danger, there was no external danger at all. Internally also, the situation was not such that there was any possibility of a rebellion. The people were simply exercising their democratic rights : public meetings were held and they would have continued to be held : demonstrations had taken place ; slogans had been shouted ; songs of protest had been sung ; there were hartals—but this happens everywhere whenever there are special circumstances. I do not accept that this demanded a declaration of emergency. Therefore I am deeply angry that for the sake of her own power, for maintaining herself in office, the emergency was imposed on the country. I have always been feeling, have been saying for years, that Indiraji's temperament is that of a dictator. I used to be asked why I said this. But now it is proved ; she has found the opportunity.

Q. :   But justifying the emergency, Mrs. Gandhi has been saying again and again that M.Ps were being gheraoed, they were prevented from carrying on their tasks, in some public meetings officials or people were persuaded to stop work and that you personally in your speech incited the army and the police to rebel. What is the reality ?

J.P. :   The correct answer to this question can be given by my speeches alone. In the specific speech that you mention, that of 25th June, 1975, I did refer to the army and police ; I also referred to them in earlier speeches. People can read them too. In that speech I only said that the Police Manual and the Army Act state that any illegal order, even if it comes from the authorities, should not be obeyed. And further that anyone who obeys such an illegal order may deserve to be punished.

9

This is what I had said. I never asked them to rebel. I have been consistently emphasising that politics and government of the country should be carried out in a democratic way. Whenever elections are due, as they are in February/March, they should be held. But they will not take place and will be put off for an indefinite period.

It is this kind of a situation that breeds violence. These are dangerous manifestations. I used to draw people's attention to them and I have appealed to the Prime Minister also that in view of such dangers she should behave like a democratic leader.

She got specially offended when after the Allahabad High Court judgement, I also said that she should resign till appeal to the Supreme Court was decided on. But she did not listen. Instead, she put me into prison and brought in the emergency.

Q. : If talks are not held, as you have just said, there is a possibility of a sudden explosion. What sort of explosion might this be ?

J.P. : Put simply, it may take the form of mass protest—people coming out on the streets to protest ; raising their voices ; demonstrations taking place ; public meetings being held ; hartals taking place ; students acting similarly. If any organisational strength is born out of it, it may organise non-co-operation with government. It may also lead to programmes and slogans of non-tax payment campaigns and similar types of protests. I have given serious thought to the matter but it does not seem to me that there is any danger of violence arising out of such protests. But if people and youth express their anger in a non-violent way and it assumes an organised form, then all these activities like no rent campaigns, non-payment of taxes, non-co-operation may occur.

Q. : A film is being shown in Bombay which depicts people like you, Morarji Desai and George Fernandes, if not in so many words, then by implication, as fascist dictators. What is your reaction ?

J.P. : What more proof is required ? What more is needed ? Power lies with Indiraji and who can deny that she does exercise dictatorial powers ? Parliament exists only in name ; all

powers reside in her. She has taken all special powers. The
Emergency continues and behind its veil her own powers and
life of the Parliament has been extended by a year. If the emergency continues for an indefinite period, the life of the Parliament is also extended without any justification. After all what
does a dictator do ?

When we have power, then whether we will (I personally
have no wish to be in the government) be dictators, history will
tell. But history has furnished a clear and a living proof that
dictatorship has been imposed on India today and that is the
dictatorship of Indiraji and the Congress party.

MERGER RESOLUTION

Meeting of the members of the Congres (O), Jana Sangh, B.L.D. and
the Socialist Party as well as members representing D.M.K., R.S.P. and
some independent political workers and Sarvodaya workers was held in
Bombay on 20th and 21st March 1976 to review the developments that have
taken place in the country after the declaration of the Emergency on the
26th June 1975. Shri Jayaprakash Narayan was available for advice and
guidance. The following statement was released to the Press on behalf of
the meeting.

The Emergency promulgated then is now being continued
though there is no sign of internal threat of any kind. Suppression of all civil liberties, severe curbs on the Press and erosion of
the authority of the judiciary still continues. To top it all, the
life of the present Lok Sabha has been extended by a year
though its five years mandate has come to an end. What has
happened during the past nine months has convinced us that
the Government has been deliberately destroying our democratic
structure brick by brick and now has established an authoritarian regime which it wants to perpetuate.

We congratulate the people of India of the peaceful resistance they have offered in vindication of their democratic rights.
We salute the thousands of detenus who continue to suffer for
their faith. We give a solemn pledge that it shall be our constant effort to restore our democratic policy in full, never allowing narrow or partisan cosiderations to stand in our way.

There was complete unanimity that democracy and democratic values as we understood them had been dealt in all but fatal blow and in our view it was of the first importance that democracy should survive if the freedoms which every self-respecting individual values—freedom of speech, freedom of association, freedom of communication and movement, freedom from fear—are to be preserved. If this first and prime objective —restoration of democracy and democratic values and restoration of civil liberties is to be realised, then those who are of that view must come together in one party with an agreed policy and programme. There was unanimity on the use of peaceful means and on the total rejection of all forms of violence.

We have welcomed the impartial and reasonable suggestions made by the Acharya Sammelan under Acharya Vinoba's guidance because it is our considered opinion that they could be helpful in evolving a national consensus on the various socio-economic problems facing the country, without destroying our democratic federal fabric. We held that firm faith in peaceful methods in and outside the Parliament and tolerance of dissent are the corner stones of a genuine democratic social order. Our co-operation will always be there to all endeavours to resist dictatorial tendencies or to formulate a code of conduct applicable to all parties for the preservation and strengthening of democracy.

With this end in view, it was decided to set up a steering committee composed of the following members with powers to co-opt : (1) Shri N.G. Goray – Convener, (2) Shri H.M. Patel, (3) Shri Shanti Bhusan and (4) Shri O.P. Tyagi, to draw up such a policy and programme for a single unified democratic opposition party. It will also be the duty of the committee to ensure that the process of integration is completed in the shortest possible time, not exceeding two months.

The following members were present :

Acharya Kripalani	Shri Krishna Kant
Shri Tridib Choudhury	Shri Mavalankar
Shri Charan Singh	Shri Nijlingappa
Shri N.G. Goray	Shri Babubhai Patel

Shri H.M. Patel   Shri Uttamrao Patil

Shri Shantibhusan   Shri Era Schelzian

Shri Om Prakash Tyagi   Shri Digvijay Narayan Singh

Shri Narayan Desai   Shri Yadunath Thatte

Shri S.M. Joshi   Shri Sequeira

Shri Umashankar Joshi

J.P.'s call to all Freedom-Loving Indians

The Supreme Court judgment on the Habeas corpus question has put out the last flickering candle of individual freedom. Mrs. Gandhi's dictatorship, both in its personalised and institutionalised forms is now almost complete. All freedom-loving Indian must face the question boldly today as to how can we reverse the reactionery course of history and regain our lost liberties and re-establish our democratic institutions. This obviously can be done only—if it is to be done constitutionally—if free and fair elections to the Lok Sabha are held, the Congress Party is defeated and a united opposition wins and forms a government. All this is easier said than done, it is true ; but it is also equaly true. If not more than all this has to be done. How, is the question. I suggest that :

(1) Meetings of the general public or of different institutions and organisations should be held all over the country demanding revacation of the emergency, release of political prisoners, holding of elections to Parliament, restoration of the freedom of the press and platform, etc.

(2) Those who believe in individual freedom and free democratic institutions must immediately, in whatever way possible even in small groups of 3 to 4 persons—start educating the people in the fundamental issues involved. Mrs. Gandhi's juggernath of the dictatorship is rolling forward because they have no understanding of what has been happening. One sided propaganda has persuaded many of them to believe that what has happened is all for their good. Therefore, re-education of the people in the fundamental of a free and democratic society is the most immediate and urgent task to be taken up. In order that this task may be carried out intelligently, it would be

necessary for the issues to be placed before the people in a series of simply written informative and instructive pamphlets. It is obvious that these will have to be published and circulated illegally. The people themselves cannot read those pamphlets but they can serve as text books and should be studied in small study classes consisting mostly of students and other youngmen and women.

It is obvious that those engaged even in this kind educational task should be prepared to be arrested, imprisoned, beaten up and otherwise tortured. But I have faith that there are enough young men and women in this country not to be daunted by these risks.

(3) Alongwith the above programme of people's education there should be also a programme of people's organisations. During the Bihar movement organisations took the form of Jana Sangharsa Samitis and Chattra Sangharsa Samatis. I suggest that in the rest of the country, the organisations be just called Nava Nirman Samatis. Qualifying words like 'Gram' 'Nagar' 'Chattra' etc. may be prefixed to the words NAVA NIRMAN SAMITI to indicate their character. I think that at this juncture this three-fold programme should taken up by the all those interested in creating through peaceful revolutionary action of the people, the new India of free, equal and self governing citizens.

To some this programme may seem rather tame. But I hope on deeper thought they will change their mind. Confrontation with the government was not the aim of the Bihar movement. It was a by-product which the movement took in its stride. If the programme suggested herein is taken up seriously and spreads and gathers strength, confronation would be inevitable, but that would not be our seeking ; it would be, as in the past, the result of society's reactionery forces led by the government trying to put down the people's revolution.

This, however, is not all that is to be done, the aim of the people's movements was and is Total Revolution, i.e. revolution in every field of individual and social life to make them better, fuller and more satisfying. These means there is a vast field of activity. In India, abolition of the caste system is in some ways even more important than abolition of the class system. Revolution in education offers another large field of activity. Examples can be multiplied, but it is not necessary as imaginative and resourceful activity can demarcate their own field of work.

Some of this work may involve confrontation with social (including caste) and economic vested interests and it is quite possible that in some of these areas of confrontation, we may get the co-operation of the state.

Bombay, 2nd. May, 1976.

N.B. Typed copy of this appeal was later published in Hindi, Gujarati and other language bulletins.

SOCIAL DEMOCRACY AND INDIA

FROM THE UNDERGROUND

Exclusive interview with George Fernandes

Since this interview with George Fernandes (Chairman of the Indian Socialist Party) was conducted the Socialist International learned that he had been arrested on the night of 10-11 June in Calcutta by the Indian Security Forces (see Socialist Diary, page 79)

Q. *How did you manage to escape when there were a huge number of arrests in the night from 25 to 26 June last yeat ?*

G.F. Partly by accident and partly with the assistance which a few of my friends gave me. I was not in Delhi on that night. After the two-day meeting of the national committees of the four opposition parties—I went to Calcutta, to Bhubaneshwar and then to Gopalpur in Orissa. My visit to Gopalpur was partly a private personal visit and I also had a few public engagements at the University and at the offices of the railway workers. I was scheduled to leave there on 26 June in the evening by train after public engagements. Around ten in the morning I was informed about the emergency and at 12 o'clock a friend who had monitored a conversation between the distric₁ magistrate and the police from the district headquarters of Chatrapur, which is the district headquarters, and Berhampur which is the police-station for Gopalpur, told me that the warrant for my arrest was all set and that I was going to be arrested in the evening after the meeting before catching another train. I was able to give the police the slip even while they kept a watch outside my house in Gopalpur.

Q. *Why did you go and stay underground ?*

G.F. My staying underground was a deliberate and positive decision which I had to take. To me when I got the news of the emergency it was obvious that we were in for a dictatorship because emergency when there was already one existing could not mean anything other short of a dictatorship. And in a dictatorship there is nothing one can do by going to jail. I think that it is very important that people somehow manage to survive, go underground, build a resistance movement and keep fighting. I think I took a right decision. Since then, my task has been to organise this underground. I have been particularly trained for this especially when people better protected perhaps more experienced have been picked up. I have been under ground in the past. But for very, very brief periods. During the 1960 Central Government Employees' strike I had not only survived in the underground but I surfaced at an hour and at a place by previous announcement while thousands of policemen were trying to locate me. On other occasions also I have had reasons and occasions to go underground.

In the underground it has been my experience that it is more often than not your own people who make a slip. But, if you are very careful with your own set-up, if you don't spread it out too far and wide in so far as your inner circle is concerned I think it is possible to survive in the underground. This is not to say that I have not had narrow escapes. I had two very, very close saves. Perhaps three. One was in Calcutta where they almost got me. They came with my picture, they talked to all the servants of the place where I had been just a few hours earlier and they almost got me.

Another time was in Madras where they were not sure about my identity but they wasted a bit of time in trying to establish it. By then I was able to escape. One time was in Ahmedabad. So there have been fairly close saves. And again it was more because of what my friends did than because of the sharpness, cleverness or the ingenuity of the policemen. But anyway that's not very important.

What I have been doing in the last ten months was primarily to organise an underground network, which is difficult. It's difficult for a number of reasons : the most important one is that trained political workers are no longer around. All of them have been picked up. So you start from scratch. You get people who either have no political background or have no ideological training. So by trial and error you keep picking up people and keep training them and getting them involved.

Q. *What are they actually doing ?*

G.F. We have people who are producing literature, people who distribute that literature, we have people who are training cadres in the trade unions, mass-organisations and elsewhere, we have people who are also helping to organise the Satyagrah, holding little meetings clandestinely and training people to go to jail. But our position has been that only such people should go to jail who are unable to do any other form of activity.

Q. *With unrest spreading can the unity of the country survive ?*

G.F. I have reasons to believe that Mrs Gandhi's dictatorship is taking the country towards balcanisation. And in fact it has been my constant appeal to the people in the North to get rid of this dictatorship if they want to preserve the unity of the country because a situation is bound to arise where people from the South are going to say that we are part of a democratic India, we are not a part of an India that is ruled by a dictator from Kashmir.

This question is being spoken. There are posters which have appeared in Kerala, which have appeared in Karnataka. I have had people from our own party—Socialists, life-long Socialists —tell me that we have accepted a democratic federal state. We didn't accept a dictatorship from Kashmir. That's not the kind of federal policy that we were talking about.

Q. *What role is the Soviet Union playing in all this ?*

G.F.   The support which the Soviet Union is giving to Mrs. Gandhi's dictatorship makes me feel that the Soviet Union also believes that this dictatorship will finally succeed in dismembering the country, in balcanising the country which has been one of the aims of Soviet foreign policy for the last years. I was going through a book on Soviet foreign policy recently and I find that the Russians do not want a united India. And perhaps it suits their politics just now to support Mrs Gandhi because they can see the inevitable break-up of the country, the seeds in any case have been planted for a break-up of the country.

Q.   *Any seccessionist movement must strengthen the underground ?*

G.F.   That's right. The resistance movement's base expands. Our base expands, whereas her forces get thinned out. We have six hundred million people to work on. She has only the police and the para-military forces.

Q.   *What about the army ?*

G.F.   I don't think the army is really involved. There is resentment against what she is doing. Resentment about the way she is behaving and about the way she is now projecting her son as the crown prince, as the 'rising sun'.

In any case these are people whose loyalties are bought. On your monthly salary you sell your loyalty. But it's not support. She doesn't trust her own people. She doesn't trust the members of her cabinet. So therefore I believe that expanding her front is not to her advantage as it is to our advantage. Though it is a logical culmination of the positions which she has taken.

Q.   *What is your objective ?*

G.F.   Our objective is the restoration of democracy, the restoration of all the freedoms and constitutional rights as they prevailed on the 25 June 1975. Of course, there is the question what does democracy mean in a country where 70 per cent are illiterate and of the 30 per cent who are literate perhaps 90 per cent are literate to the extent of just being able to sign their name ?

I believe that a country like India needs democracy more than perhaps a country where there are certain built-in guarantees of fundamental rights, where certain social and economic standards have been acclaimed. The whole working class movement of India is suppressed today. The workers need democracy. If there is no democracy there are no free trade unions. If there are no free trade unions there is no collective bargaining. If there is no collective bargaining there is no improving the standard of living of the workers.

There is also corruption —it is the ordinary man, the most helpless man who is the victim of corruption. It's not a man like me, it's not an educated man who is so much a victim of corruption as the smallest and most helpless man in the rural areas. It was the political leadership in the country, the democratic leadership in the country, the newspapers—who articulated the problems of these people. A dictatorship means that all this articulation is finished.

Q. There are reports of secret radio stations in India ?

G.F. We have aquired a transmitter, a short-wave transmitter. We have also aquired small transmitters which will operate at a radius of 30 kilometers.

Q. Does the Socialist Party still exist ?

G.F. Mrs Gandhi's real target has been the Socialist Party. My entire National Committee is in jail. All the people in my State Committees are in jail. I have 200,000 people of the Socialist Party, in jail all over the country. It has been the most massive clean sweep.

Q. So the structure is completely broken. Just a few people are kept out ?

G.F. That's right. That's what the Party's position is.

Q. What is your agrument against Mrs Gandhi posing as a socialist ?

G.F. Well, I suppose, a man called Adolf Hitler also had a National Socialist Party and a socialist programme. But I suppose, every fascist invariably has a socialist image, or at least tries to create a socialist image.

Q. Where do the students stand ?

G.F. There is activity in all the universities and the colleges in the country. Although there has been a major crackdown on professors, lecturers, teachers, principals of colleges, former Vice-chancellors, who are all now in detention. Large numbers of student leaders are also in jail. Presidents of almost all the students unions in the country are in jail. So again we are having the same problem. When the trained leadership is away from the field it takes a little time to reorganise. But students are engaged in producing literature, they are setting up cells. They are also moving into the rural areas and it is a very interesting development that students from Delhi, for instance, are now organising resistance among the peasants. Only recently we had a meeting of our youth leaders. Forty student leaders met and had a two-day conclave, and planned certain actions amongst the students all over the country.

Q. *How do you operate in the trade unions* ?

G.F. As I said, trade unions are being taken over. But we are setting up our cells within the unions, but not only in unions with which we have been associated, but also in unions with which we were not politically associated.

Q. *Do people in the rural area realize what is going on* ?

G.F. Oh yes, I think, the average Indian is politically a very, very conscious being. In fact, I think, Indians are by and large politically more conscious than most people that I know of anywhere in the world. I am not saying this just with a sense of pride about the people. But, we don't have anything else. Go to a village. What is their entertainment ? There are no movies, there is no TV, there is no theatre, there are no cultural things. It's politics, it's constant infighting of some kind or other. Then Party politics comes in. Then we have had these five General Elections. Umpteen State Elections, and Local Elections, then Gandhi's movement which were all rural based, then the socialist movement in the country which is primarly a rural based movement. Contrary to most people's understanding that the Socialists are a kind of urban-based party, we are not. We are primarily a rural-based party. A few of us may be involved in trade unions and in urban politics. But primarily we are a rural party. Therefore there has been tremendous political education that has gone on in spite of the fact that the people are illiterate. And don't forget that for all the illiteracy in this country, for all the so-called lack of communication and non-understanding of issues, and whether democracy is relevant or not to the hungry and the poor and the illiterate—at no point in time in India's post independence history has the Congress Party ever got more then 45 per cent of the vote. 55 per cent of the people have voted against the Congress.

It is a tragedy that these people could never create really a big enough movement that could pose a genuine alternative. It was a failure of leadership. But it was not the failure of the people. Those people are very conscious. And in the rural areas their response to the fight against the dictatorship has been magnificent.

Q. How do you finance your work ?

G.F. The trade unions, the working people, and also a large number of people who are sympathising with our underground activities are helping us. Without their help and support we wouldn't be able to do a thing. But so far, the bulk of our money comes from the trade unions and the working class base that we have. Primarly from this source.

Q. The Socialist International has not been allowed to visit India, especially to see Jayaprakash Narayan (JP) in jail. What can they do for you ?

G.F. The Socialist International has been doing magnificent work. I really don't have words to express my gratitude to them. It is not just the resolutions, it is not just their wanting to meet JP, it's not just the kind of things that they have been saying. But the real emotional involvement of a large number of people in the international has been a source of tremendous encouragement. It's the fact that there are people around the world who really care, who are concerned, who are emotionally and spiritually involved in the movement here—these are things that really sustain us. They have sustained me, I must say that.

Socialist parties and trade unions around the world have also spoken up for us. I would want them to get more involved in a number of ways : keeping themselves informed. Not from what the dictator has put out but from independrnt sources, from sources that are dependable. Well, keeping themselves informed about what is happening. Not taking the position that it's just the Socialist Party and we that are involved but it's the whole country, the country's freedom, it's what happens to India to day. I want them to get involved by keeping themselves informed. I also want them, where they are in Government, to take more positive steps, to pressurise the Government of India. Take the question of aid, take the question of providing money, providing her with technical know how.

I just can't understand—it beats me—how a Socialist Government anywhere in the world could go along with a system that is imposing a naked fascist dictatorship. I am not saying they should break off diplomatic relations and say go to hell. But I could not understand the argument that if they don't give her the assistance she needs she will go to somebody else. I would want that where socialists are in government that they adopt a policy where they really don't have much to do with Indira Gandhi's Government. People have asked me, if I were Prime Minister of India, what would I do vis-a-vis autocratic Nepal? I said if I were Prime Minister of India I would do everything possible to encourage the forces of socialism and democracy in Nepal. Because I am opposed to totalitarianism. I am opposed to all autocratic rule, whether it is a Raja's autocratic rule or whether it is Idi Amin's autocratic rule. I am opposed to it. I am opposed to fascism anywhere in the world.

And I want socialists in government to do the same. And where they are in opposition I would want them to put pressure on their government. For instance, in France, in Italy, in other parts of the world. Where the socialists are influential, I would want them to pressurise their governments not to go along with this dictatorship, with this fascist dictatorship in India. But we also need material help.

Money is an important question. We are producing a fortnightly journal, called 'Swaraj' from London. But we are facing tremendous problems. We just don't have money to produce that journal. Now, we print a few copies, some of which are smuggled into the country and they mean a lot to us because they give the ordinary people in the country information of what the Western world, the free world, is doing so far as the Indian situation is concerned. We want to set up more information centres. We would like to set up a centre in Hong-Kong from where we could disseminate news to the Far Eastern press. Again this calls for money.

N. B. This interview was first published in Socialist Affairs, London the organ of Socialist International. Later, photostat copies were circulated.

INKWORLD

Journal of the National Union of Journalists (India)

Vol. IV January 1976   No. 1

WBUJ holds annual

The West Bengal Union of Journalists, one of the largest units of the NUJ (I), held its annual general meeting at Student Hall, Calcutta, on December 14, 1975.

"This meeting expresses its concern over the treatment meted out to Shri Nishit Dey, a journalist and member of the WBUJ, by taking him tied with rope through the public streets. Shri Dey has been released as he was found innocent. This meeting condemns in unequivocal terms the treatment meted out to this innocent journalist by the police during his arrest.

"This meeting expresses its grave concern over detention without trial of Gour Kishore Ghosh, a noted journalist and writer. This meeting urges the Prime Minister to intervene and to ensure that justice is done to Mr Ghosh."

Socialist International Appeals for Release of George Fernandes

Cable to Indira Gandhi

Upon learning of George Fernandes' arrest the General Secretary of Socialist International sent the following cable to Prime Minister of India, Smt. Indira Gandhi :

"Deeply concerned arrest George Fernandes, Chairman

Indian Socialist Party. Strongly urge his release on behalf of Bureau Socialist International which declared its solidarity with Indian Socialist Party in their struggle for democracy."

On June 15, the General Secretary of the Socialist International issued a statement protesting against the arrest of George Fernandes by the Indian government.

The following joint statement by Willy Brandt, Chairman of the German Social Democratic Party, Bruno Kreisky, Federal Chancellor of Austria and Chairman of the Austrian Socialist Party and Palme, Prime Minister of Sweden and Chairman of the Swedish Social Democratic Party, was issued on June 16, simultaneously in Bonn, Vienna and Stockholm.

"It is with great concern and dismay that we have learned of the arrest of George Fernandes, Chairman of the Indian Socialist Party on the night of June 10-11 in Calcutta."

"We strongly appeal to the Indian Government and in particular to Prime Minister Indira Gandhi to reconsider their action in the interest of India's reputation in the democratic world."

From *People*, August 9, '76

International Transport Workers' Federation

(I. T. F.)

London (U.K)
Circular No. 100/A. 16   Dated 13.8.1976.

Affiliates will be well aware of the conditions of repression which exists in India as a direct result of the seizure by Mrs. Gandhi of dictatorial power of Government.

Much of her attention has been concentrated on the Trade Union movement as she can see, in the existence of organisation devoted to the advancement of social justice and eradication of governmental abuse and corruption, a threat to her power. Where and when it has been possible for her to imprison those opposed to her mal-practices she has done so.

Fortunately, not all of her critics are within the graft of her police and those include the ITF which has been one of her strongest critics. Particularly following the arrests of J.P. Narain and George Fernandes, the President of the All-India Railwaymen's Federation (AIRF). Nevertheless, the Indian Government appears to be under the impression that it can silence ITF criticism by attaching one of the officers of the ITF who happens to be a citizen of India.

Mohd. Hoda has worked for the ITF since 1965 (since 1968 as the Secretary for the CIVIL AVIATION Section) and that appears, in the eyes of Mrs. Gandhi, to be a crime which warrants seizure by the Indian High Commission in London of Mr. Hoda's passport which was impounded on 2nd August, 1976 on instructions from Delhi. In return he was offered a document which would enable him to return to India to undoubted imprisonment without specific charges being made against him and without the right of appeal to any Court.

DESPITE several telephone calls to the Indian High Commission the only reason given for impounding Hoda's passport was "in the interest of the general public."

We would like Mrs. Gandhi to know that, so far as the work of the ITF is concerned this particular example of dictatorial venum is only a minor irritant, but for Mohd. Hoda this puts him in the position of being an exile from his homeland. This should serve to strengthen the resolve of affiliated Union to assist the Indian people and Trade Unions to achieve a society in which social justice prevails, in which abuse and corruption have no place and in which freedom of speech and democratic actions are not denied.

Affiliates are requested to give publicity to this circular in their Trade Union publications and the Press of their country.

Yours fraternally,
Sd/-
(C.H. Bliblyth)
General Secretary.

N. B. : ITWF circulated this throughout the world to its affiliated unions. Underground leaflets and bulletins used its excerpts to gear up the resistance movement.

DEMAND FOR POSTPONEMENT OF CONSTITUTION AMENDMENT BILL

STATEMENT BY INTELLECTUALS

The following appeal was submited to the President of India, the Prime Minister, the Speaker of the Lok Sabha and the Chairman of the Rajya Sabha on October 25, 1976, the opening day of the session of Parliament convened for the passing of the controversial Constitution Amendment Bill (termed the 44th, later 42nd Constitution Amendment Bill) :

The Government of India proposes to make sweeping amendments to our Constitution at the forthcoming session of Parliament on October 25, 1976.

We, the signatories to this statement, are not opposed to changes, even sweeping changes, being made in the Constitution. As concerned citizens, however, we feel that matters of such vital importance must not be decided in haste without the widest possible public debate in the country, as the Prime Minister herself has often stressed.

We also unanimously and firmly believe that the present Parliament has neither the political nor the moral authority to enact such fundamental changes in the Constitution. First, Parliament was expressly elected by the people of India for a period of five years, and that period expired in March 1976. Secondly, in the General Election of 1971 the ruling party had neither asked for nor was given any special mandate for making the changes now proposed. Thirdly, the country has been in a state of Emergency. Press censorship and other restrictions imposed by the Government have prevented legislators from fully and freely airing their views among their constituents. The people, too, have not had the opportunity of a full and free debate, without which they cannot comprehend the full implications of the proposed changes. It is clear, therefore, that the present Parliament is unable to discharge its constitution-making functions adequately and properly.

For these considerations of procedure and the enormity of the substantive changes contemplated, we feel that it is improper and unwise to rush the Constitution (44th Amendment) Bill through Parliament. A Parliament which has outlived its term and yet proceeds with such drastic amendments bears the grave responsibility of undermining the very democratic foundations of our society and state which were laid during a long struggle for national freedom led by Mahatma Gandhi, Jawaharlal Nehru and other revered leaders. The democratic alternative readily available at hand is to seek a clear mandate in a free and fair election so that the will of the people truly prevails.

The signatories to this statement appeal to the President, the Prime Minister, the Speaker of the Lok Sabha and Chairman of the Rajya Sabha and the Members of Parliament, to postpone the consideration of the proposed constitutional changes by the present Parliament. The Constitution does need changes, but such must be made only after the established democratic procedures have been fully and effectively utilised whereby the people expressly empower their representatives to make the changes. The ultimate power to shape the destiny of India must continue to be vested in the people of India.

Signatories to the statement are noted below :

Delhi University

Andre Beteille, Veena Das, R. K. Dasgupta, Mrinal Datta Chaudhury, G.D. Deshingkar, K.P. Gupta, Raj Krishna, Jaidev Sethi and others.

Institute of Economic Growth (Delhi)

B. B. Bhattacharya, T. N. Madan and others.

Gokhale Institute of Politics and Economics, Pune

V. M. Dandekar, Nilakantha Ratha and others.

Pune University

Ram Bapat, V. M. Sirsikar

Bombay University

Vasant Bapat, Usha Mehta

South Gujarat University, Surat

M. B. Dave, H.J. Desai, D. B. Gupte, R. I. Patel and others.

Vishvabharati, Santiniketan

M. Das Gupta, Ashim Das Gupta, Shyamal Sarkar and others.

Aligarh Muslim University

Hussain Ahmed, Muhammad Ahsin, Iqbal Husain, H. A. S. Jafri, S. T. R. Zaidi and others.

Allahabad University

Manas Mukul Das, V. D. N. Sahi, R. C. Tripathi and others.

Meerut College

Dharm Yash Deva, R. S. Yadava,

M. S. University, Borada

G. M. Sheikh.

Punjabi University (Patiala)

S. Teja Singh Tiwana, S. Ajit Singh, S. K. Bajaj and others.

Jawaharlal Nehru University, New Delhi

Anil Bhatti, S. Gopal, Romila Thapar, Parimal Kumar Das, S. C. Gangal, K. P. Misra, Urmila Phadnis, Satish Saberwal and others.

Columbia University, New York

Rajni Kothari

Writers, Artists, Film Directors

Mulk Raj Anand, Sekhar Chatterjee, Nissim Ezekial, Jainendra Kumar, Uma Shankar Joshi, Mani Kaul, Prabhakar Padhye, Annada Shankar Ray, Kaa Naa Subramanyam, Mrinal Sen, Paritosh Sen and others.

Journalists

G. S. Bhargava, Ajit Bhattacharya, Nikhil Chakravarty, E. P. W. De Costa, Harji Mallik, D. R. Mankekar, G. G. Mirchandani, V. K. Narasimhan, Kuldip Nayar, Cho S. Ramaswamy, A. B. Shah, Romesh Thapar, B. G. Vergese and others.

Advocates and Lawyers

M.C. Chagla, C.K. Daphtary, Ram Jethmalani, M. Hidaya-tulla, Shanti Bhushan, Soli Sorabjee, V.M. Tarkunde and others.

Educationists

Gouri Ayub, Bina Bhowmick, V. V. John and others.

Trivandum

K. N. Raj

Bombay

B.P. Godrej, Anand Kanekar, V. B. Karnik, K. K. Mahajan, D. G. Nadkarni, Shanti Patel, Dinkar Sakrikar, Sophia Wadia, Rajmohan Gandhi, Gulabdas Broker, Jehangir Sabawala and others.

Calcutta

Shaibal Kumar Gupta (retd. I.C.S) and others.

Delhi

S.K. Dey, Dharma Vir (retd. I.C.S.), Amiya Rao, B. G. Rao Pyarelal Nayar.

Indira's Emergency And The Working Class

Mrs. Indira Gandhi and her tycoons, through their mono-polised media shout from the top of their voice that everything is going on well in India. She claims as the champion of the downtrodden and declares that the poorer sections of the society are on the way to economic gains. She even declares that the emergency has been proclaimed for the benefit of the weaker sections of the society. But the facts are different. The 'gains of emergency' have benefitted the rich and the poor have become poorer.

The following excerpts from the inaugural address of HMS General Secretary, Shri Mahesh Desai at the 15th Annual Conference of Maharashtra Hindu Mazdoor Sabha at Nasik on 12th December 1976 will reveal the real state of affairs about the conditions of the working class after emergency.

1. The Government of India in a statement prepared for the 28th Labour Minister's Conference in Delhi in October 1976 had stated that in the one year between July 1975 and June 1976 one lakh and twenty thousand (1,20,000) workers had lost their jobs due to retrenchment and closure and seven lakh workers (7,00,000) had been subjected to wage erosion due to varying periods of lay-off.

2. The Conference of State Labour Commissioners which met under the auspices of the union Labour Ministry in October, 1976 expressed its concern about the loss of mandays due to lock-outs and closures, which far exceeded the loss of mandays due to strikes, in spite of the amendment to the Industrial Disputes Act, 1947 which stipulated three months' notice and prior permission of the appropriate Government before lay-off and/or closure.

3. The return of the first annual instalment of compulsory deposit of wages and dearness allowance operative since July 1974 has been slow, irregular, incomplete and unsatisfactory. But the Compulsory Deposit Scheme itself, which was to expire this year, has been extended by one more year.

4. The 1975 amendment to the Payment of Bonus Act, 1965 which had halved minimum bonus last year has all but taken away the minimum bonus from the overwhelming majority of workers in overwhelming majority of establishments in all industries in all parts of the country.

5. On the national scale so widespread and deep rooted has been the malaise in the industrial sector that the Government of India has made a special provision of rupees two hundred crores (Rs. 200) for special soft term financial assistance for rehabilitation and recovery to the growing number of sick units in cement, sugar, jute, cotton textile and engineering

industries which together in their prime employed nearly four million workers.

6. After registering production increases of 15% and 17% respectively in the last year the coal and steel industries, employing together about a million worker, have not only not been able to reward the workers for their performance but are concerned about the accumulation of pithead stocks of coal and unlifted steel in the stockyards with the inevitable consequence that their annual as well as plan targets are being substantially revised, limiting the scope of expansion of employment. The 242 mini-steel plants, with capacity of utilisation of 50% on the average, show the most aggravated symptoms of sickness.

7. The Government of Maharashtra has stated on the floor of the Legislature in December 1976 that there were 330 sick units in Maharashtra whose workers are out of employment and where production has ceased.

8. The conclusive indicator, so far as the working class is concerned, is the number of unemployed on the live register of the Government Employment Exchange. This figure has now almost reached one million.

9. Some of the more distressing aspects adversely affecting the standard of living of the Indian Worker are :

a) Increase in absolute unemployment.

b) Erosion of the monthly pay packet due to :
    (i) Price rises unreflected in the cost of living indices.
    (ii) Continued deduction under compulsory deposit scheme.

c) Denial and diminution of annual income augmentation on the bonus account.

d) Undermining of job security on account of closures and retrenchment.

e) Interruption of work and earnings on account of lay-offs and lock-outs.

Late News

All the detenus in Dhulia District Jail, Maharashtra went on hunger-strike on 19-12-1976 as a protest against inhuman and callous policy of the Government of Maharashtra regarding release on parole of detenus when their relatives are seriously ill.

Mrs. Joshi, wife of Shri Vithal Parshuram Joshi, a detenu in Dhulia District Jail was seriously ill. The parole application was pending before the Government for more than a month. The reminder was also sent but had no effect. Only after the death of the unfortunate lady, the parole of 15 days was sanctioned. What a torture ! One more 'gain of emergency' !!

CHAPTER IV

REPORTS AND ARTICLES

Cases of Torture and Harassment of Satyagrahis by Police

Extract from the letter written to Madam Prime Minister by Sarvashri T.N. Singh, Mohan Dharia, Samar Mukherjee, Jagannath Rao Joshi and Digvijaya Narain Singh, all Members of the Parliament on 21-10-75.

a) In Muzaffarpur a lathi charge was made on 9.9.75 by the Jail authorities and criminals were let lose. A large number of them received injuries, some of them serious. The injured persons include : Prof. Thakur Prasad Sinha, Head of Math. Deptt. of S. R. D. College, Prof. Shyam Sunder Das of D. S. College, Sh. Yoshwant Singh Chaudhari, Ex. MLA, Vice-President, Sinar BLD.

b) Another case of lathi charge in Begusarai Jail is reported where Shri Ram Jiwan Singh, Ex. MLA who was recently operated for HARNIA received head injuries. Another Ex. MLA, Shri Hukamdev Yadav and Sri Ram Bahadur Sharma of Bachwara were badly injured in Jail.

c) On 15th August, police arrested one Shri Anand Rau whose son is a Jawan in Indian Army. He was brutally assaulted while being taken to prison, as a result of which he died on 26th August, 1975.

EXTRACT from the letter addressed to Sh. B. Reddi, Minister for Home Affairs by M/S. T. N. Singh, K. Mathew, D. N. Singh, Jagannath Rao Joshi......

d) On Sept. 25, when a student was arrested and said to have been dragged to a waiting Ambassador Car by some police men in plain clothes who had entered the University Campus with the permission of Vice-Chancellor. The name of the student is Shri Prabir Purakayastha and the incident is reported to have taken place near the School of Languages in the University Campus. Later in the evening of Sept. 26th the DIG

Delhi informed the University authorities that they were holding this student under MISA. (Jawaharlal Nehru Un.).

EXTRACT from the letter addressed to Sh. Reddi on 24.9.75 by M/s. Tranib (Tridib) Chaudhary, N. G. Gorey, Jagannath Rao Joshi, T.N. Singh and others.......

e) Shri Bhairav Bharati an Ex.MLA, Trade Unionist and fredom fighter of Nagda (M.P.) who was detained under MISA following the proclamation of Emergency has died in person. According to our information, even relatives of Shri Bharti were not informed either of his illness or about the circumstances of his death. Shri Bharti was arrested on 26th June. He suffered from Jondice in the first week of August in Ujjain Jail. His son Babu Lal Bhartiya, Advocate, brought the situation to the notice of Madam Prime Minister, Hon'ble President and others telegraphically on 4.9.75.

EXTRACT from the letter addressed to Madam Prime Minister on 2.9.75 by Shri Samar Mukerjee, M.P.

f) Com. Than Singh, Leader of Textile workers of Pilakhua and his family members are being harasssed. Police took away from their house articles of daily use without sparing a saree for his wife or utensils for boilng milk for the small child.

EXTRACT from the letter addressed to Madam Prime Minister by A. K. Gopalan, M. P. from his camp office in Cannanore in Aug., 75.

g) Our party MLA Com. M. V. Raghavan and other leading comrades were stripped naked and assaulted in public under the direct supervision of Cannanore D. S. P.

h) After declaration of emergency on 21.7.75, Com. Sahadevan was taken to Cannanore Police Station and brutally tortured. Now he is undergoing treatment and his condition remains critical.

i) On 21.7.75 at about 11 p.m. Circle Inspector Balaram and party broke open the House of Valluvakandy of Maloor Panchayat. Policemen entered the house and indiscriminately assaulted the inmates as a result of which his daughter, Janu, a village school teacher sustained injuries.

j) On 9.7.75 two of our party workers, Mohanan and

Salan from a place called Jravachal were arrested by Kuthu-paramba Circle Inspector without any reason. They were kept in custody for six days and subjected to inhuman torture.

k) On 10th July, Payyannur Circle Inspector and party entered the campus of Payyannur College and picked up 16 students. They were brought to the police station and brutally tortured. Later all of them were produced in court framing charges under D.I.R.

l) On 11th July, 19 students belonging to S.F.I. & K.S.C. were arrested from Sir Syed College Campus at Taliparamha. All of them were brought to the police station, stripped naked and cruelly beaten up.

EXTRACT from the letter of Shri E.M.S. Namboodripad MLA from his Camp office Shanti Nagar, Trivandrum on 11.10.75 addressed to Madam Prime Minister.

m) Com. P. Vijayan, MLA was brutally assulted in police lock-up before he was taken in the jail for detention. The assault was so brutal that he sustained such grievous injuries that he had to be hospitalised.

APART FROM THE ABOVE CASES REFERRED TO Madam Prime Minister and others by the Members of the Parliaments, the CENTRAL HEAD QUARTERS of Lok Sangharsh Samiti is in receipt of reports from various State Quarters narrating the cases. Some of the torture and harassment cases are reproduced below : —

Goa :

13 persons are detained under MISA and their relatives are allowed to meet only once a month. A sum of Rs. 2.70 paisa per day is spent on them for fooding etc. They are not given "A" CLASS. The relatives of the detenues have appealed to the Government and the members of Parliament.

Madhya Pradesh :

On 5.12.75, 8 persons belonging to JAN SANGH took part in Satyagrah at DEWAS. They were beaten and were forced to sleep naked. They were tortured to do unnatural acts

(SODOMY) with each other. This all was done in the presence of S.P.

Delhi :

1. *Shri Hemant Kumar Vishnoi*, Secretary, Delhi University Students Union which represents one lakh students, was arrested with his fellow students while in a picnic in the Budha Gardens in New Delhi. He was hung upside down and beaten. Burning candles were applied to his bare soles. Chilli powder was smeared into his nose and rectum.

2. Another Delhi University student, *Mahavir Singh* was arrested, taken to the police lock up, hung upside down, stripped naked and beaten up so badly that even three months later his skin reacts against the touch of a shirt.

3. *Mr. Shiv Kumar*, student of B.Sc. Final was arrested on December 11, was taken to the police station, beaten with rods, shoes and gun butts. Later he was made to inhale chilli smoke.

4. *Harish Kumar* of Tilak Nagar was arrested and beaten mercilessly. *Shri Suresh Jain*, student of LLM (Law) was similarly treated. They were disallowed medical test and proper treatment.

5. *Rajesh and Anil*, aged 15 and 18 who were picked up for distributing pamphlets at a function addressed by President Ahmed, along with other boys were mercilessly beaten and made to sweep entire floor of the big police station.

6. *Satya Parkesh* of Fathepuri Delhi was beaten with rods and shoes at the Hauz Qasi Police station on 23.11.75. He was tied with a bundle of iron chairs. The bundle was then hung by the ceiling fan whirrled around and his body was beaten at every turn till he finally broke down.

7. *Om Perkesh*, aged 21 was arrested for offering Satyagrah and was denied sleep, food and water for two days on stretch was mercilessly beaten, specially on the neck. He was thrice hung up upside down, chilly solution poured into his nose. Later he was made to stand for two days at stretch. This happenend on November 25, 26 and 27 while in lock up at Timarpur Police Station.

8. *Rasik Agiwal* aged 20, Commerce Graduate was tortured

at Timarpur Police station on Nov. 28, 29 and 30. Every method stated above was applied to him. He ultimately succumbed and gave out the name of *OM PARKESH* (other than the one mentioned above) as his associate. Police went to his house but he did not happen to be there. His wife was kicked and abused.

9. On December 3, *Vasudev* was picked up for offering Satyagrah along with *Para*s *Ram*. From among the batch these two (aged 52 and 48) were specially selected for police torture.

They were made to stand in open during the cold winter night, were hit hard and legs with hands up and a rod tied to their neck.

10. *Prof. O.P. Kohli*, President, Delhi University Teachers Association, who is a lame person was made to stand for 24 hours at a stretch in the Police lock up while the policemen showered him with abuses, shoes beatings and even pushed him from side to side with abusive remarks.

11. *Shri Madan Lal Khurana*, Secretary, Delhi State Jana-sangh was picked up on 19.12.75 from Darya Ganj. He has been mercilessly tortured by police in the special cell at Nazafgarh. He was arrested at about 11.00 A.M. and was produced before the Court the next day. He was tortured in various ways overnight in an underground cell. Shri Khurana is a sitting Member of Delhi Metropolitan Council and a leading politician of Delhi.

12. *Shri Surendra Jain*, B. Com., *Shri Shyam Bihari, Praveen and Mahesh* offered Satyagrah at Red Fort (in front of Appolo Circus) on 16.11.75. They were beaten up by the police at Kotwali Police Station. They were detained under DIR. Shri Surendra Jain has been subsequently transferred under MISA.

13. *Sarva Shri Kishan Lal Katpiecewala*, Ex. Member, Delhi Metropolitan Council, *Dr. Mulak Raj Juneja, Govind Chalani*, Municipal Councillors and about 150 detenues of ward 15 of Tihar Jail sustained injuries due to the brutal lathi charge which was ordered by the Jail Superintendent on the 2nd October, 1975, the birthday of Mahatma Gandhi. The lathi charge was ordered in the presence of Shri Krishan Sarup, Executive Councillor (Jails), Shri Rajender Tanwar, Congress (Indira)

Member to Metropolitan Council. Lala Hans Raj Gupta,
former Mayor of Delhi and Industrialist (Sangh Chalak of
Punjab Province which includes Delhi, Punjab, J & K, Haryana,
Chandigarh and Himachal Pradesh) made a strong protest to
Shri Reddy, Minister of Home Affairs in a letter dated 3.10.75.

14. Two minor childs named Suneel and Manoj were
picked up on 17th Nov. at about 10 p.m. from Jogiwara by the
Hauz Quazi Police just to oblige some local Congress (Indira)
workers. They were beaten up till they finally broke out to
make a planned (by police) confession. They were taken to
various residences and were forced to call names. Since the
called persons did not appear to be in at one place the father
(aged 60 years) and the wife were taken to Police Station. They
were made to sit in cold throughout the night along with two
months old baby without milk. They were later produced
before the Duty Magistrate under DIR.

15. On 15.11.75, three students, S/Shri Surendra Jain, Ravi
Narain Khanna and Naresh Sadiyala were picked up by the
Daryaganj Police at about 4 P.M. They were produced before
Magistrate after 30 hours. They were mercilessly beaten in the
police lock up.

Haryana :

1. At Yamuna Nagar, *Shri Malik Chond, Satya Paul and
Pawan Kumar* who were arrested on Nov. 23, were kept in
unlawful detention till 27th Nov. and were paraded on the
streets with their shoes on their heads. Policemen beat them with
rods and kicked on way and later humiliated them further by
urinating into their mouths.

2. At Ambala, five Satyagrahis led by *Jai Parkeh* were
arrested on Nov. 25. Before being produced before the Magistrate on 29th were made to stand naked on the road-side on
29th Nov. Bucket full of water were poured over them during
the cold wintry night. They were not allowed to sleep even for
a minute and so were his comrades. On Nov. 28th, Jai Parkesh
was tied in ropes and placed in a cycle rikshaw with face paint-
ed black. He was then paraded in the town and was spat and
beaten by policemen.

3. At Karnal, *S/Shri Sultan Singh, Dhan Pal, Ravi Datt and Lekh Raj* were arrested on 14th Nov. for offering Satyagrah. In addition to the usual merciless beating, they were stripped naked and made to lie on the floor with faces touching the ground for hours at stretch. Over them climbed three policemen with their boots on and kept on jumping over their bodies.

4. At Rohtak, even a seventy years old man, *Dulichand Gautam* was not spared. He was very mercilessly beaten.

Rajasthan :

1. At Jodhpur, demonstrators paraded with the placards "WE ARE TRAITORS". Nothing can be more insulting than to be paraded as a traitor.

2. On Dec. 8, 75 at Jhunjunu right before the Chief Minister, Hardev Joshi, *Shri Suresh Chandra Tiwari* who is a Research Scholar was mercilessly beaten up. He was taken to Police Station and made to stand with his hands up for 34 hours and his sensitive parts were poked with rods.

Kerala :

1. On 19.9.75 one CPI (M) Branch Secretary at New Mahi *Abdul Rahiman* (at a Saw Mill where he works) and members *T. Vijayan, K: Gangadharan and S.K. Sukumaran* (at Dinesh Beedi Company where they work) were arrested and beaten mercilessly.

2. On the night of 21.8.75 Coms. *K.K. Balakrishnan and P. Narayan* were arrested. On 14.8.75, Com. *Ponnan Kunhiraman* was arrested from his house at Kanhapuram under DIR and was beaten.

Andha Pradesh :

Karimnagar Dist.

1. Satyagrahis were brutally beaten in Karimnagar Police Station and Jugtilal Police Station. Two of the men arrested at Godavarikhan were tortured and their bodies were burnt by lighted candles nearly at 200 spots, by the S.I. at Police Station. The wounds were very severe and the Jailor refused to admit them without Medical Ceritificate (Photo enclosed—now preserved).

Nalgonda Dist.

2. On 14.11.75, *Shri Gopi,* a Satyagrahi beaten severally (severely) in Police custody in Nalgonda, could not urinate and so was taken to a private Doctor. *Shri Suresh Chandra Reddi,* was beaten to unconsciousness. *Shri Suresh Reddi* was beaten severelly in CID Office, Nalgonda.

3. *S/Shri Krishniah and Narsimha Reddi* were severely beaten in illegal police custody by Muralidhar Rao, S.I. Shri Krishnayya was admitted in Nalgonda Govt. Hospital for swollen things and twisted ankles.

4. On 8.12.75 nearly 33 persons kept in police custody for 3 days in a small room, not leaving them even for passing urine. 3 of them were kept in illegal police custody for 15 days and even a 12 year old boy was beaten to unconsciousness by Badri Rai, S.I. and Anand Rao under the supervision of Bharatchand, S.I.

5. On 22.12.75, *Shri Voikuntha Chari* was beaten in police custody for 4 days.

Hyderabad Dist.

6. *Shri Krishnayya and other Satyagrahis* at Vikaroad were severely beaten, stripped off their clothes and made to sleep in the biting cold, were denied food.

Warangal Dist.

7. On 26.11.75 at Hanumakonda P.S. the following police officers tortured the stayagrahis throughout the night. The satyagrahis are *S/Shri Venkat Rao, S. Reddi, Veera Reddi, Venkatnrama Reddi and Sampath.*

Hyderabad Dist.

7. *Shri K.Narsimha Reddi* aud other were brutally beaten in a room in Salarjung Museum by G. Venkata Reddi, S.I., Shri Narsimha Reddi was later operated upon in Osmania Hospital for the injuries. This incident is dated 4.11.75.

8. On 5.12.75 at Charminar P.S. Dabirpura Police out-post and Saidabad P.S. : S/Shri Manendra, Rajawardhan

Reddi, Bapi Reddi, Madhusudhan Reddi and Ashok Reddi were severally (severely) beaten by S.I.. Shri Bapi Reddi was kept in illegal police custody for 3 days.

Shrikakulam Dist :

9. Brutal beating even on the private parts of *Shri Edida* Raman, Shri Nraleti Krishna and Karra Appla Narsimha Murthi, Shri Trinadan and Shri Simhachalam from 7 P.M. to 3 A.M. by AZEES P.C. at Srikakulam P.S. This incident is dated 14.11.75.

Visakhapatanam Dist :

10. On 15.11.75 *Shri Erraji,* a worker found writing slogans on the walls was given electric shocks in I. Town P.S. in Vishakha.

East Godavari Dist :

11. In Kakinada P.S. on 14·11.75 *Shri Koka Kurma Rao* leader of the batch of satyagrahis and Shri Krishna Prasad were severelly beaten and hang them by hair and as a result they became unconscious.

12. For sticking wall posters, *Shri Satyanarayana Chair* was brutally beaten in Kakinada P.S. on 2.12.75 for 4 days. Shri K. Ranga Rao Engg. student was also beaten.

Karnataka :

1. *Shri Srikant Betgeri* a youth of Belgaum offered satya-graha on 12.11.75 along with a batch led hy Shri Ganpatee Kulkarni, the chief Belgaum branch of RSS. He was separated from the batch, was beaten brutally by the police at the police station. His back became blue and green.

2. *Shri Ashok Mutgekar* a young college student on 30.11.75 was taken to police station and badly beaten. He was put on "aeroplane", a third degree method whereby the entire body is subjected to excruciating agony.

"AEROPLANE" specialised by the Karnataka police is : The victim's hands are tied behind his back with a rope. The rope is taken over a pulley at the roof and the victim is pulled

up a few feet above the ground. The victim tangles in mid-air hanging by his hands tied at the back.

3. *Shri Srikant Desai* of Hubli State Jt. Secretary of the Karnataka unit of Vidyarthi Parishad was put on the "aeroplane" and inhumnly beaten.

4. *Shri Padmanath* of Harihar (Chitradurga Dist.) Secretary of Dist. RSS and *Shri Puttuswamy* RSS worker were taken from home on 27.11.75 and were kept in police lock up for 2 days. They were beaten and put on "aeroplane."

5. *Shri Nagendra* and 3 other students wete brutally beaten by the S. I. in the Devaraja P. S. on 2.12.75.

6. *Shri Ravi* leader of students satyagrah was arrested at Mysore and beaten and kicked on 2.12.75.

7. *Shri Uday Shankar*, a student of Canara Collage, Bangalore was arrested from his house on 1.11.75 and brutally caned at Bunder P.S. His body turned red and blue. This was done in the presence of S.P. Chopra.

8. *Shri Anant Hegde, Pandurang Hegde and Ganesh Kudwa* were arrested without warrants on 13.11.75. They were kept at Bunder P.S. for 3 days without proper food and sanitary arrangements. They were caned so much that they could neither bend their knees nor walk.

9. At Bidar on 14.12.75. *Shri Shivraj Nillagi and Shri Sharanappa* and 3 other satyagrahis were cruelly beaten up with lathis.

10. *At Bellary Shri Garanath Kulagari* was illegally detained in the police station for 10 days and beaten.

11. *Shri Pullikeshi* who offered satyagraha on 14.11.75 was brutally beaten at City Market P.S., causing several wounds on his body.

12. Five Vidyarthi Parishad workers at Bungalore, *S/Shri Puresh Naik, N.H. Suresh, Goverdhan, D.S. Srivaram and Somashekher* were treated inhumanly and brutally beaten up in police lock up. They were put on "aeroplane" and for 4 days they were not produced before the Magistrate. To avoid their production before the Court they were put behind MISA after 4 days.

13. Shri Srinata of National College, Bangalore was arrested on 27.11.75 and put on "aeroplane".

14. *Shri K.N. Krishna Murthi,* reader in Maths. in an Engg. College Bangalore was beaten in black and blue.

There are 20 more cases from Karnataka itself and this is not all. PLEASE circulate it and send detailed reports to Centre.

N.B. Cases of torture and harassment, arrest etc. were collected by Lok Sangharsha Samity. Typed copies were sent to the states. Later, a booklet titled 'Tortures in Indian Jails' was published from Bombay. It contains specific cases of inhuman tortures with demonstrative drawings.

AMNESTY INTERNATIONAL FIGHTS
FOR HUMAN RIGHTS

Amnesty International's campaign is designed to bring greater support to prisoners of conscience throughout the world.

Amnesty International is a worldwide human rights movement which is independent of any government, political faction, ideology, economic interest or religious creed. It works for the release of men and women imprisoned anywhere for their beliefs, colour, ethnic origin or religion, provided they have neither used nor advocated violence. These are termed "prisoners of conscience".

Amnesty International opposes torture and capital punishment in all cases and without reservation. It advocates fair and early trials for all political prisoners and works on behalf of persons detained without charge or without trial and those detained after expiry of their sentences.

Amnesty International seeks observance throughout the world of the United Nations Universal Declaration of Human Rights and the UN Standard Minimum Rules for the Treatment of Prisoners.

ANNESTY INTERNATIONAL REPORT 1975-1976

INDIA

The large scale arrest of members of all opposition parties in India (except the Communist Party), which followed the declaration of a national state of emergency on 26 June 1975, was perhaps the most significant event of the year in terms of human rights in Asia. The state of emergency was declared because of "internal distrubances". It added a new dimension to the emergency declared for external reasons which had existed since the Bangladesh war in 1971.

The declaration followed a growing anti-corruption campaign led by the widely respected veteran politician, Jaya Prakash Narayan, a follower of Mahatma Gandhi, which had attracted support from most opposition parties. The immediate cause for the imposition of the emergency was a call by the opposition parties that Prime Minister Indira Gandhi resign pending a Supreme Court appeal against her conviction by the Allahabad High Court on charges of electoral malpractice.

On the day following the emergency declaration, 27 June, Amnesty International made a public appeal to Prime Minister Indira Gandhi to free all political prisoners arrested under the MISA. In a cable, AI said the arrests constituted a "departure from the long standing traditions of democracy in India". AI national sections visited Indian embassies to express their concern. One month later, on 16 July 1975, AI proposed to Foreign Minister Y.B. Chavan that an AI mission should visit India to discuss the measures taken under the emergency. However, no response has yet been received.

On learning of the first arrests, the Research Department began to collect data on individual prisoners as the basis for a large scale adoption program. AI groups are now working for 120 adopted prisoners, a figure which is expected to rise in the near future.

On 6 October 1975, five members of Parliament presented a report to Minister of Home Affairs Brahmananda Reddy requesting an independent inquiry into reports that political prisoners had been seriously beaten in New Delhi's Tihar Jail on 2 October. On 8 October, AI launched an urgent action campaign through its national sections asking parliamentarians to send telegrams to the minister requesting that a full and independent inquiry be made into allegations of ill-treatment.

The Indian authorities have shown considerable sensitivity in the face of these approaches.

In August, in an interview with *Socialist India*, Prime Minister Gandhi charged that AI was "very active in the hate India campaign". Deputy Secretary General Hans Ehrenstrale, in a letter of 15 August, replied that the work of AI was well known to the Indian government. He said AI was concerned about the detention of political prisoners in all countries, irrespective of political, ideological or geographical considerations. "Any suggestion that we are engaged in a hate campaign against any country is totally unfounded", he said. But on 29 September the Prime Minister charged that AI was among the organizations "not at all worried over events in countries under open authoritarian rule where people were killed, but raised its voice if some people were detained".

The strict censorship regulations in force, by prohibiting publication of news on political imprisonment, have encouraged widely varying unofficial estimates of the numbers detained, which range as high as 175,000. Government claims that many detainees have been released are certainly true. Equally, although there is no comprehensive official figure for arrests under the emergency, the Government has conceded that a large number of political prisoners remain in detention.

On 23 August 1975, Minister of Information V.C. Shukhla stated that the total of arrests since the emergency did not exceed 10,000. He claimed that the majority of arrests since the emergency had been made among economic offenders, of which a number of arrests were made on purely political grounds. In one of India's 22 states, Maharashtra, alone, Chief Minister S.B. Chavan stated on 17 November 1975 that 3,000 persons remained in detention out of the 13,500 originally arrested in that state.

But large scale arrests continued to take place over the year. More recent examples include the arrest of thousands of persons taking part in a *satyagraha* (non-violent) program which was initiated in November 1975, the arrest of 16,000 persons in West Bengal, mainly trade unionists, on and after 6 January 1976 for participating in strikes against the government's Bonus Act, and the arrest of hundreds of opposition members in Tamil-

Nadu following the recent imposition of President's rule on 31 January 1976. Most recently, Minister of State for Home Affairs Om Mehta announced on 17 May the arrest of more than 7,000 people in a government move to stop circulation of clandestine literature opposing the emergency.

On the basis of these and other official figures made in various states, AI is certain that a minimum of 40,000 persons are now detained without trial under emergency regulations for political reasons, although many more may actually be held. Reports by independent observers, estimating the total of dissidents at 100,000, possibly indicate the true scale of political imprisonment. On 16 March 1976, AI published a list of parliamentarians in prison in all countries. More than half the names on the list are of 59 Indians, members of the *Rajya Sabha*, the *Lok Sabha* and state legislatures.

In a letter of 30 April 1976 to the Prime Minister, AI appealed for a return to full constitutional rule on the first anniversary of the emergency declaration. It urged the government to consider announcing a general amnesty for political prisoners held without trial on that occasion. The letter reviewed legal and constitutional developments which appear to contravene the provisions of the United Nations Universal Declaration of Human Rights and asked for verification of reports regarding the detention under which some of the political prisoners were arrested and detained. Reports were cited that former Deputy Prime Minister Morarji Desai and Mrs Mrinal Gore, a socialist member of the legislative assembly, are among the political prisoners being kept in total isolation from other political prisoners.

AI also requested the Indian government to investigate reports of ill-treatment of political prisoners. These reports allege that the prisoners have been severely beaten after arrest on sensitive parts of the body, hung upside down or suspended with hands tied behind their backs, and also that prisoners had been burned with candles. AI sought assurances from the Indian government that the provisions of the UN Resolution on Torture and the General Assembly resolution on torture would be implemented.

On 5 December, AI cabled its deep concern at the hanging of two members of the Communist Party of India (Marxist), commonly known as Naxalites, who are executed on 1 December 1975. Kista Gowd and Jangam Bhoomiah, both peasants from Andra Pradesh, who had awaited execution for nearly three years, were hanged for participation in politically motivated killings in the state. AI had earlier made several representations for clemency on their behalf.

The substance of the allegations made in the *Report on Prison Conditions in West Bengal* (see *Annual Report 1974/75*) concerning prisoners held in Bihar and West Bengal for alleged involvement with extremist leftwing political activities were substantiated by Mary Tyler, who was released from five year's detention without trial in Bihar Jails. Her detailed account confirms that such prisoners are held in insanitary and overcrowded conditions (for example, Jamshedpur District Jail, built for 137, house 1,100 prisoners in the summer of 1975), that political prisoners in Bihar have very little chance of ever being brought to trial and that, when released, political prisoners are often re-arrested under preventive detention laws like the MISA. Her report confirms that some prisoners, alleged Naxalites, have been kept in iron fetters in Bihar Jails for four years.

N.B. This printed report was circulated to underground sources.

HUMAN RIGHTS AND DEMOCRACY IN INDIA

Major Events in Mobilizing International Opinion

Indians for Democracy (IFD), the Free J.P. Campaign and the Committee for Freedom in India (CFI) worked in close cooperation in mobilizing international opinion for restoration of human rights and democracy in India following the emergency decree by Mrs. Gandhi's government. While IFD and CFI concentrated on North America, the Free J.P. Campaign concentrated on U.K. and other European countries. All three groups worked in coordination with one another.

1. *Demonstration, Vigils and Meetings :* The three groups

organized many demonstrations, a march for freedom, and meetings on many occasions such as Independence and Republic Day, visits of Government officials (e.g. Foriegn Minister Chavan's visit to Chicago) to increase awareness of the loss of human rights and freedom in India and to keep this issue alive.

2. *National Conferences :* Indians for Democracy held several national conferences in various cities in the United States such as Washington, D.C., New York, Chicago and Hartford, to discuss the latest situation and formulate strategies for continuing the mobilizing of public opinion.

3. *Newsletters and Publications :* The Free J.P. Campaign Committee was the first to publish a newsletter "Swaraj," edited by Satish Kumar, immediately after the emergency. Indians for Democracy started publishing its bi-weekly newsletter "Indian Opinion", edited by Ravi Chopra, in October 1975. The readers of these newsletters were not only supporters and admirers of India and its democratic traditions all over the world, but also freedom fighters in India who continued their heroic resistance to Mrs. Gandhi's dictatorial rule.

These organizations brought out several publications including the underground document, "Anatomy of Dictatorship" by George Fernandes, and speeches of opposition members in the Parliament.

The most notable publication was an 80 page booklet entiltled "Democracy or Dictatorship in India ?" edited by Ananda Kumar and published by the Committee for Freedom in India in August, 1976. This publication includes, among other things, a letter from Loknayak J.P. from Chandigarh Jail, uncensored documents from India, resistance to Mrs. Gandhi's emergency rule by freedom loving people, Indians and non-Indians all over the world. The booklet has received wide acclaim.

4. *Petition to the United Nations Commissions on Human Rights :* The Indians for Democracy in cooperation with the International League of Human Rights submitted a thoroughly researched 73 page report to the United Nations Commission on Human Rights charging the Government of India with a consistent pattern of gross violations of human rights. The

report was compiled by Faruk Presswalla and several of the documents of human rights violations for this report were provided by the Lok Sangarsha Samiti in India. This received world wide publicity.

5. *Meetings and Speaking Programs of Prominent Dissidents from India and IFD Activists :* There were nationwide speaking programs of prominent dissidents from India such as Ram Jethmalani, former Chairman of All India Bar Council and Subramanian Swamy, a Member of Parliament. In addition, Mr. C. G. K. Reddy, who travelled extensively in Europe and North America was able to mobilize a great deal of additional support from trade unionists, Socialists and prominent leaders. He also was responsible for a resolution of Socialist International denouncing Mrs. Gandhi's emergency rule and calling for restoration of democractic processes.

In addition, activists of IFD went on speaking programs to further increase the support for their activities, to establish better communication and coordination among similar minded groups and individuals. Mr. Anand Kumar, a doctoral student at the University of Chicago, went around the United States immediately after the emergency to mobilize support for the activites of the Indians for Democracy.

Later, as a Representative of Indians for Democracy, the Committee for Freedom in India and the Free J.P. Campaign, Mr. S. R. Hiremath, Chairman of IFD, Chicago, travelled extensively in Europe and met with various groups such as Amnesty International, International Commission of Jurists, U.N. Commission on Human Rights, and Socialist International and spoke to several human rights groups in London, Brussells, Amsterdam, Bonn, Berlin, Munich, Vienna, Zurich, Geneva and Paris.

6. *Hearings in the U.S. Congress on Human Rights in India :* Congressman Donald Fraser, Chairman of the Sub-Committee on International Organizations started the hearings on Human Rights in India on June 24, 1976, on the eve of the anniversary of the declaration of emergency by Mrs. Gandhi. Prominent dissidents from India, Ram Jethmalani, Leila Fernandes (wife of George Fernandes) and others such as Dr. Home Jack who

worked with J. J. Singh of the late India League which championed the cause of India's independence prior to 1947, testified before this Congressional committee.

The hearings had dramatic impact and further shattered the credibility of Mrs. Gandhi's propaganda.

The Committee for Freedom in India, under the leadership of Rev. G. G. Grant, worked to mobilize the opinion of the U. S. Congress and has been in contact with prominent Senators such as Sen. Edward Kennedy, and Senator Charles Percy and Congressmen such as Abner Mikva, Donald Fraser and Edward Derwinski, especially for the release of imprisoned parliment-arians. The Committee worked closely with another group, Ad Hoc Committee for Human Rights in India under the leadership of Dr. Homer Jack, which did a very good job of mobilizing the opinion of the U. S. Congress.

7. *Worldwide Events on the First Anniversary of Emergency :* The three groups, in cooperation with other groups, held meetings, demonstrations, and issued statements of concern in various places around the world.

The Indians for Democracy held meetings and demonstrations in over 20 places in various parts of the U. S.

The Committee for Freedom in India released a statement on the first anniversary of the emergency, June 26, 1976, calling for restoration of human rights and democratic processes in India signed by over 130 prominent Americans. Some of the signatories to the statement included Herbert Marcuse, philosopher and Author, Nobel Laureates George Wald and Salvador Luria, Ralph Abernathy, President of Southern Christian Leadership Conference, Prof. Noam Chomsky of M. I. T., Rev. G.G. Grant, Chairman of World Association of World Federalists, Collin Gonze of United Auto Workers, and Congressman Abner Mikva.

8. *Impoundment of Passports and Merit Scholarship :* Angered by the successful campaign of the Indians for Democracy against the emergency rule, especially the submission of a petition to the U. N. Commission on Human Rights, the government of Mrs. Gandhi first cancelled the Merit Scholarship of Anand Kumar in March, 1976, and later, in July, 1976, impoun-

ded the passports of Ram Gehani, S. R. Hiremath, S. G. Nandi and S. K. Poddar, all leaders of Indians for Democracy. Far from intimidation, this action of the government only helped the IFD further intensify its efforts. In a similar move, the Indian Government also impounded the passports of M.S. Hoda of Free J. P. Campaign and Mr. Harish Sharma of Indian Peoples' Association of North America.

9. *Walk for Human Rights* : To protest the state of emergency and the impoundment of passports by the Indian government, the Indian for Democracy organized a 14-day walk from Independence Hall in Philadelphia to U.N. Headquarters in New York. Well known Quakers, academics, peace and labor leaders and others joined this walk. At the end of the walk, several copies of a well documented memorandum to Mrs. Gandhi were mailed to over 100 prominent persons and activists in India. This was a symbolic act of asserting that the restrictions on the freedom of conscience and information are evil and must be resisted by each individual. Mr. Ravi Chopra and Dr. P. K. Mehta played leading roles in organizing this walk.

10. *Ads in the Newspapers* : There were advertisements taken in leading publications such as the "London Times" and "New York Times" and publications such as "India Abroad", serving the Indian Community, on such important occasions as the Indian Independence Day (August 15th) and the birthday of Mahatma Gandhi (October 2nd). The most notable one was the full-page ad taken by the Free J. P. Campaign on August 15, 1975 in the London Times which was signed by well known leaders all over the world.

11. *International Organizations* : All the three groups worked with well-known international organizations such as Amnesty International, the International Commission of Jurists, Socialist International, World Federalists and several prominent trade union organizations all over the world. While Amnesty International was helpful in working on the release of political prisoners, the Socialist International was very helpful in mobilizing the support of most of the prominent Socialist leaders of Europe.

These three organizations worked in cooperation with several other groups such as Indian peoples' Association of North America (IPANA), Friends of India Society International (FISI), George Fernandes Defense Committee and the Ad Hoc Committee for Freedom in India.

This summary of major events has been prepared by the Indians For Democracy and the Committee of Freedom in India, 67 East Madison Street, Suite 1417, Chicago, Illinois 60603 U. S. A.

FIGHT TO THE DICTATORSHIP

A Brief Report of the Movement for the Year
26 June '75 to 26 June '76

Clamp down : On the night of 25-26 June 75 JP and number of leaders of the LSS group of opposition parties were arrested. It was in the morning of 26th June and through the broadcast of the PM that the country came to know that the president had declared emergency for internal security reasons.

Spontaneous Protest : Stunned by this onslaught, political activists and enlightened citizens could not make out what exactly had happened. Yet, there was sense of anger and indignation in majority of the urban populace. In the capital, posters were pasted all over the city announcing the news of the leaders' arrest. Bandh was attempted at a number of places like Patna, Agrah, Muzzafarpur, Varanasi, Allahabad, Kota, Bombay, Puna, Dhule, Jalgaon etc. But for want of adequate preparations and due to the confusion as well as fright, it was not successful. Public rallies were held at few places because the police had not received full instructions immediately. From the next day, repressive machinery was started in full steam.

On the 1st of July 75 PM broadcast her new economic policy in the form of 20-point programme. This was intend to further confound the vocal elements of the nation, who could be enamoured by the talk of progressivism. ("If something good is likely to be done to the poor, why grumble about the loss of liberty ?") Within four days 26 organisations were banned and their members arrested. The CPI was trumpetting all this as "a triumph of progressive forces over the monopoly capital backed by imperlialist forces".

As many leaders were jailed and communications with the remaining was difficult, the LSS could not meet and formulated its stand. Nor could it issue directions to the caders of the constituent parties. Nevertheless, people under the leadership of Smt. Vijayaraje Shinde, offered satyagraha on 29th June. It continued for a few days. At some other places, it was decided to launch individual satyagraha from 16th July 75 to mobilise the public opinion on the demands of : (1) Withdrawal of emergency (2) Release of Political prisoners (3) Withdrawal of censorship. The DMK organised a huge rally at Marina Beach, Madras, on 6th July, 75 at which about six lakhs men and women took a pledge to defend democracy. Demonstrations were organised at various levels in Kerala between 9th and 13th July. Individual satyagraha was offered at a number of places in Bihar, U. P., Punjab, Maharastra etc. between 16th and 25th July. It was reported that the demonstrations in Bihar were so intense that the police had to resort to lathi-charge and firing at 72 places. In U. P. people hnd gheraoed police chowkies at two places. In Gujrat, hartal was observed at a number of urban centres on 26th July.

A number of individuals registered their protest again the draconian measures of Smt. Gandhi. Shri N.A. Palkhivala withdrew from the election case of her. Shri S.V. Gupta resigned from the post of the Solicitor-General while Prof. M.L. Dantwala resigned from the directorship of RBI. Bomday union of Journalists passed a resolution demanding the withdrawal of censorship, and the executive committes of the All India Union of Journalists passed a similar resolution a little later.

Lawyers of Allahabad had passed a resolution on the 26th comdemning the imposition of emergency. Similar resolution was passed by the Western India Bar Association at Bombay and the lawyers there boycotted the functioning of the courts that day. In Gujarat the lawyers held a number of conferences to condemn the imposition of emergency. In other states also, similar protests were recorded.

University and College teachers of Bombay sent a memorandum to the President demanding the immediate withdrawal of emergency, release of political prisoners etc. University and college teachers in Marathwada and Puna areas also followed suit.

CPI not only continued support to her but reinforced their propaganda against the "right reactionaries and the imperialists."

Muslim league, who was wavering in extending support to JP movement, came out with whole-hearted support to Indira. Minor parties like Hindu Maha Sabha and Shiva Sena did the same. Republican party of India and Zarkhanda Party of of Bihar were ambivalent in their support to JP movement ; on the proclamation of emergency, they changed sides and supported Indira. Peasants and Workers Party opposed the emergency but wanted the genuine leftist forces to join hands to fight the dictatorship, but as long as that was not possible they preferred to keep aloof from the struggle. Revolutionary Socialist Party and Forward Block are divided on the issue. The W. Bengal branches of the two parties are opposed to it while the Kerala unit of the former and Maharashtra unit of the latter have extended support to the Govt. (In the last week of July 76, Shri Jambmantrao Dhote has demanded release of political prisoners and holding free and fair elections as early as possible.)

The constituent parties of the LSS remained steadfast in opposing Indira and characterised the emergency as the begining of the dictatorship. DMK and Akali Dal took similar positions but continued to remain outside the LSS. CPM described Indira rule as semi-fascist and decided to oppose it but not to align with the rightist forces. CPI (M.L) described the Indira rule as compradore capitalist and fascist dictatorship and decided to cooperate with all those who were ready to fight it. Some Marxist groups like Lal Nishan Party of Maharashtra did not either support or oppose Indira rule but decided to fight back if the workers are denied political rights. Dalit Panthers, who were opposing the powers that be on the ground of injustice meted out to the scheduled casts, overnight changed sides and supported Indira.

From amongst the organised labour, the INTUC and AITUC enthusiastically supported Indira rule while HMP, CITU, BMS and sections of the HMS opposed it jointly as well as severally.

Akhil Bharatya Vidyarthi Parisad, Tarun Santi Sena and Samajwadi Yubajan Sabha opposed the emergency while some groups like SFI, Yuwak Kranti Dal, Magova etc., have decided to organise the down-troodden and the dalits for justice and equality.

Some individuals in the public life, who had earlier supported JP movement changed sides. But they are outnumbered by those who were, prior to 25th June 75, critical of the programmes and methods of agitation of JP, came out boldly against emergency. There are many more who share these views but prefer to keep silent.

Organised compaigns : Though the spontaneous reaction of the constituents of the LSS and of a number of unaligned democrats was to oppose the authoritarian rule, there was utter organisational confusion. The LSS could not convene a meeting to chalk out a plan of action. Activities (activists) had to take decision individually.

A number of bulletins have sprang up all over the country and the Govt told the Parliament that more than 7,000 persons were arrested for publication and preservation of prejudicial matter : The LSS could not make arrangement for collection and distribution of the news about the movement.

From July to November, there were many programmes organised by the local groups e. g., gathering before the statue of Lokmanya Tilak and pay tribute individually through wearing the badge of 'Nirbhaya Banc' (Fear Not) on the birth anniversary of Gandhiji organising a Kavi Sammelen and sing patriotic songs, etc., some leaders like S.M. Joshi and N.G. Goray visited a number of places and discussed the situation in the country with the citizens. A public meeting was also held in Bombay in Sept. 75 in which Goray spoke about the present situation and criticised the emergency. Subsequently, the Govt. banned all gatherings even inside the hall. In U. P. efigies of the P. M. were burnt in a number of towns. In Kerala a committee consisting of the leaders of CPM and SP tried to

organise a Civil Liberties Conference, but the Govt banned it
and put the leaders in jail.   In Karnatak, students of a number
of colleges observed hartal on 25 Sept. 75. At Delhi on 2nd Oct.
a batch of 11 youth staged demonstration against Indira, while
in the evening a pravachan was organised in which veterans like
J. B. Kripalani, H.V. Kamath, Sushila Nayar, etc. participated.
Kamath and a few others were prosecuted under DIR and acquitted by the magistrate but in the process nine activists had to
spend seven months in jail.   Individual satyagraha continued to
be offered at a number of places in Bihar, U.P., Punjab, Tamil-
Nadu, Maharashtra, Gujrat etc.

Battles were also fought in the law courts. Shri M. R. Masani
had filed a suit petition against the order of the censor. Another
journalist R. Y. Oltikar of the Maharashtra Times also filed
similar petition.   Habeas Corpus petitions were filed by a large
number of political detenues.   High Courts of Delhi, Bombay,
Karnatak and U.P. had overruled the preliminary objection by
the Govt that since the President had suspended Articles 13 and
19, the courts cannot entertain all these petitions.   Editors and
and publishers of Bhoomiputra (Gujrati periodical) and Sadhana
(Marathi) had also to approach the high courts against the
orders of the respective state Govts.   A number of lawyers like
Chandrakanta Daru of Ahmedabad and C. R. Dalvi of Bombay
took the briefs of these liberty-fighters and fought bravely in
the courts without caring for the pecuniary gains. Citizens for
Democracy Commitee had organised a Civil Liberties Conference
at Ahemedabad in the second week of Oct. Eminent jurists like
J.C. Shah, M.C. Chagla, Solly Sorabji, V. M. Tarkunde etc.
participated.   Bhoomiputra published a report of the speech by
Chagla for which the Govt served seal order on it.   The matter
was taken up in the High Court which gave a very fine judgment
in the defence of liberty and laying down stringent guidelines
for the censor.

Some lawyers of Bombay under the leadership of Justice
Nathwani, former judge of the Bombay High Court, tried to
organise a lawyers' conference on the issue of emergency and
Civil Liberties. The Commissioner of Police banned it. The
lawyers, aggrieved by the order, approached the High Court

which gave them relief. The Govt. however preferred an appeal to the Supreme Court.

Political prisoners were harassed and tortured in a number of states like Kerala, Delhi, Madhya Pradesh, U. P., Bihar, and Maharashtra. Mass hunger strikes were organised in many jails to protest against the inhuman treatment meted out to them and also to get demands like more interviews per fortnight, more letters to be allowed to be received and posted etc.

In the meantime, the LSS had planned nation-wide satyagraha campaign from 14th Nov. It started with a bang in hundred of places, accompanied by writing on the walls, posting of thousands of posters, and distribution of laks of leaflets. At some places, it lasted for a month while at a few places, for two months. Exact number of those who courted arrest is not available. The figures given by Shri Subramaniam Swamy in his London interview, were as follows : Karnatak-15,000, Kerala-9,000, Bihar-8,000, U. P.-8,000 Delhi-5,000. Obviously the list is incomplete. In Maharashtra, there were more than 5,000 satyagrahis, while more than 1,000 had offered satyagraha in Tamil Nadu and Andhra Pradesh each. Gujrat had mustered more than 5,000 satyagrahis. From the reports in the New Age (CPI weekly) it seems significant number had offered satyagraha in Assam, Orissa and M P., which even the paper had described as "The reactionaries are turning their head in these states."

Due to the press black-out there was no glamour in courting arrest. It was feared that the Govt. may detain persons offering satyagraha under MISA which meant indefinite detention, and actually, it so happened in a number of cases. Many also felt that if the attempt was not going to be made known to the people, it was useless to go to the prison. However, the satyagraha campaign helped in lessening the fear psychosis. At many places, the spectators responded cheerfully to the slogans shouted by the satyagrahis, but since the people at large were not proposed by the cause of civil liberties, as they were in the national liberation struggle, impact was not deep enough.

There were a few encouraging features of the campaign. Young boys and girls, particularly the college students, were preponderent in number. Some of them are members of the RSS and ABVP ; but many of them were not aligned with any party before 25th June. Participation by women was also on significant scale. Not only in the metropolitan centres like Bombay, Delhi, Nagpur and Puna, but at a number of small towns like Nanded, Buldhana, Sangli, Palghar and the advasi area of Javhar, did the ladies offered satyagraha, some of them with babes in arms. Hawkers of Bombay and a few other self-employed workers of big cities also participated in the campaign. It is a fact that the RSS had contributed a lion's share in this campaign for which the organisation must be congratulated. However, it may be noted that it tried to focus attention on the injustice in banning the RSS only, and not on the wider issue of civil liberties.

Shri Madhu Limaye and Shri Sarad Yadav resigned from the Lok Sabha as a protest against immoral extension of its life.

Protest by the men of literature and academic

It was around this time that men of literature recorded their protest. Shivaraman Karanth of Karnatak had returned the Padmabhushan award. In Gujrat, eminent poet Umashankar Joshi had been campaigning against the dictatorship. In Maharashtra, Durga Bhagwat, President elect of the Sahitya Sammellan voiced her indignation in clear terms. In the first week of December, strong views against restriction of freedom of expression were voiced by the eminent men of literature like V.S. Khandekar, Laxmanshastri Joshi and P. L. Deshpande besides Durgabhai in the Marathi Sahitya Sammellan. On 7th December the whole Sammellan stood in silence and prayed for JP's health. Gujrath Sahitya Sammellan held only a few days after, adopted a resolution demanding withdrawal of emergency and restoration of civil liberties.

But it should also be noted that Hindi Sahitya Sammellan decided to confer the degree of 'Sahitya Saurakahak' on Smt. Gandhi despite the fact that Phanishwarnath Renu and Nagarjune were in detention.

About 200 literatures (litterateurs), academicians and journalists from Maharashtra signed a memorandum demanding withdrawal of emergency.

Eminent political scientists, Rajni Kothari in an article in Seminar (Jan. '76) unequivocally condemned imposition of emergency and came down heavilly on the tendencies towards centralisation exhibited recently by Smt. Gandhi.

Shri Manubhai Pancholi, veteran Freedom Fighter returned the Tamrapatra while Vishnubhai Pandya, noted Gujrathi Literary figure, declined a state award.

First Anniversary of Dictatorship

JP had appealed to the citizens, and the youths in particular, to give a lie to the claim of Indira that she is safeguarding democracy. He had suggested that processions may be taken out, meetings organised and leaflets distributed. The LSS sent instructions to the activists. Accordingly, lakhs of leaflets were distributed all over the country. Small meetings were held at a number of places, and big ones at a few. At Ahmedabad in particular, a huge rally was addressed by Shri Asoke Mehta, Babubhai Patel and others. A procession was also taken out for which Babubhai and others were arrested and released later. In Maharashtra hundreds observed one-day fast and thousands wore badges with the mementos of JP and M. Gandhi for which sources were arrested and prosecuted. Around a thousand were taken in preventive custody on 25th June.

Efforts at Mediation

Soon after the proclamation of emergency, a few eminent citizens like Madame Sophia Wadia, V. B. Karnik, M. R. Masani, etc tried that a dialogue between the P. M. and the opposition be held. The attempt received indifferent response from the authorities.

JP when interviewed immediately after release, had said that the movement would continue till the following demand were met : (1) withdrawal of emergency (2) lifting the press censorship (3) release of political prisoners (4) holding free and fair elections.

After the Supreme court verdict in Smt. Gandhi's Election case, Acharya J. B. Kripalani wrote an open letter to the president urging revocation of emergency, since one chapter is closed and oposition demand for PM's resignation lapsed, it evoked no response.

Many hopes were entered on Vinoba who was to break his year-old silence on 25th December 1975. The LSS had addressed a memorandum to him enumerating various repressive measures of the Government. Vinoba, however prefered to restrict his observations to this much. India is an independent country and in a democracy, satyagraha will have to be resorted to if the state did not respond to the councels of the Acharya who are fearless, impartial and hostile to none (Nirbhaya, Nishpaksh and Nirvaira).

Shaikh Abdulla, the Vazire Asam of Kashmir, also pleaded for reconciliation, but in vain.

In the meantime, in response to the speech of the P.M. in the Rajya Sabha in the second week of January, N. G. Gore and H. M. Patel, leaders of the recently formed Janata Morcha in the Rajya Sabha and Lok Sabha respectively, addressed a letter to the P. M. saying that if the Government was inclined to have dialogue with the oppositions, the latter were prepared to talk and that as a first step towards normalisation the MPs in detention may be released. A few days later, they also addressed a similar letter to Vinoba welcoming the statement of the Acharya Sammelan. At the instance of some senior colleagues, JP also sent a letter to the PM dated 19th January, saying that if he was to do something towards conciliation, he may be given an opportunity to discuss the matter with Morarji Desai, Charan Singh, Madhu Limaye and Nanaji Deshmukh. The letter remind (remained) unanswered. All this indicated that Sm. Gandhi did not want any kind of dialogue or reconciliation with the LSS.

Gujarat and Tamil Nadu

Since the proclamation of Emergency, Smt. Gandhi had been frowning upon the non-congress Government of Gujrat and Tamil Nadu. Particularly, the former, because it came into

power by defeating her party at the polls. Right from the beginning, the Cong (R) opposition there tried by all means fair and
foul, to pull down the Janata Morcha Government.

On the proclamation of Emergency, Babubhai had to make
a different choice to resign as a protest against the repression or
to remain firmly in saddle and become instrumental in continuing the repression. With great courage and prudence, the
Janata Morcha decided not to resign. At the same time it also
decided not to enforce restrictions on the civil liberties as far as
it could help. Press censorship was entirely in the hands of the
Central Government, but the State Government decided not to
detain activities (activists) of the political parties under MISA
and not to impose ban on public assemblies etc.

The most dangerous aspect of the situation is that only a
small minority (consisting of a few lawyers, journalists, political
activists and other public spirited individuals) is aware of this.
As it is, common man is averse to learn the intricacies of the
State craft. The khadi curtain, pulled over by the press restrictions, has made the things more difficult.

In addition, the Govt. has resorted to various methods,
cruder as well as subtler, of repression. Some of the activists of
the opposition parties were pressurised to desert their parties
and join the ruling one or at least to welcome the 20-point prog-
grame publicly. In U. P., a number of educational institutions,
presumed to be under the influence of the oppposition parties,
particularly JS, were taken over by the Govt. under DIR. In
Maharashtra and in some other states, employees & teachers in a
number of colleges were asked to give an undertaking in writing
that they would not participate in political activity. The vice-
chancellors of all the Universities in Maharashtra have formulated a code of conduct which says that the university/college
teachers cannot propagate views even in conference and
seminars.

It is a sad fact of Indian political life that an overwhelming
majority is not politically alert or articulate. In the rural areas,
the political consciousness is very little and communications are
difficult both because of the shortage of means of communication and the illiteracy of the masses. They could not grasp the

import of the events of 25th-26th June 75. According to the survey conducted by a semi-official agency in eight states, it was found that 95% of the rural population were not knowing that emergency was proclaimed or 20-point programme announced.

Problems before the movement

1. Smt. Gandhi has shrewdly used the term 'Emergency'. It indicates ad hoc nature of the measure. And also ideological neutrality. But her intentions are more than clear. She wants to strangulate impersonal, institutional framework of democracy and perpetuate dynastic rule.

Leaders of the movement against dictatorship should unequivocally expose the true nature of Indira rule. People will have to be educated in the essence of democracy, and the vital role various institutions have to play in its functioning and how Indira has eroded those institutions.

2. Smt. Gandhi and her henchmen have been denigrating civil liberties by saying that they are the obstacles in the path of Garibi Hatao. Leaders of the movement will have to spell out the true content of civil liberties and their relevance for the poor and the downtrodden. More attention will have to be paid to the rural areas.

3. Systematic efforts will have to be made to persuade the minoirties (minorities) and the scheduled caste and tribes to join the forces of democracy.

4. Long-term perspective of the movement should be formulated in clear terms. People should be told how they can dislodge dictatorship by peaceful means, if free and fair elections are not held and the electorate do not get chance to change the rulers peacefully. Not only the common man but many an activist of LSS group of parties feel that the fight against dictatorship is unequal and it is not within the reach of the unarmed common people to dethrone the dictator. Clear guidance should be provided to buttress the faith of the people in the efficacy of the peaceful means.

5. As pluralism is the essence of democracy, anti-dictatorship movement may be developed on the multi-central lines.

Various voluntary groups and organisations may be encouraged to propagate democratic value and undertake programmes that would promote fearlessness amongst the people.

But all this cannot be treated as a substitute for building a strong organisation to run the movement in the main. It must be born in the mind that democrats were defeated in a number of countries because they were weak organisationally. Truth can prevail only when backed by strength. Keeping this in view, LSS should be revitalised and, as suggested by JP, its branches be organised in different mohallas of cities and towns, in schools, offices, colleges and factories and in the villages. All agitational activity should be coordinated through it.

Resource-raising will have to be paid special attention. Internal communications will have to be strengthened. Channels of mass communications to be built up systematically. Cadrebuilding should be the main plane of organisational efforts.

6. Forms of recording protest, etc., should be so revolved as to make possible for maximum number of people to participate in it.

7. Mass organisations of various classes and section will have to be built and the existing ones to be strengthened. More so in the rural areas. Various sections to be encouraged to conduct limited agitations to get their specific grievences redressed.

N. B. This typed report was prepared by Socialists and Lok Sangarsha leaders and distributed by Socialist Action Council.   J. B. 1-7-76

REPRESSION BY INDIRA

Jack Anderson

Despite the dictatorship Indira Gandhi has imposed upon India, threatening the extinction of democracy in its largest and most challenging setting, the democratic spark still flickers in that teeming land.

It can be found in the courageous letters and speeches of

dissident Indian leaders, including members of Parliament, who still dare to speak out against repression. Their words cannot be published in India, so the suppressed statements have been smuggled to us.

We stood up for India when its soldiers liberated the dreary, impoverished piece of earth now called Bangladesh. We condemned our own government for its deception and duplicity during the India-Pakistan conflict.

For exposing the secret works of Richard Nixon and Henry Kissinger, we were hailed in India. Jack Anderson rallies were held there, thanking us for telling the truth. Now it is our mournful duty to expose the secret works of Indira Gandhi.

The smuggled documents tell a depressing story of political intimidation, press censorship and prison abuse. Yet the letters and speeches reveal that India, too, has its Alexander Solzhenitsyns.

The undaunted opponents still speak out, even as their colleagues are arrested in the halls of Parliament. In an angry letter to the Indian Speaker, one outspoken member of Parliament, Era Sezhiyan, decried the arrest of colleagues during actual committee sessions.

"Several leading members of Parliament, both from the opposition side and the ruling party," he protested, "are incarcesated for reasons best known to the government." This strips Parliament, he charged, of "its meaning and purpose." ; it "loses its basic character as a debating body." Concluded Sezhiyan : "With a press silenced and members prevented, the House becomes a muted museum."

A similar cry was raised in the Indian Senate by another bold member, N.G. Goray, who shouted out the names of colleagues who had been arrested : L.K. Advani, A.B. Vajpayee and Madhu Dandavate.

Still another, A.K. Gopalan, charged that "34 members of Parliament have been detained without trial." This had reduced Parliament, he cried, to "a farce and an object of contempt."

These speeches, of course, were never mentioned in the censored Indian press. "The press is often called an extension

of Parliament," explained Sezhiyan. "Hence for effective functioning of a parliament, there should be full facility and freedom for the press to cover the proceedings and to publish all
that is said. Any curb on the activities of the press, overtly or
covertly, will make a Parliamentary debate...unreal."

Goray hurled a challenge directly at Indira Gandhi's supporters : "Why are you afraid of the press ? I would like to ask
my friends, are you going to make democracy a woman in
purdah that nobody should look at her, nobody should touch
her and only you people will speak to her ?"

Some of the jailed Indian legislators, meanwhile, allegedly
are suffering from atrocious prison conditions. One of the
letters smuggled to us, was written by three members of Parliament to India's Home Minister Brahmananda Reddy.

The letter complains that their colleague, Jyotirmoy Basu, is
held in solitary confinement in a dark, insect-infested jail cell.
He wasn't told the reason for his arrest, nor was he permitted
to see his wife and son, the letter protests.

"We understand," the letter declares, "that he (Basu) has
been kept in complete isolation in a solitary cell in Hissar Jail.
No person other than those on duty are allowed to go in. The
cell has no window or door excepting a small ventilator at
ceiling height and a grilled iron gate.

"When there is a dust storm, he has no protection from such
storm. The cell also gets flooded when there is a downpour.
We further understand that to make the isolation complete, the
jail authorities have fixed two thick blankets on the courtyard
gate so that nothing outside is visible for him...

"For a number of days, there were no switches for the lights
that were in the cell, so he had to sleep with a powerful bulb on
throughout the night, which attracted thousands of insects.
Subsequently, the bulb was removed, but he had to live and
eat in darkness."

Other protest letters paint a similar picture. One letter,
signed by 19 members of Parliament, condemns the Gandhi
government for its "highhanded and inhuman treatment of the
political prisoners who have been arrested." Estimates have
placed the number of political prisoners as high as 50,000.

At the Indian Embassy, a spokesman acknowledged that the press is now censored in India and conceded that many speeches in Parliament, therefore, go unreported. But the reports of prison atrocities, he said, were "absolutely untrue."

The spokesman insisted that India remains a democracy because it has an elected Parliament. This recalls the words of George Orwell : "It is almost universally felt that when we call a country democratic, we are praising it ; consequently, the defenders of every kind of regime claim that it is a democracy."

Footnote : Indira Gandhi's acquisition of dictatorial powers hasn't stoped the flow of U.S. aid to India. President Ford has asked Congress for another $ 76 million for India this year. On Capitol Hill, there is some sentiment to cut off aid to India, but the U.S. has financed many a dictatorship worse than India.

State Journal Register : Springfield, Illinois   10.7.75

N. B. Reproduced from SWARAJ.

INDIA'S NEW POLITICAL INSTITUTIONS

Myron Weiner

For many months we have been reading reports of the steps taken by Prime Minister Indira Gandhi to dismantle India's democratic institutions, particularly the steps she has taken against the opposition parties, the press and the judiciary. Less attention has been paid to the kinds of institutions that are taking their place or to the effects of these changes on the government's promised efforts to accelerate economic growth and to create greater equity for the poor.

These institutions actually grew in importance even before the emergency was declared. They each reflect the trend toward the centralization of authority that has taken place since 1971 as a response to the erosion of Congress party support, the rising dissidence within Congress, and the resurgence of the opposition. The growth of these institutions provided the central government with the capacity to take decisions it took on June 26th and thereafter. Four institutions are of increasing importance :

1. *Centralized intelligence organisations.* Of these the most important are the Research and Analysis Wing (RAW) organized directly under the Prime Minister's secretariat, and the Central Bureau of Investigation (the CBI), located in the Home Ministry. The decision to declare an emergency would hardly have been possible had Mrs. Gandhi not strengthened and centralized India's intelligence organisations. It is widely believed in India that RAW has built up dossiers on government opponents, on critics within the governing Congress party, journalists, businessman and bureaucrats. The intelligence provided by RAW made it possible to arrest thousands of opponents on the night of June 26th, to dismiss or early retire many civil servants, and to keep a watchful eye on India's growing underground.

2. *Central government police forces.* In the past decade there has been a major expansion of the Central Reserve Police, the Border Security Forces, the Central Industrial Security Forces, and the Home Guards. These centrally controlled police units, which total well over 600,000, are independent *both* of the state police (an estimated 750,000 men) and the armed forces (estimated at 900,000). The government could thus declare and maintain an emergency without deploying India's armed forces and without relying upon state police units.

3. *The Prime Minister's secretariat.* The secretariat, created by Lal Bahadur Shastri, but considerably expanded by Mrs. Gandhi, has emerged as an independent executive force more comparable to what exists in a presidential than parliamentary system. Members of the secretariat take responsibility for intelligence, for monitoring the paramilitary police forces uuder the Home Ministry, and for shaping the country's basic domestic and foreign policies. The appointment and promotion of senior administrative personnel is now handled by the secretariat rather than, as in the past, by the Home Ministry. Frequent shifts in recent years have underscored the importance of the Prime Minister's secretariat in the making of police. The government's twenty-point program to create more discipline in the country

emanated not from the Congress party or the cabinet, but from the Prime Minister's own staff.

4. *The Youth Congress*. In recent years the Youth Congress has been emerging as a militant cadre-based organization taking over many of the functions of the regular Congress organization. Initially a force in Calcutta where government funds enabled the Youth Congress to attract many of the tough elements in the city in a campaign to break the popular hold of the Communist Party of India (Marxist), the Youth Congress, under the leadership of Sanjay Gandhi, the twenty-nine year old son of the Prime Minister, has been building local units elsewhere in the country. It is a growing force in the southern state of Kerala, in Bombay city, and in New Delhi, and efforts are now underway to build the organization in the country's major cities.

In the past half-dozen years Mrs. Gandhi has actively sought to prevent the emergence of powerful state political leaders who might threaten the person or program of the Prime Minister. She has appointed the Chief Ministers in most of the states, rather than permit the local state Congress party organizations and legislative assemblies to choose their own leaders. While a decade ago, when Mrs. Gandhi first took office, there were a dozen or so state leaders who were widely regarded as important national figures, today there are hardly any state leaders with independent political power.

Not only have the powers of the state governments declined, but there has also been a decline in popular control over India's cities. Many of the country's municipal governments have been suspended. In Bombay, Calcutta, Delhi, Hyderabad, Madras and Bangalore, municipal power is in the hands of officials appointed by the state or central governments. In Delhi, this has enabled the Delhi Development Authority to summarily remove thousands of squatter slum dwellers and sidewalk shopkeepers from the city. Similar programs to remove the poor are planned for several of India's other large cities.

New legislation has been passed which strengthens central authority. The Maintenance of Internal Security Act (MISA) has been amended so that the government has the authority to detain and arrest individuals without producing charges before a court of law. Recent acts by parliament also prevent the press from publishing articles inimicable to the interests of the government. Statements made by opponents of the government in parliament or in the courts can no longer be freely reported in the press. These various acts thus give the government authoritarian powers even if the emergency is terminated.

It seems likely that the constitution will be amended to permanently institutionalize the present limitations on civil (or as they are called in India, "fundamental") rights and to further restrict the power of the courts. Mrs. Gandhi's decision to postpone elections for at least another year ensures the government of the two-third parliamentary majority that is required to amend the constitution.

As with most countries in the Third World, power in India has become both more centralized and authoritarian. There has been a marked shift in power from popularly elected officials to government bureaucrats. It is the state apparatus that is now growing, while the Congress party, the opposition, the press and the independent judiciary are declining in importance. Like so many Third World leaders Mrs. Gandhi aspires to create a political order where policies are initiated by her supporters in the national bureaucracy, are implemented by centrally appointed politicians and bureaucrats whose careers are dependent upon her support, and—she hopes—will be backed by popular acclaim.

Mrs. Gandhi has pointed to the improvement in the performance of the bureaucracy as one of her greatest accomplishments since the emergency was declared. Corruption is down, government bureaucrats come to office on time, government-run trains leave and arrive on schedule, the administration is enforcing anti-smuggling and anti-hoarding laws and is collecting previously untaxed "black" money. But programs to accelerate the country's economic growth and to deal with the problem of poverty require more than an efficient bureaucracy. Can the bureaucracy carry out land reforms or can agricultural laborers obtain higher wages when tenants, laborers, and small farmers are not allowed to organize themselves ? The local Congress organization, which continues to rest on the support of the local landed classes, is hardly willing to support an agrarian reform program. And as for accelerating economic growth, there is no evidence thus far that the Prime Minister and her advisors have a program that might unleash the forces of productivity that are latent within India—for without a major expansion of domestic private investment, or a massive infusion of foreign assistance or investment, where are the forces to accelerate the country's economic growth or improve the opportunities for India's poor ?

Mrs. Gandhi can centralize authority under her leadership, but she does not lead a revolutionary mass party capable of pushing the country in a revolutionary direction. Nor is she ideologically willing to stimulate private investment and savings though for short-term tactical reasons the government may pursue a pro-business policy. India is not at present organizationally capable of moving to the left, nor ideologically prepared to move to the right. Instead, India retains the organizational structure of a right-of-center government and the ideological outlook of a left-of-center government. Thus far, the emergency has left India's political economy fundamentally unchanged.

Both development and distributional policies will be shaped by Prime Minister Gandhi's overriding need to consolidate her power. Whatever policies she pursues and however she amends the constitution, it seems likely that the era of multiple centers of power and decision by consensus in India is now over.

*Adapted from a talk presented at the Annual Meeting of the Association of Asian Studies, Toronto, March 20, 1976.

THE INDIAN POLITICAL CRISIS IN PERSPECTIVE

Rajni Kothari

I have been in this country for more than three months now and am amazed at both the naivete and the ignorance that prevails among large sections of Americans as well as among a majority of Indians living here about the breakdown of demo-cracy and the erosion of human rights in India. Even the liberal press — including some dispatches in the *New York Times*—is not free from this. There is a growing ambivalence towards what has happened in India and this often takes the form of a supercilious attitude based on studied disinterestedness and even a degree of disdain. Indians that have lived here for long years share the same attitude and indeed seem to have outsmarted their American employers and colleagues in their contempt for their own country over the years, and now seem to welcome the end of democracy and the rise of what seems to them a strong-willed dictatorship—the so-called "hard state"—that will some-how "deliver the goods."

As I hold a completely opposite view (to me what has happened to India since June 1975 is a great tragedy not just because I value liberty and democracy, which I do, but because I believe that any other form of government will be unable to manage the affairs of this highly diverse and continental size polity and will lead to its disintegration and ultimate demise) I shall first examine the assumptions on which the view that favours or at least condones dictatorship in India is based, and then argue why I think each of them is misplaced.

First, it is held that democracy in India had failed to solve the problems of that country, especially in respect to poverty, food shortages, population growth and the condition of the mass of the people. Second, it is argued that there was massive inflation and economic disorder and that this had to be stem-med. Third, it is alleged that in June 1975 the Indian Govern-ment faced political chaos and disruption which threatened its survival. Fourth, that the curtailment of civil liberties, the free-dom of the press and constitutional rights have affected only the well-to-do sections of the middle class and have no relevance to the illiterate and toiling masses in the rural and urban areas who are likely to be the beneficiaries of the new regime. Fifth, that drastic programmes like enforced family planning would not have been possible under a democratic form of government. Sixth, that following the imposition of a state of emergency, the Government in India has been able to not only bring order and stability to the land but also improve the economic lot of the people, stem rising prices and control population growth.

Underlying these more specific assumptions are certain beliefs about the suitability of democracy to a developing country like India. (These beliefs extend to the Third World as a whole and have became stronger with India's deciding to join the ranks of authoritarian governments in the Third World.)

Three such beliefs are widely prevalent, including among many who may not agree to all the specific points about India mentioned above. First, that a dictatorship is better to undertake radical economic and social changes than a democracy : it is too bad that civil liberties and intellectual freedoms have to be trampled but this is necessary for economic development. Second, in any case democracy is unsuited to developing societies as it brings large masses of the people into the political process and raises their expectations and this leads to unrest and instability. The third argument, which I find to be a peculiar mixture of non-interventionism, unconcern and ethnocentric arrogance runs as follows : why should we try to impose our values and institutions on alien cultures which may be better suited to more primitive forms such as a dynasty with its courtly order and forms of coercion that are meant to secure compliance of the people ? Democracy, being a special form of governance that arose in Western Europe and North America and deeply embedded in the cultural milieu of these societies (individualism, Protestant ethic, pluralism, moderation of conflict, bargaining culture, etc.), is unlikely to succeed elsewhere. It was an unnatural outgrowth in India and other countries and we should not shed tears at its demise which was bound to come sooner or later.

Now, I believe that these assumptions and beliefs are without foundation and are based on a mixture of ignorance, lack of historical perspective, prejudice against the Third World, and a basic lack of faith in their own long cherished values among Westerners. Let me first deal with the more specific assumptions and then come to the more general belief structure.

1. The first argument, that democracy had failed to produce results in India, can be rejected right away as it is contrary to

available evidence. True, there is still a lot of poverty and malnutrition in India. The battle against illiteracy has slowed down and population control has not made as rapid a stride as may be considered desirable by many. But on each of these the heyday of democracy in India—which lasted from 1950 to 1965 —had shown significant improvements. The rate of economic growth was, with one or two setbacks due to particularly bad harvests, consistently way above the rate of population growth (between 4 and 4.5 percent as against a 2.5 percent rates of population growth which had gradually begun to slow down). Agricultural production had more than doubled, industrial output had risen dramatically, and the country had moved from a largely primary goods producer that was dependent on external markets and imports of manufactured goods to a broad-based economy with a large measure of economic independence and the beginings of a considerable export potential. Furthermore, this period was also marked by a considerable spurt in rural development, the constructions of a fairly developed transport and communication network that integrated the economy, and on balance a transfer of resources from urban to rural areas and from the upper to the middle and lower middle castes though not yet to the lowest deciles of the population except in very small ways.

This process would have gone further if only the leadership after Nehru had maintained his perspective and moderation and allowed full scope to the political pressures that had begun to emerge from the lower levels of polity in the form of demands for a more decentralized and employment oriented economic policy. Instead, after the 1967 elections and the split in the Congress party in 1969 (which resulted from a confrontation between the state-based leadership made up of less sophisticated but more rooted politicians and more urban and English-educated politicians who employed a "radical" stance and found an at first hesitant and undecisive Mrs. Gandhi willing to become their instrument) the democratic process suffered a series of set-backs, the fine balance on which economic performance was based was also upset, and the country was pushed towards a highly centralized, insensitive and bureaucratic form of government.

13

It is not just a coincidence that the period of political con-
solidation through the democratic process from 1950 to 1965
was also the period of steady economic growth and social justice
whereas the period since then has been marked by a decline in
both the democratic content of politics and the social content
of economic performance. The Emergency put a seal on both
and those who hope that erosion of the political process can be
accompanied by an improvement in the economic condition of
the people are simply prisoners of their own fantasies.

2.   The second argument about inflation is simply based on
misinformation. The Government of India undoubtedly succeeded in taking steps that curbed inflation and gave rise to an
era of stable prices. But this was long before the declaration of
the state of emergency and the latter cannot claim any credit
for it. The situation has no doubt been further helped by two
exceptionally bountiful harvests and to an extent the benefits
of good rains were maximized by the Government's support of
irrigation projects and increased production and import of
fertilizers. But once again the credit cannot be claimed by the
post-emergency regime during which, if anything, stocks of
fertilizers have been piling up and grain surpluses are not finding
their way to the most needy strata of the population (thanks
largely to the Government's failure to raise employment and
incomes and purchasing power among the mass of the people).

As a matter of fact, apart from favourable monsoons and a
striking improvement in the balance-of-payments the Indian
Government has, since the Emergency, been following policies
that are anti-labour, against employment generation, far more
liberal to the upper middle classes than to the lower classes, and
generally successful in maintaining prices (except of late) only
by allowing considerable retrenchment of labour and the holding back of working class bonuses and equity earnings of fixed
income groups. There has also been a sizeable cutback in
production in a number of industries, a piling up of inventories
and redundant plant capacities, and a sagging morale among
both the labouring and the middle management cadres as well
as in small and medium scale business. As for the peasantry, it
is finding out that its market is shrinking too, and the govern-

ment, which is dominated by urban interests, is not allowing a fair price for agricultural produce. As for the claim that the wages of agricultural labourers have been raised through state legislation, this has only to be weighed against both violation of the law in practice and a net reduction in employment of agricultural labour.

Generally speaking, the economy presents an apparently optimistic picture only due to the two good harvests, but there is no sign that the government has utilized this opportunity to any great advantage. And this is hardly surprising. There have been almost no structural reforms that could have generated the necessary momentum for change from below, for there are no grass roots pressures to do so. An authoritarian government is under no compulsion to perform—untill a large attack on it mounts, as is bound to happen sooner or later when the economic situation worsens. But by that time it will be too late for this particular government as it is not likely to survive such a storm.

3. As for the charge that in June 1975 the Indian government faced a lot of disorder and violence and threat to its survival, this again is not true. If anything, the situation had distinctly improved from the point of view of the Government, with the movement led by Jayaprakash Narayan virtually fizzling out, with inflation coming under control, and with everyone preparing for the next general election which was just a few months ahead. As a matter of fact, Mr. Narayan had accepted the Prime Minister's challenge of testing out his movement at the next poll and the Prime Minister had also shown a degree of sensitivity by holding the state election in Gujarat following Mr. Morarji Desai's fast unto death on that issue. In the state election, the results of which came out on the same day as the Allahabad High Court's judgment on Mrs. Gandhi's election case, the Congress party lost by a narrow margin. But all signs suggested that it will come through the national election as it was the only nationwide and organized party and as even in Gujarat—where the opposition movement had first started and the Congress was a discredited party with its record of corruption and highhandedness—it had done rather well. (It got 40

percent of the votes, just a few points below its normal vote in earlier elections.) There is really no doubt that there would have been no Emergency had it not been for the High Court's unfavourable decision unseating Mrs. Gandhi from Parliament and the interim judgment of the Supreme Court which, by imposing restrictions on her participation in the Parliament, humiliated her and took away her standing and legitimacy as the nation's political leader. Once this happened, the opposition parties went on a (to my mind unthinking and impatient) rampage of demonstrations asking for Mrs. Gandhi's resignation, matched only by Mr. Sanjay Gandhi's even more vociferous demonstrations on behalf of his mother. In the event the leaders of the opposition who demanded the resignation were arrested and the forces masterminded by Mr. Sanjay Gandhi have since been reigning the roost.

For those who justify the Emergency not so much on grounds of the unrest and the instability but on grounds of the massive poverty and rising economic discontent, it would be better for them to ponder on the government's own record in this matter. Between 1969 when Mrs. Gandhi's group ousted the senior leadership of the Congress from the party and the 1971 election when she got an overwhelming mandate for radical economic reforms, and since then till almost the end of 1973, she and her government enjoyed enormous popularity and no one stood in its way if it had introduced the necessary structural reforms for radical transformation. Nothing of this kind was done and if anything the genuinely radical groups in the Congress felt more and more frustrated and began to move closer to the movement led by Mr. Jayaprakash Narayan. To expect that the same ruling group, under a still more centralized and authoritarian regime, would take up the cause of the masses is, as suggested above, to expect the impossible.

4. The view that restrictions on civil rights and democratic freedoms affect only a small middle class and the mass of the "poor and illiterate" could not care less about them, not only shows a certain disdain for the latter but also misses the whole point about the role of the democratic political process in social change in country like India. The openness of the political

process was an essential prerequisite of the struggle for social and economic justice. The open democratic process was the only means available to the lower castes and deprived strata of India for staking their claims and backing these up with the power that they themselves possessed (instead of relying on a condescending elite from above). The possibility has now been taken away and the results are there for everyone to see. We have already indicated how the policies of the present government are anti-labour, against employment of the large masses of unemployed (indeed a large number of already employed have been thrown out of jobs), and on balance against the agricultural interests except for the very rich among them. Add to this the fact of massive slum clearance in the main cities and the rounding up of beggars and squatters and hawkers and their forced eviction to distant areas, in the process creating hardship, destitution and often unemployment for them. Even the much-boasted of programme of forced sterilization affected the poor and the vulnerable sections of the people, the government often using brutal methods and meeting the backlash that resulted by further repression and firing at those from the minorities and the rural communities which resulted in a large number of deaths. The present government in India is not just anti-intellectual, it is also anti-people.

5. The sympathy towards the present Indian regime on the grounds of its determination to enforce population control measures, based on the widely-held belief among Westerners that the root cause of all the problems of the poor countries is population, exemplifies how dictatorial regimes can play upon deeply held prejudices in the West—and among the Westernized sections of Third World societies—and draw support and legitimacy from them. The fact of the matter is that such an attitude is based on a misconception of both the "population problem" and the steps needed to deal with it. Compulsion of the type employed in India in recent months led to an adoption of means that were not just inhuman and discriminatory as indicated above ; they also turned out to be highly inefficient. They led to massive backlash from rural communities, minorities and the poor, leading at first to brutal repression and then, when this

did not work, to a withdrawal of the whole strategy. In the process the entire family planning programme in India, which was making steady headway earlier and promised some real breakthroughs in the years to come, has been discredited and the slow gains that were being made by a large number of official and unofficial agencies have suffered a setback. Population policy depends on a delicate interplay of individual, family and social norms and cannot be changed by resort to administrative fiat only. In the absence of open communications and efficient feedback, this can only turn into thoughtless fulfillment of "targets" by hook or crook (such as sterilization of young unmarried boys or of people beyond the reproductive age). This is what happened in parts of India and led to an outbreak of violence which forced the government to backtrack and led to frustration and disillusionment all around.

6. I have said enough to indicate that the various claims made by spokesmen of the Indian government are not only exaggerated but are simply not true. The two remarkably good harvests have helped the government in holding the price line and ensuring supplies of essential commodities, at least in the main urban areas. (Even here there are reports that indicate a reversal.) Meanwhile, there has been a cutback in production and lay-off of workers in a number of industries, demand has been falling (one reason why grain stocks have been piling up is that the poorer strata have no money to buy the food), and the much needed fresh investment is not forthcoming in any effective manner in either agriculture or in employment-oriented industries. The economic picture of only a year from now appears bleak, especially as the monsoon is not likely to be as bountiful as in the last two years. As for the claim that there is "law and order" in the country in place of former chaos and disorder, which seems to have been uncritically accepted by almost everyone, this too is not quite correct. There has been a spate of communal violence and anti-government riots, and even strikes and demonstrations of protest are once again on the increase. Even the so-called "discipline" among government servants and and other employees is no longer strictly observed, bribery and corruption are on the increase, and standards of civic behavior,

even in things like cleanliness and sanitation, have distinctly disappeared as public accountability has declined and the fear of "losing the vote" in the event of discontent of the people is no longer there. The hordes of unemployed are on the increase, and both the unionized labour and the ranks of unorganized and casual and migrant labour is seething with a desire for revenge, while the small shopkeepers and self-employed poor people like hawkers and petty traders feel terrorized as they are subject to incessant pressure for donations and contributions of various kinds which they must comply with for fear of their business being closed down or physically attacked. Highhandedness and arbitrary use of power are on the increase. One has only to step out of the posh shopping and residential areas of the main cities to see all this. Unfortunately very few visitors, including newspaper reporters, are willing to do this. The local journalists know all this but their reports cannot see the light of day.

Having dealt with the specific claims made on behalf of the Emergency rule in India and the widely prevalent assumptions about the efficacy of such rule, let me turn to more basic beliefs that lend support to such claims and assumptions. For it is not simply that miselading and often false claims are made by spokesmen of the Indian government ; such claims would not have made much headway were it not for the fact that there already existed deeply held prejudices and beliefs that provided hospitable ground for making such claims. Indeed, far more serious than the propaganda on behalf of dictatorial regimes in India and other Third World countries is the framework of thought and belief that has all along been present (in these countries as well as in the West) and which now lends credibility to such regimes.

1. Three such beliefs were mentioned above and they all pertain to the suitability of democracy to developing countries like India. The first of these is that whereas curbing of civil liberties is to be regretted, a strong and centralized government with dictatorial powers is better suited for undertaking rapid economic development and radical measures aimed at removal of poverty and inequity among the mass of the people. Evi-

dence from both India and a number of Third World countries does not support this belief. Most of these countries present a picture of a large degree of economic mismanagement coupled by an increase in disparities and deterioration in the condition of the poorer sections of the people. Even where, either through the help of large-scale foreign corporate investment or through a brutal process of internal exploitation by a local industrial and bureaucratic elite, a high rate of economic growth has been achieved for a few years, the benefits of such growth have been limited to a small elite. In India there is little sign of even this happening though there is a good deal of talk of moving to a free enterprise economy, inviting foreign capital, and adopting something like the Brazilian model of development. But, as with most other such countries, there is practically no thought given to initiating basic structural changes which will lead to a better distribution of land or of incomes and employment and, if anything, the condition of the ordinary people is likely to deteriorate.

The economic justification of authoritarian regimes has always been illusory. In a country of the size and complexity of India it can turn out to be much worse as it ignores the need for involving different sectors and strata of the people in the productive process, generating the necessary demand for goods and services among the people, and undertaking reforms in the structure of economic relations that can stimulate both an efficient system of production and an equitable system of distribution. There are no signs of any of this happening. The only time this happened was from 1950 to 1965 when an open and democratic political and administrative process was at work. Since then, with growing centralization of these, the economic picture has been steadily on the decline. The Emergency has led to much further growth of centralization and arbitrary power and this can not augur well for the economic well-being of the people.

2. The second widely held belief against democracy in India and other developing countries is more political and has to be distinguished from the economic justification of authoritarianism. This is the belief that democracy is unsuitable to developing societies as it brings large masses of people into the political process, raises expectations and leads to unrest and instability.

It is held by a number of conservative thinkers in the West, especially in the United States, whose main concern is with sources of instability and conflict in the Third World which they are likely to upset the fine balance on which the international system rests. They would rather put up with dictatorship that can maintain control and order and compliance of the people than encourage a free and open competition for power which may, according to them, lead to rising expectations and class conflict. Apart from the low regard for freedom and dignity that is exhibited by these thinkers (who, of course, value democratic freedoms in their own societies), they seem to underrate the possibility of greater cohesion and stability that an open political process is likely to bring to societies that are so full of diversity and plurality of allegiance and identification.

The Indian case shows cleary that the only way of managing various forms of conflict and diversity that are inherent in a far-flung and plural society is by allowing their open expression and and gradual absorption at various levels of society, thereby both allowing a sense of participation to various segments of society and at the same time containing conflicts of interest and preventing their aggregation at the national level. And it was found that even expectations were prevented from rising too much and too rapidly. Indeed, if anything, it is with centralization of political and economic decision making and the erosion of self-government at state and local levels over the last ten years, and now with the virtual elimination of the party system and elected bodies and the emergence of demagogy and a plebiscitary form of leadership, that both expectations and discontent are directed upward and the load on the central apparatus of government has greatly increased. Now even a slight rise in prices or a small demonstration or riot makes the government nervous and leads to irrational behavior both in the management of the economy and in the management of demands from the people. If anything, the rise of dictatorship is likely to produce a sense of instability and continuous firefighting at so many points, with a disproportionate use of coercive power and repression. The present regime in India is already shaky and unstable and is likely to become far more unstable with the passage of time.

3. Alongside the economic and political arguments against the suitability of democracy in a developing society like India, there is a more subtle argument that has been growing among Western commentators which on surface appears to be fair and sensitive to the cultural diversity of the world. Why, it is asked, should we Westerners try to impose our values and institutions on alien cultures which may be better suited to other forms of governance (such as a dynasty or a monarchic form)? It is argued that democracy, being a special form of governance that arose in Western Europe and embedded in the peculiar cultural and historical conditions of Europe and the United States with their individualist ethos, Protestant ethic and pluralist conception of society, is unlikely to succeed elsewhere. I find this to be a specious argument which under the garb of respect for diverse cultures is in fact more ethnocentric and supercilious. As I mentioned earlier in this article, it is based on a peculiar mix of isolationist psychology and racial arrogance. It is based on perhaps a genuine urge to be noninterventionist in other peoples' affairs following the extremes of interventionism to which this country went in various parts of the world in the preceeding quarter century. Subtly, however, this feeling has taken the form of isolationism and unconcern for the fate of human beings outside one's own society. Examined closely, it turns out to be an attitude of callous disregard for peoples who were first robbed of their autonomy and dignity and the resources with which they could have built their own distinctive ways of life, and then asked to look after themselves and stew in their own juices, and told that the values of freedom and justice and dignity are not for them.

It is also highly arrogant to assume that individualism and pluralism are specifically Western values whereas in fact not only are these values found deeply ingrained in other cultures but are lately found to vanish from the West under the impact of the utilitarian calculus and a model of development, technology and mass communication that insists on straitjacketing all diversities into one common mould. The peoples of the Third World have to struggle against these tendencies if they are to preserve their integrity against these encroachments as well as against encroachments from within their own societies from interests and elites that seem to have become accomplices of the global managers of power. It is only by returning to the democratic path and restoring autonomy and dignity to the people that these societies will be able to become truly independent and work out their distinctive personalities and modes of development.

The rise of dictatorship and the decline of democracy in various parts of the world appear to be part of a new global trend towards fascism. In this the incompetent and insecure elites of the Third World, the philosophy that economic development necessitates authoritarianism, and the structure of global power in which the two superpowers support dictatorial regimes and often give tacit approval to the overthrow of democratic regimes have all played their part. The latest and most disturbing manifestation of this global trend is the penetration of intelligence agencies of the superpowers into the Third World and the reverse penetration of intelligence and surveillance agents of Third World regimes into the United States, England and other countries for persecuting and intimidating the dissidents from these countries. The activities of the South Korean CIA that have come to light, the openly admitted presence of the agents of the Shah of Iran's secret service, the murder of an ex-diplomat of Chile in this country, and the reported presence of the Indian government's surveillance agents are all signs in this direction. It is not yet known how far the authorities in this country are knowledgeable of these activities and, if they are, what is the degree of deliberate tolerance of, if not complicity in, such activities by them. Nothing short of the building of global public opinion, backed by organized pressure against fascist tendencies everywhere, can change this state of affairs. There is need for a new movement for human rights the world over, a movement that is not confined to restoration of civil liberties but is seen as an essential prerequisite in the struggle for a just and equitable social order. But such a movement cannot even begin to be effective until there is conviction among intellectuals and opinion makers of the world in the values of freedom and democracy as essential conditions for promoting well-being of all and building a humane and just world order.

Chapter V

CARTOONS : LOCAL AND FOREIGN

Another attractive feature of the underground literature was cartoons. Sometimes cartoons published in foreign magazines were reproduced in raw form (see Cartoon No. 1). Besides printed bulletins and photostat clippings of foreign newspapers, cyclostyled bulletins also carried cartoons. The local ones (Nos. 2-6) were printed in *Pabanaco Bulletin* published by the West Bengal Citizens Commitee, a breakaway group of Congress (O) in West Bengal. Those cartoons were drawn on stencil papers by sharp pencils and were cyclostyled. Cartoons Nos. 7-12 were published in foreign newspapers.

The underground sources reproduced these in photostats and circulated among the activists and sympathisers of the resistance movement.

1.

August 7, 1975

2.

August 21, 1975

3.

Inscription in Bengali says—verdict ! you give it that.
I am majority against them.
Bulletin No. 20. Aug 28, 1975

4.

September 23, 1975

5.

No. 25 of the same Bulletin

6.

Three faces of Mrs. Gandhi. After Mujibar Rehman's
murder Mrs Gandhi's reactions are shown.
Bulletin No. 27. Nov. 7, 75.

7.

'Who's the fairest one of all?'.

8.

'Indira's Press'

9.

OK CHILDREN, REPEAT AFTER ME.

10.

"I find myself not guilty."

11.

Inscription says : Better shape it to fit my
figure, buster !

12.

Chapter VI

LETTERS

Shrimati Indira Gandhi,
Prime Minister of India,   New Delhi
1, Safdarjang Road,   23rd July, 1975.
New Delhi.

Madam Prime Minister,

Ordinarily a Prime Minister's time which is precious in the extreme should not be encroached upon. But since, of late, you have been making yourself available for close personal contact with all shades of public opinion quite freely, we have been encouraged to draw on your valuable time.

2. We are amongst the very humble of your follow (fellow) countrymen, just ordinary citizens interested chiefy in constructive work, none of us belonging to any political party. We have no political axe to grind nor are we interested in any political office or power. Our chief interest is in upholding the freedom and dignity of the individual.

3. We regard Pandit Jawaharlal Nehru as one of the priencipal architects of Indian democracy. He used to say : "No one, however, great he may be, should be above criticism".

It was he who gave the memorable slogan when the British came down heavily upon us in the freedom struggle : "Freedom is in peril ; defend it with all your might." We sorrowfully remember him for, had he been alive today, we have no doubt that he would have given the slogan "Democracy is in peril ; defend it with all your might".

4. We do not dispute the right of the Central Government to invoke the aid of the emergent provisions of law as contained in our Constitution. The intiative for summoning the emergent provisions of law to its aid has also to be with the Government

14

for the time being. But that is not all. A lot more remains to contend with.

5. The people's government has to satisfy the people who give it life, that a recourse to the emergent provisions of law was absolutely unavoidable. This is not possible without a free and open public discussion of the matter in issue. As it is, no freedom for doing this is at present available to the general public. On the contrary, special interests enjoying or endeavouring to enjoy government pleasure, are wholly free to demonstrate their support in favour of the Government decision. Is it fair to the people ? The tragedy of it all is that the Press has been muzzled, except when registering support for Government policy and Government measures and promoting government party's propaganda. The government of the people must listen to all sections of the people with equal solicitude.

6. We do not, we repeat, challenge your right to arm yourself with additional powers even when ample powers are with you already for dealing with offenders against law ; what, however, we fail to appreciate is the denial of normal opportunities to the people—to all the people—to discuss openly the merits of government or government measures. Our democracy is not yet out of the woods and many are bound to feel puzzled over what meets their eye.

7. Opposition leaders and the dissentors in your own party have been behind the bars without the chance of a trial in a court of law. We hope with all our heart that the arrested Members of Parliament will not be deprived of the opportunity to have their say in the current session of Parliament. Was it really necessary......to withhold from the public even the names of the political leaders and workers you have arrested and to deny facilities to their near and dear ones to meet them and arrange their legal defence, if any such defence is at all possible in the midst of present ordinances. Some of the persons arrested were, not so long ago, Ministers in your Cabinet and Chief Ministers and Ministers in the states. Did they really turn traitors overnight that even their names and whereabouts do not deserve, to be intimated to the public or their relatives ?

8. Apart from your political supporters, the common people

of Delhi now talk in hushed tones as they do in communist societies ; they do not discuss politics in the coffee house or at the bus stands and look over their shoulders before expressing any opinion. An atmosphere of fear and political repression prevails and politically conscious citizens differing from your view-point prefer to observe a discreet silence, with some of them afraid of the mid-night knock on their door.

9. Must the monster of fear deavour us again, the monster for the annihilation of which our beloved Pandit Jawaharlal Nehru had sacrificed his all—his riches, his comforts, his parents and even the dearest deity of his heart. He held fear to be enemy No. 1 of India's destiny. It is well to seek fresh inspiration from his memorable words :

"The greatest gift for an individual or a Nation, so we had been told in our ancient books, was *abhava* (fearlessness), not merely bodily courage but the absence of fear from the mind. Janaka and Yajnavalka had said, at the dawn of our history, that it was the function of the leaders of a people to make them fearless. But the dominant impulse in India under British rule was that of fear pervasive, oppressing strangling fear ; fear of the army, the police, the widespread secret service ; fear of law meant to suppress. It was against this all-pervading fear that Gandhi's quiet and determined voice was raised : 'Be not afraid".

10. The present situation looks every citizens in the face enquiringly and the old surviving freedom fighters in particular. We must respond to the call. Accordingly we propose, with effect from 9th August, 1975 and regardless of consequences to ourselves, to advocate openly the right of public association and freedom of the Press, for discussing the merits and demerits of the Government arming itself with extraordinary powers. The intention is not to embarrass authority or to cause any unnecessary stir. Our self-suffering will just be an humble offering at the foot of the Motherland, in the breaking of whose chains we had been privileged to play our small part inspired by the mighty lead of the Father of the Nation.

Sd/-	(1) Bhim Sen Sachar	20, Tughlak Crescent, New Delhi—11.
„	(2) S. D. Sharma	A-312, Defence Colony, New Delhi—24.
„	(3) J. R. Sahni	Adhyatma Sadhana Mendra, Chattarpur Road (Mehrauli) New Delhi—30.
„	(4) Vishnu Dutt	WZ 1282, Nangal Raya, New Delhi—46.
„	(5) Kishna Lal Vaid	Najaggarh, New Delhi—43.
„	(6) Sevak Ram	New Delhi—24.
„	(7) K. K. Sinha	B-79 Neeti Bagh, New Delhi—49.
„	(8) K. Sharma	B-999, Shastri Nagar, Delhi—52.

P. S.   Immediately the letter was addressed all the signatories were arrested and detained under MISA.

PABANACO BULLETIN—17

Mrs. Indira Gandhi,
New Delhi.

I note that I have been particularly singled out for a lot of publicity ever since you assumed the role of a Dictator.

First, the railway strike of May, 1974 is still haunting you. You see in it the grand design of reactionaries to overthrow you.

You know that the railway strike was for the legitimate demands of railwaymen. You know that your own CPI and AITUC who are sworn to defend you and your dictatorship to the last drop of the people's blood were active participants in the strike. When you still keep raking up the railway strike issue and indulge in your perverted and false propaganda after shutting us out from replying your wild accusations, you are also doing great disservice to CPI Chairman S. A. Dange who hailed the May 1974 strike as a great struggle of the working people and compared you to the medieval period rulers of Europe, to CPI MP Parvati Krishnan who spent a week in prison and to the thousand of your big and small puppets in the CPI.

And, when the International Transport Workers' Federation (ITF) to which your own Congress scab-unions are affiliated decided to send a fact-finding mission to India, your government in true fascist style, refused permission to the ITF Mission to enter the country. So, please stop lying on the railway strike.

Second, you have charged that I received large foreign funds during the railway strike in May-June 1974.

That is the damnedest lie you must have uttered in your whole life of lies, if this were the case, why the hell did you wait for one whole year to make the charge ? Produce the evidence, put me on trial, and get me shot if what you say is true. All dictators are congenital liars, but you Madam, excel them all.

Third, your publicists including the Russian patriots in India have written that I have received dollars from Japanese institutions and American Institutions. You have cited two drafts, one for 68,000 dollars and the other for 17,000 dollars cleared by the Bank of Tokyo in June 1975. You jolly well know that these two drafts were presented to the All India Railwaymen's Federation by two Unions of Japanese railwaymen at the fiftieth annual conference of the Federation of Jodhpur on May 27, 1975. The Japanese Railwaymen's Union (KOKURO) presented the Cheque for 68,000 dollars and the Japanese Locomotive Engineers Union (DORO) presented the cheque for 17,000 dollars. This money was the contribution of individual Japanese railwaymen to their Indian colleagues and though was earlier meant to provide relief to the railwaymen thrown out of employment by you in May, 1974, was actually presented by them for trade union education activities of Indian railwaymen. Six leaders of these two Japanese railwaymen's Unions, all militant trade unionists and socialists attended the AIRF Conference as fraternal delegates along with a three-men delegation from the railwaymen's union of Turkey. How dare you accuse the Japanese railwaymen of being American stooges ?

And what perversity of mind you and your propagandists display when you charge me with receiving foreign money? Every paisa of the gift received by the AIRF have been deposited in the bank and is lying there. Madam dictator, can you not show even a semblance of respect for truth and decency, even assuming that in your desperate quest for power, you have to indulge in the most caluminous campaign against me.

Fourth, I am supposed to have written to Chairman Mao of the Republic of China complaining about the suppression of the railway workers strike by you in May last year.

Before dealing with Mao, let us have the facts straight. Are you suggesting that you did not suppress the railwaymen's struggle by using repressive measures unheard of the recent history of our country which made even President V.V. Giri get disgusted with you and which were condemend by the working people all over the world including the WFTU of which your patrons the Russians, are the god fathers.

And, Madam Dictator, will you please publish the text of my letter to Mao and provide further evidence of your perverted mind in dealing with your political opponents.

In December 1974, there was a news report in the Indian press datelined Hongkong that the Chinese railwaymen were on strike to press their demands and that the army had refused to break the strike. The All India Railwaymen's Federation staged a demonstration before the Chinese Embassy to condemn the reported efforts of the Chinese government to break the strike by using the army and to extend moral support to the Chinese railway workers. I led this demonstration. A memorandum addressed to Chairman Mao was sought to be handed over to the Chinese Embassy officials, but the Embassy had closed its gates on us. On the advice of your police which was guarding the Embassy gates, the memorandum enclosed in an envelope was thrown into the Embassy compound. The memorandum extended support to the Chinese railway workers, called upon Chairman Mao not to suppress the workers and urged that the railway workers' demands should be met. And in that context, the memorandum referred to your suppression of the strike of Indian railwaymen.

(Incidentally, in January 1975, I was to learn that the story of the Chinese railway workers' strike was a Russian canard planted through your courtesy in the Indian press with a view to damn the Chinese Government).

And Madam Dictator, if your effort is to suggest that I am a Chinese agent too, besides being an American agent, may I remind you that I am the same George Fernandes about whom your father publicly apologised to China's Prime Minister Chou En Lai. The white paper on the India-China dispute contains your fathers' letter to the Chinese Premier.

Fifth, you have in a letter to some leader of the Muslim League in Kerala refuted my charge that you are the most communal-minded person. My charge against you has been publicly made during the last three years, both in my speeches and writings and has been carried by the national press on many occasions. But you waited till you became a dictator and imposed censorship to refute my charge that during the last war with Pakistan, you as the Home Minister issued a secret circular which requried all public sector undertakings and government departments to see that Muslims were not employed in the key installations and positions. Accordingly, Muslims working as Controllers in the BEST Undertaking in Bombay were removed from their positions and put to work as Inspectors. Muslims employed at Vaitasna Water Works of the Bombay Municipal Corporation were removed from their positions and transferred to the city, away from their families. Muslims in the Bhave Atomic Centre were terminated from service with one month's pay in their hands. I intervened on behalf of these Muslim workers with the managements to no avail.

I also repeat my charge that Muslims in India are denied equality of opportunity and in the matter of jobs in army, police and other public services, they are discriminated against. I can prove this by facts and figures. The point is how to do it in a dictatorship.

Lastly, may I demand that you show the courage to publish this note and be damned.

Sd/-

July 27, 1975.   GEORGE FERNANDES

LETTER FROM A FATHER

My dear Son,

For some time now I have been thinking of having a few words with you. About myself. For about two months now something has been troubling me. I find no remedy for it. The only relief that I can expect is to unburden my mind to you.

At your age—you are only thirteen now much of what I shall say now may sound as incomprehensible. Yet, the reason for my writing to you alone, about my trouble, is that you also should know of it.

Now about my trouble. Do you remember how upset you were, seeing my clean-shaven head when I went to see you last, quite a few weeks ago ? "Father," you asked me then, "why have you shaven your head ?" I told you in reply that the Government had proclaimed an Emergency and had thereby taken away my freedom to write. Now I cannot write and publish what I really think and feel. I am allowed to write only such things as would please the Government. I told you, I remember, that I considered this act of the Government as an unjust encroachment on a writer's freedom, and that I had shaven my head only to register my protest against the wrong done by the Government ; that I would not let hair grow on my head until I got back my freedom of expression as a writer.

I am not certain if you could understand everything that I said, but I still remember that your face darkened. And later, when your mother was at your side, you asked her : "Will they not allow father to write any more ?"

In reply, I can tell you this much : unless freedom of expression is restored in this country, your father will never have a chance to write.

You can thus understand that I very much resent the fact that my freedom as a writer has been taken away ; I am unable to reconcile myself to this state of affairs. Not merely that ; I want also to register publicly my protest against this wrong. But whenever I think of protesting, faces appear in my mental vision—your face as well as the faces of your sisters, mother and grandmother. Some among you are too young. Some helpless and some old. All of you are dependent on me. All these years I have tried to provide you with a secure home. Should I do anything which may result in the loss of this secure shelter for you all, just for satisfying my 'whims' or 'fancy' ? If I recognise as the supreme end of my life the task of providing you all with a secure shelter, then the question of my taking the risk of registering my protest does not arise, for such registration of protest is surely going to endanger your security. But then I have to meekly submit to the injustice done by the Government and make a compromise with untruth. That means that I have to sell my honour as a writer and adopt the profession of a hired quill-driver. In other words, I have to stifle in me the urge for asserting myself as a man.

On the one hand I have to think of you—of your security ; on the other hand, I have to think of myself—of my self-respect as a man. Which of the two shall I preserve at the cost of the other ? It is this dilemma that torments me every day, every moment. This is the root of my trouble, which I mentioned at the outset.

It is an irony of fate that I am confronted with this tormenting question not under a communist regime, but in a democratic set-up with Mrs. Gandhi at the helm of its affairs. But choose I must, since circumstances have thrust upon me the difficult task of making a choice. Bypassing the issue makes no sense to me.

I have therefore to make my decision known to you. I strongly protest against the deprivation of my freedom.

I feel that by taking away my freedom of writing, my freedom of expression, they have done violence to my very being. Hence I declare that the censorship that has been imposed on us is an affront to all principles of justice and morality ; it is anti-democratic and violative of freedom.

All my life I have fought for human justice and morality, for democracy and freedom. My writings will bear testimony to it as you will find for yourself, provided you get an opportunity to read them when you grow older.

It is for this very reason that I raised my lonely voice in

those dark and chaotic days of Naxalite violence. Time and again, I sought to persuade those misguided young men that violence and hatred could not bring freedom. They only result in the replacement of one kind of tyranny by another. Democracy alone keeps individual freedom alive. For democracy is the only system which makes room for, and respects, dissent.

After a long period of experiment in history with various types of social systems, the wise amongst us have, by and large, come to accept the democratic way, for it is the only way that ensures peaceful change of rulers, without resort to violence and terror. The most humane and effective way of peaceful transformation lies in reasoned persuasion. Not the way of bullets and dagger. It is for this reason that I prefer the democratic way, though I am fully aware of its many imperfections.

I have talked of change—of change of society and change of rulers. It is in the nature of man to seek change. It is also a kind of vulnerability in man which ennobles him. Man is both a householder and a wanderer. He sets up a home and assumes the responsibility of a sheltered life under the sovereign compulsion of necessity. At the same time, a mysterious and compelling urge calls him away from home and makes him a wanderer. This is the nature of man. To build anew and to destroy what is built. These two opposing tendencies dwell in him side by side. Hence what man builds today he must pull down tomorrow, and the same man who was found busy destroying yesterday, will come forward today for creating anew. Man can never remain content with what he has created. This perennial discontent is the impulse behind his progress. As man is ever dissatisfied, so is his society in perpetual unrest. This is so because society is created by man. Hence we must first understand man before we try to understand society. Man, by nature, desires change.

In the ever-changing society created by change-loving man, no system can therefore be permanent and absolute. We would do better to realise this truth. Of the various methods of changing social and political systems, the constitutional method appears to me as more humane and therefore acceptable. I cannot bring myself to believing that, in the long run, we can ever achieve any good through bloodshed. This is what I tried to

convince the Naxalite youths, who once proclaimed my death
sentence. I directed my efforts towards persuading them to see
the futility of their programme of senseless murder. Violence
and ferocity pertain to that nature of man which was once
shaped in the jungle. Civilization has made us more tolerant
and believers in co-existence. This is what I call the democratic
approach.

Ferocity belongs to our primitive nature. Democratic tolerance is the gift of civilization. Dictatorship is nothing but
primitive ferociousness in modern guise. That is why dictatorships have to resort to force continually in order to survive.
And dictators can hardly be removed from power without
bloodshed.

In a democracy, it is much easier to replace the rulers because
opposition (to the rulers) is recognised and respected in this
system. The leader of the Government today gracefully occupy
the place of the leader of the opposition tomorrow, upholding
thereby the dignity of civilized conduct.

From my repeated emphasis on the merits of democracy you
can see how dear democracy is to me. No other system recog-
nises the dignity of the individual so much as democracy.

It is therefore with profound sadness that I have now to tell
you that the democratic system in which I breathed for the last
twentysix years and in which you have grown up, has now been
defiled. The threat to our democratic system now comes from
our present rulers who are lacking in foresight. Democracy has
been reduced to a farce by proclaiming an Emergeney. Our
fundamental rights have been taken away on the pretext of
doing good to the people.

My right to express views has been taken away. No one can
now talk freely except the fawning flatterers of our Prime
Minister.

If these words, which I write now, happen to appear in print
you may even come to know very soon that your father has
been arrested by the police for the crime of expressing his views
so candidly. Yes, it is a crime these days to say all these things.

It will grieve you when you come to know of my arrest. But
don't be afraid. It is small incidents like these that teach a man

to be firm, and make him think. And such thinking helps a man grow up. Surely you will have many anxious thoughts. But pray, don't give yourself up to the mood of desultory thinking. It scarcely helps. The only fruitful kind of thinking is that which raises questions and makes one restless in the search for their answers. Entertain, therefore, only such thoughts in your mind as are productive. You must not be perturbed at whatever news you get about me. Always bear in mind, my dear, that your father has discharged his responsibility. If you really love your father, you too must learn to discharge your responsibility.

In addressing this letter to you, I am performing a duty. I had to do something in this situation or else I could not justify my existence to myself.

I alone know the intensity of the anguish in which I passed the days since the 26th of June. Every moment something prompted within me to ask our Prime Minister : "What led you to take this road to ruin ? This way leads to no good for you and me and our future generations. This is the lesson that history has taught us time and again. Prime Minister, please turn back ; do retrace your steps." This is all that I wished to tell her.

I am no conspirator. Party politics is not my line. I am a mere writer. I am conscious of my responsibility to society, and am generally guided by reason. I try to be honest. When therefore I found that our Prime Minister was planting her feet on quicksands, I thought it my duty to warn her against the disastrous outcome. I have no pretentious notions about myself. So I know that the Prime Minister will scarcely design to pay heed to what I say. But that is of little moment to me. I see doom ahead, so I must speak out.

It is this trend of thought that prompted me to shave my head. They have taken away my freedom to write by imposing censorship, and thus shorn me of my human dignity. Hence I have registered my protest by having my head shorn.

But I did not want to stop at that. I had to proceed further in order to defend my rights. I must tell our Prime Minister that this way can never lead to any good. Please turn back, I implore her.

My dear, I feel somewhat relieved after writing this letter to you. I want this letter to be read by many others. That may encourage others to speak their minds. So I have decided to publish it. My only desire is that you grow up in a democratic atmosphere.

Your loving father
Gour Kishore Ghosh

N. B. For this letter published in special political issue of *'Kolkata'* a literary little magazine, Sri Ghosh was arrested on 6th October, 1975. This letter was again re-printed in underground leaflets and circulated widely amongst the political cadres and intelligentsia groups. Shri Ghosh, a renowned writer and journalist, is the Asst. Editor of *Ananda Bazar Patrika.*

NOT SLAVERY, NOR SERVITUDE, BUT FREEDOM

Dear Countrymen :

This is the first time that I am addressing you from behind the prison bars. This may be the last occasion too, because I know that even if this letter finds its way to some of you at last, after crossing all barriers of censorship and other restrictions, my dear, dear friend, Sriman Siddhartha Sankar Ray, Chief Minister and a fancy puppet of the political puppet-show of West Bengal, will not view it with much pleasure. As a consequence, I fear, I may be subjected to a greater measure of persecution. If I have yet come forward, even at this risk, to send you a note of warning, it is because I consider this to be my duty as an humble servant of Bengali literature, as well as a conscientious journalist. It is also my moral obligation as a committed democrat.

Some of my writings, published under my own name, or under my pennames (Roopadarshi or Gourananda Kobi), may have at times come to the notice of some amongst you. Whoever of you have read these, know that my pen was all along engaged in an incessant and untiring struggle against terror and violence as well as anti-democratic forces. Even then, early in the small hours of 6th October, 1975, Indira's detective police raided my house and arrested me. They did not consider it necessary even to produce a warrant of arrest. And later, on that very day at night, I was detained in jail for an indefinite period, without trial, on false charges of treason, on the strength of an Order made under Emergency MISA. Ever since then I have remained in prison. For you and me today there are no such fundamental rights, by dint of which I may seek redress in a court of law against this unjust highhandedness of the government, and to regain my freedom. The situation has now reached a stage when, not I alone, but every Indian is an inmate of a vast prison. Indira and Sanjay are the only exceptions.

Today, at the instigation of power-hungry Indira, citizens of India have been robbed of all freedoms, by issuing a Presidential decree, or with the approval of a brute majority in the Lok Sabha. The Constitution has been murdered. And the Supreme Court, too, has been turned into a *Brihannala**. It is all suppression and oppression.

Indiscriminate use of MISA Orders. On this alone stands today the edifice of Indira's much-coveted power. Alas, instead of the spontaneous support of the people, Indira has to rely today on the secret police, and the secret police alone.

I have been astounded to find, scattered through prisons, numerous examples which show how cruel the widespread abuse of MISA can be. Innumerable indeed are these instances. They do not lack variety. Detention without trial for five to seven years. Even boys and girls of thirteen to fifteen detained without trial for years. Never before had I seen such massive insult to human dignity. It is your brother or sister, or son or daughter, to whom they have meted out this treatment.

And yet, there happens to be no remedy for all this. From newspapers you must have learnt what the Prime Minister is offering us as this year's Republic Day present ! Slavery. Unmitigated slavery.

*According to the Mahabharata, a curse from Urvashi, a courtesan of the gods, rendered the hero Arjuna impotent for a year. During this period of impotency the hero adopted the name Brihannala.

The President has, by exercise of special powers, taken away from you and me and millions of our countrymen, the right to move a court of law granted under Article 19* of the Constitution. Similar, the exercise of our fundamental rights, guaranteed under Article 14, 21, 22 of the Constitution, has been suspended.

Dear fellow-citizens ! These rights are not merely an array of lifeless words printed on paper. They constitute a citizen's natural rights to live as a human being. These are the safeguards possessed by citizens—like you and me—of a democratic state. It is by virtue of these that a citizen enjoys the "right to live" and the right of "protection against tyranny of the strong" Article 19 alone confers seven freedoms : the right (a) to freedom of speech and expression ; (b) to assemble peaceably and without arms ; (c) to form associations or unions ; (d) to move freely throughout the territory of India ; (e) to reside and settle in any part of the territory of India ; (f) to acquire, hold and dispose of property ; and (g) to practise any profession, or to carry on any occupation, trade or businsss.

All these rights have been taken away from us. In addition the Government has moved the Supreme Court for taking away the rights to make an application before a Court of Law for a writ of *Habeas Corpus*. It was the only safeguard which protected a citizen against illegal detention or torture by the Government. The very arguments submitted in this case by the Additional Solicitor General of the Central Government clearly show how dangerous the Government's attitude is in this regard. The Additional Solicitor General submitted before the Court : A citizen has absolutely no recourse to any redress or legal or Constitutional remedy through courts to safeguard his right to personal liberty during the period of the emergency, even if he is totally innocent and is illegally and wrongfully detained on wrong and false information and on non-existent grounds. (*The Statesman*, 10 July 1976, Page 7 Column 4).

*A misquotation ; the "right to move the Supreme Court" is guaranteed not by Article 19, but by Article 32. While in prison, Ghosh obviously had no access to a copy of the Constitution.—Translator

My dearest friends, it is now for you to judge for yourselves what rights are left after all this to enable us to live as self-respecting human beings. Remember that, before 26 June, each one of you had been a free citizen of the Indian Republic. And in the course of just seven months, each of you has been transformed into a chained slave in *Indiracratic India*. No rights for you any more. Only seven months back, you were a free, self-respecting human being. And today ? Your position is becoming worse than that of a faithful domestic animal. Whoever you are, whatever the status you enjoy in society, where is your security ?

Are you a government officer of high rank ? What is the guarantee that you will not be the victim of the jealousy or envy of an officer of your rank, or of the ambition of an officer of a lower rank ? Are you a journalist or a creative writer ? However servile you may have become, are you sure that colleague of yours is not busy removing an obstacle from his path by a display of greater servility ? Remember : at the instance of Indira, the President has armed the police with unbridled powers, to "arrest and detain illegally, unjustly or by mistake" anyone on the basis of wrong information or false charges. Are you a lawyer ? A physician ? A professor ? A school teacher ? A student ? An industrialist ? A worker ? A businessman ? A statesman ? A Congressman ? Where is your security ? One who no longer serves Indira's end is no more worth to her than a pair of tattered shoes. Even allegiance and loyalty of the constantly tail-wagging type are no more precious to Indira than a bit of counterfeit coin. Sardar Swaran Singh is a case in point ; so are Umashankar Dikshit, Bahuguna, and Priya Ranjan Das Munshi.

Dear compatriots ! What are you thinking, sitting on the fence ? That this is a temporary measure ? That Indira has taken this measure out of anger at the insolence of oppositionists ? That as soon as her rage subsides, she will, like a good girl, return all the rights snatched away from us ? Or, are you thinking of saving your skin today, by putting on the chain of slavery around your neck, leaving the future to take care of itself ? Or is it that you think we would better sacrifice our rights for the prosperity of our country ? If this be the trend of your thought, then I shall urge you to learn from the history of the rise of Hitler and Mussolini ; to be on guard, and to prepare at once for freeing yourself and your guiltless children from the chains of slavery. And as for prosperity ? The sixty year's history of our new-found friend Soviet Russia has clearly exposed the naked truth that even a crude type of prosperity cannot be brought about in twentieth century society by denying the people all kinds of freedom, and by reducing them to slaves. Soviet Russia today is a cordial host to big American capitalist industrial cartels and the most resourceful wholesale buyer of American capitalist grains. The paradise of the proletariat will for the next five years, meet its deficit in food, and feed its hungry millions, by importing grains from the "most hated" capitalist market.

A nation cannot be built by resort to wholesale oppression and lies. What can thus be created is a mere illusion of development. The fount of human creativity cannot be opened up by persecution and forcible imposition of slavery. This is proved by the retarded growth of Soviet consumer goods industries. Its proof lies also in the huge failure of Soviet agricultural production. Besides nature's wrath and bureaucratic mismanagement, another factor has been revealed by the Nobel Peace prize-winning Soviet scientist, Andrei Sakharov. In his recent book *"My Country and the World"* (published by Collins, Harville), Sakharov has described the poverty ridden, despondent, dejected way of life led by the Kolkhoz serfs in Soviet vilages. Unwillingness for work, and excessive addiction to drinking are progressively on the increase among able-bodied male agricultural workers of the country. Young people are leaving their jobs on the farms, and fleeing to towns. Farming there resting largely on old people and children. In Sakharov's opinion, this is one of the major reasons for seasonal and extensive failure of Soviet agricultural production.

This shows how big a hoax it is to claim that, floods of milk and honey will flow merely by chanting the *mantra* of the Prime Minister's pet twenty-point economic programme, after perpetuating slavery in the country by proclaiming Emergency, gagging

15

the press, depriving the people of their freedom, and large-scale detention. The claim is as deceptive as a mirage. The power-mad tyrants and Fascists raise the edifice of their power on lies alone. Hence the need for so much trumpeting to make false-hood appear as truth. And this is why an autocratic and des-potic regime crumbles like a house of cards as truth comes out, removing the veil of falsehood. Because autocracy has no moral power.

Hence, very educated citizen must take upon himself the moral responsibility of exposing lies. It is the dictate of his conscience, it is what he owes to his humanness. Will you not undertake this reponsibility ? Taking full advantage our vacil-lations, doubts and passivity, Indira's dictatorship and shameless fascism will forge the chains of slavery around our necks, and around the necks of our future generations. Are you going to submit to this slavery just for the comforts of today ? Remem-ber, passivity too is a sin, because it, too, amounts to collabora-tion.

Remember : Sanjay the Crown Price is not our saviour ; the democratic rights that have been taken away from us, alone can save us. As much as rights cannot be gained without earn-ing them, so rights that are not defended do not survive. Hence it is we who have to struggle for regaining our lost liberties. And in this struggle, let truth alone be our only weapon. Let conscience be our leader.

Come, let us uncover falsehood and bring truth. Come let us, defeat terror by suffering persecution with a cheerful mind. Come, let us non-cooperate with the despotic administration in all possible ways. Come, let us bestow all our love upon free-dom. Come, let us take a vow of non-violence, since non-violence alone possesses the power to reinstate democracy. And on this day, the Republic Day, come, let us loudly proclaim that we demand freedom, not slavery, not servitude.

Not despotism, but democracy is what we want. Come, let us sing in chorus ;

"Tell me who, with freedom lost,
To life soulless wants to cling.

Tell me what man, round his feet,
Wants to have that slavery's ring."*

Let Democracy prevail, Let Love prevail. Let man prevail.

Yours in all humility,
Gour Kishore Ghosh

Presidency Jail, Cell 10,
Republic Day, 1976

*First stanza of a song composed at the turn of the century
by Rangalal Bandyopadhyaya (Translator).

This letter smuggled out from the jail was published in Bengali underground leaflet *Khabar*.

LETTER FROM GEORGE FERNANDES,
CHAIRMAN, SOCIALIST PARTY

To
Shri JYOTY BASU, Member of Polit Buruau, (Bureau)
Communist Party (Marxist) of India

Dear Com. Jyoty Basu :

Your interview to the Statesman (May 1) cleared many a
doubt that had arisen during these past several months and
particularly during the last few weeks about your Party's atti-
tudes and programmes. I am aware of the various problems
that beset you, especially in West Bengal and now, Perhaps
also in Kerala. But I am still not convinced that the low Profile
adopted by your party is the best answer to them. Of cours<.
one has to protect ones cadres and lives to fight another day,
though for some of us it may become necessary in the circumstances to decide to fight today and pay the price. But do you
belive that self preservation should be our sole concern ?
What about the masses ? Should they not be educated simultaneously ? Are they to be allowed to be swallowed up by the
dictator's wolves ? Is it not only through constant struggle

that we shall be able to protect the masses and at the same time educate them ?   I am speaking of mass struggle here.   May be, the time is not propitious for them and, in any case, a lot of prepratory work will be required.   But should we not make it obvious to them one hand and to the fascist rulers on the other that we are uncomproising in our opposition to the fascist state and shall do all that we can, in the circumstance, to overthrow ? I belive that it is not we who should seek after the fascist rulers to talk to us.   We should creat a situation in which the rulers should beg to talk to those who are fighting to restore demo-cracy and the rule of law.

I am happy to note your statement that, as things stand, you will not participate in the elections.   I had sent you a note on this subject a few months ago which I had also circulated to other parties. I am aware that it had a mixed reaception (recep-tion), for which there are still a large number of people among the opposition parties to whom a seat in the legislature (and for many, an attempt howsoever futile and hopeless, for a seat, is the Alpha and Omega of political activities.   Could your party formulate a definite position on the election and circulate it among all other parties ? The minimum position. The sine qua non for participation in the poll. It may help the other parties to arrived at certain decision.

Though the Statesman interview does not speak of left and right parties, I had a few days ago (Perhapes after your meeting with the dictator in Delhi) read you statement that your had no quarrel with the dictator's fight with the right. Who is the right and, in any case, in the present circumsrance, what is the right ? Even if you have some reasons, I fail to see them which, (perhaps ; is my misfortune, to call tha Government semi-fasist (fascist) is it suggested that it is also semi-manarchist (monar-chist) and there for, semi-fasist) can there any party in the country at the present moment which is worst than the ruling party ? Which part in the country has democracy ? Must the Communist continnue to stick to certain phraseolagy that is totally irrelvant to the time and to the situation ?

No, I am not trying to sweep under the carpet all the ideological and pragrammatic difference that exist between the

many parties of the opposition. They are there and they/remain.
But when look arround us realistically, who are the enimies of
the Indian people to day ? Morarji Desai, Atal Behari Bajpayee,
L.K. Advani and all those who are in the prison refusing to sign
a compromise with the dictator ? You know that a large
number of Congress (O) and Jana-Sangh workers and legislators have been brow-beaten or bribed into joining the dictators
party since the Emergency was declared. So they have become
progressive by the touch of the petticoat. Are we going to
judge progressivism by the standered set by an unscupulous,
corrupt, unprinciple fascist, monarchist oligarchy in Delhi ?
Should any one who is prepeard to fight fascist and help in the
restoration of democratic and trade union rights and the rule
of law be our ally today ?

Now that the committed Judges of the Supreme Court have
finally put their stamps of approval on despotism in India,
What is that we are still waiting for ? The Gas Chambers ?
But don't they have in the other form ? How many of your
party comrades have been tortured and killed during the last
five years ? How many thousends of boys and girls have been
tortured and killed in prisons and outside by being branded as
Naxalites ? The fumes of the gas chambers would at least
attract the attention of the World. But the way things have
happened and are still happining even the world liberals have
been lulled into cynicalslum (cynicism). And not that the courts
have that unbridled despotism shall rule the country, are we still
to adopt a low profile which may be termed as cowardice ? I
dont know if will agree with this secarion and the quality of
respons have a familiar ring-like what happened when Hitler
came to power.

There is more point about which I have written to your
party. You know Madhu Limaye and Sharad Yadav resigned
from Parliament since the Lok Sabha ceased to have the legitimacy when its five years terms expired. All efforts were made
to persuade other parties to have their members also resign
their seats from the prisons seems to be far better than any
commitment to long term socio-political goals. Even assuming
that it is stupid to talk of idealism to hard-boiled politicians,

what about some manliness and courage ? Dose a seat in Lok Sabha require jettisoning of certain basic human qualities too ? I wish you would take up this issue in your party and withdraw all your members from the Lok Sabha.

For obvious reasons, it is not possibla for my party to take formal decisions or even positions on any issue. Almost the entire National Committee of my party is in prison, as are most members of States and Districts Committee all over the country. Hardly any active Socialist is out, though a few seniors like N.G. Goray and S.M. Joshi have not been arrested. But that is not because of any thing they have said or not done. (That is a party of dibolical style of the dictator.) I would, howevar, like to assure you that my party stands fully committed to all our mutual agreements.

With greetings,

From the underground   Your sincerely,
somewhere in India, May-2-1976   Sd/- George Fernandes
Com Jyoty Basu   Chairman, Socialist Party
Communist Party of India (Marxist)

N.B. This letter was printed and circulated by sympathisers. It is printed here in its original form. No correction has been made.

AMNESTY INTERNATIONAL

International Secretariat

53 Theobald's Road
London WCIX 8SP
Telephone : 01-404 5831
Telegrams : Amnesty London

Mr Sukumar Ghosh   28 May 1976
Acting Secretary
Socialist Party
86A Lower Circular Road
Calcutta 700 014, India

Dear Mr Ghosh,

Amnesty International, as you may know, is a worldwide human rights organization which is independent of any government, political faction, ideology or religious creed. It works for the release of men and women who are imprisoned anywhere for their beliefs, colour, language, ethnic origin or religion provided that they have neither used nor advocated violence ; these persons are termed "prisoners of conscience".

We would very much like to be in touch with you concerning members of the Socialist Party who are imprisoned in West Bengal. If you know personally any Socialists who are in prison, we should be most grateful if you could supply us with details concerning the date of their arrest, the legislation under which they were arrested, their present place of detention, and some personal details, such as the names and addresses of their family or relatives.

I look forward to hearing from you.

Yours sincerely,
Janet Hunting
Asia research department.

From :   Sukumar Ghosh, Acting Secretary,
        Socialist Party West Bengal,
        86A, Acharya Jagadish Bose Road,
        Calcutta-700 014—West Bengal (INDIA)

15th June, 1976

Dear Mr. Hunting,

Thanks for your letter of 28.5.76. After promulgation of Emergency many Socialist cadres were arrested or offered Satyagraha. The Satyagrahis have been released after 8 months. Some prominent leaders are still detained, their details are given as follows :—

1. Prof. Samar Guha (56), a Member of the Parliament detained in Rohtak Jail in Haryana. A well known politician and educationist he fell ill 4 times during imprisonment. A cardiac patient as he is, imprisonment since June, 1975 is telling upon his healh. His wife is also a political worker and has got a daughter of 14 years. Address : Mrs. Basana Guha, Central Park, Calcutta-32.

2. Biman Mitra (55), Chairman, Socialist Party, West Bengal, 48, Sambhu Babu Lane, Calcutta-14. Detained since June, 1975 in Hooghly Jail 30 miles away from Calcutta. A patient of diabetis and low blood pressure. Denied all facilities due to political prisoner, no sufficient medical facility is available.

3. Swaraj Bandhu Bhattacharya (55), Secretary, Socialist Party West Bengal. Detained since June, 1975. Received special honour for his contribution in the freedom struggle. Now in Burdwan Jail 80 miles from Calcutta. He is now kept in a condemned cell of 8′ × 4′ size, denied movement within Jail, not allowed to see co-prisoners. Every morning he is awakened by armed guards who would undress him for a thorough search. His old mother aging 95 appeal to the Prime Minister of India and Chief Minister of the State for proper redress against inhuman torture goes unreplied. Address : K.B. Bhattacharyya, 371/8, Asoke Nagar, P.O. Asoke Nagar, Dist. 24-Parganas.

4. Prof Sandip Das (40). An important leader of Socialist Party detained since January, 1976 in Presidency Jail. He is now on hunger strike with some 60 other political prisioners for the last few days against the inhuman treatment of the Jail authority. Their grievances have not been taken into account.

5. Ashoke Dasgupta (50). Detained since June, 1975. Now in Suri Jail, some 130 miles away from Calcutta. An employee of New India Assurance, is suspended for his imprisonment.

All these prisoners are detained under Maintenace of Internal Security Act (MISA) under which no trial is executed. Several amendments have been made after Emergency, as a result none can question or challenge the legality of Government action. Government is not liable to show reasons for detainment, detention may continue for indefinite period without any trial.

With respectful thanks,

To

Mr. Janet Hunting,
Asia Research Department
Amnesty International
London.

Yours sincerely,
Sd/-
(Sukumar Ghosh)
Actt. Secretary, Socialist
Party, West Bengal.

N.G. Goray
Editor, Janata

1813 Sadashiv Peth,
Pune 411030
Date 3-7-76

Dear friend,

Once again they have hit Janata hard, this time on the head. Last time the Government had told Janata's printers in Bombay not to print anything that came to them from Janata Office. So we approached the Bombay High Court for redress. That case is still to be decided.

In the meanwhile we thought of having Janata printed in Sadhana Press, Pune. The welcome that was extended to Janata on its reappearance was really heart-warming. Janata had never believed in abusing the Government or the party in power but it did not believe in flattery either. Its credo has been fearless advocacy of truth and defence of the underdog.

Evidently Indira's government was not amused. They wanted to silence the voice of Janata, which they have tried to do now by preremptorily laying down under D.I.R. that Shri N.G. Goray, the Editor and Shri G.B.S. Choudhary, the publisher be "prohibited from making or publishing the said English Weekly Janata and also from using any press for the purpose aforesaid".

And still our great Prime Minister wants us and the world to believe that in India the press is free. Can there be greater travesty of truth ? On this occasion also we propose to approach the Court for redress, but we are not sure whether the Court under the new dispensation has the power to give us relief.

So good-bye dear friend till Janata comes again to meet you—may be in a new avatar.

Yours sincerely
Editor, Janata

George Fernandes to J. P.

My dear Jayaprakashji,

There are certain aspects of the present situation that have disturbed me and alarmed me. First, there is this orchestration of statements by many sundry leaders and some leader writers urging you to call off the movement. Second, one sees constant efforts by some busy-bodies to somehow or the other secure an invitation to sit across the table with Mrs. Gandhi. Third, there is a stubborn refusal to realise that Vinoba's first loyalty is to the Court and that he will never lift a little finger to help the fighters for freedom and democracy in the country. Fourth, there is reluctance to make an honest evaluation of the changes that have taken place in our body politic since Mrs. Gandhi turned dictator on June 26, 1975. Concomitant with all this is the delusion that Mrs. Ganhdi is still not a dictator. A recent refrain from those who seek to have a dialogue is that the first task before JP and others is to secure the release of those in prisons.

I had hoped that this growing cacophony of normalisers is but only a manifestation of the frustration and despondency of some of the leaders and not one of those diabolical moves of the dictator to drive a wedge in the ranks of those opposed to her dictatorship, sow confusion among the masses and demoralise those who are uncompromising in their fight. This move to negotiate has, I believe, been motivated by a desire to prevent or in any case postpone the creation of a one party through merger of various parties of the opposition by presenting a new set of priorities.

The frantic efforts that are being made, and a series of meetings that have been arranged of opposition party leaders have confirmed my fears of a "sell-out". I could not believe that any reasonable leader from any party could formally put down the kind of terms that are reported to have been suggested as the basis for talks that are scheduled for the next few days. Neither the demand to revoke the Emergency nor for release for all political prisoners surprisingly is set for negotiations. Whatever the result of these talks, it would affect the already low morals and sagging determination of political workers and others who have been opposing the dictatorship.

I must say the opposition parties in India have neither learnt nor unlearnt anything since June 26, 1975. When will they realise that they are facing a woman who will never surrender power ? Can they not see that if Nehru went about grooming his daughter in a subtle and sophisticated way to succeed him, the mother lacks even a modicum of shame while indulging in a crude and vulgar exercise to annoint her son as the succcessor ? This is not to say that Nehru's method was commendable or was less dishonourable, but only to point out that like then so now the opposition refuses to understand the designs of the ruling clique. Over the years, opposition politics in India has been of reacting to the initiatives of the ruling party and of never taking the initiative on its own and make the ruling coterie run for its chairs. In the mid-sixties, Dr. Lohia took the initiative, united the opposition by dragging them literally by the scuff of their necks and routed the Congress in 1967. But since then, except for the initiative which the youth took in Gujarat and later in Bihar, there has already been no effort to confront the Congress by the opposition parties. The developments since June 26, 1975 indicate that the opposition leaders lack not only in perspective but also in nerve. Or else how can anyone say that the primary task today is to secure the release of those in prisons ? This is not the stuff that can oppose and overthrow a dictatorship ; if anything this is the stuff that breeds and nourishes dictators.

I am aware of your own frustrations with the opposition leaders, and also of the kind of pressures they are building on you. But I want you to know that there are people who are committed to carry the fight against the dictatorship to the bitter end and for as long as is necessary. I believe that there can be no compromise with the dictatorship. I believe that there are certain issues which are simply non-negotiable. These are : Revocation of the Emergency and scrapping of MISA ; Release of all political prisoners and others held without trial ; Freedom of the Press ; Independence of the judiciary ; Immediate dissolution of the illegitimate Lok Sabha and the holding of election after fulfilling certain preconditions to ensure a fair poll ; and repeal of all Constitutional amendments adopted since June 26, 1975.

I know that Mrs. Gandhi will accept none of these terms. If she can accept these conditions now, she need not have, in the first place, usurped power and become a dictator. And it is not merely that it is impossible for her to reverse what she has done. With an opposition that does not show much will to fight, what is there for her to be worried, about ? So what precisely do the "negotiatours" want to "negotiate" about, even if they realise at this last moment to add to their demands for discussion at the negotiating table ?

Instead of spending their time drafting statements seeking negotiations with Mrs. Gandhi and being over enthusiastic at the prospect of talks on whatever terms, I with the opposition parties applied their collective mind to build an effective movement among all sections of our people to resist the dictatorship. The time appears to be favourable for such efforts to be successful.

For all her bombast, Mrs. Gandhi is today more isolated from the people than she ever was. Her credibility is at its nadir. I am told that recently in Delhi, even doctors rushed to the schools and took their children away believing that Mrs. Gandhi is sterilising them. She and her propagandists say that prices are falling, while in Delhi in the four weeks beginning from the first week of November to the first week of December, there has been an increase of ten to twenty per cent in the prices of consumer goods. Even in Delhi's Super Bazar, the dictator's much touted fair price shop of the Capital, musterd oil was selling at Rs. 12.15 a kg. on December 1, compared to Rs. 10.20 on November 1. In this one month Vanaspati has gone up from Rs. 8.15 to Rs. 8.50 a kg., packed Vanaspati from 9.90 to 10·15 a kg. pure ghee from Rs. 25·50 to Rs 26·50 a kg. Two hundred grams of coconut oil cost Rs. 4·85 on December 1 compared to 4·25 in the last week of November. The same with the prices of dals. In the above period of one month, a kg of Moong (whole) is up from Rs. 2·15 to Rs. 2·30, urak (whole) from Rs. 2·65 to Rs. 2·80 Masur (Red) from Rs. 2·45 to Rs. 2·80, Ranma Chitra from Rs. 2·60 to Rs. 2·95. The Economic Times index of wholesale prices of commodities (base 1962-70) : (100) which was 159·5 on December 9,1975 stood at 179·2 on December 9, 1976, an increase of 13·5 per cent.

Her radio has become a permanent joke. The censored press and the Samachar news do not fool the people any more. The all pervading fear that she succeeded in instilling among the people is still there ; but in Bombay, Poona, Bangalore, West Bengal and Tamil Nadu, there has been a series of strike actions by industrial workers. The number of police firings in Uttar Pradesh alone during the last few months of the sterilisation drive are said to be more than one hundred with over a thousand fatal casualties. Last month, in a speech in the Lok Sabha, Shibbanlal Saxena said that in his constituency of Gorakhpur police had opened fire on people in several places to force them into sterilisation camps. Of course, the speech was censored. In West Bengal and Orissa, her sycophants are fighting like hungry dogs over a bone. In Maharashtra and Karnataka, her party is an house divided. In Gujarat, her party legislators came to blows on who should be the Chief Minister. Her ministers in Orissa and West Bengal are issuing press statements accusing each other of being "anti-social elements" who indulge in "anti-social activities". This is the house Mrs. Gandhi lives in. Granted that the bureaucracy and the repressive organs of state power are continuing to prop her petticoat dictatorship, are there not enough signs to indicate that like all dictatorships everywhere her dictatorship too finally will be consigned to the grabage heap ?

I am sorry if I have rumbled a bit. But I think it is necessary to record my total disenchantment with some of our friends. It is my conviction that the future of our country will be shaped by those who are willing to stake their everything to restore democracy and the rule of law. The compromisers and others who are seeking the soft options will succeed only in giving some legitimacy and hence credibility and respectability to Mrs. Gandhi's dictatorship.

In this context, I am at a loss to understand the minds of

those who continue to maintain their membership of the Lok Sabha even while they criticise for the record that it is a House which has lost it mandate. Why should anyone take cognizance of their criticism when they have no qualms in deriving whatever pattly privileges they can as member of that illegitimate Lok Sabha ? This split mind of the opposition is Mrs. Gandhi's real strength.

I am glad that the Socialist Party's special convention that met in Bombay at the end of November has resolved to give all support to your efforts to unite the four parties of the opposition. If such unity is not forthcoming, the party has said that it will go along with you in the formation of a new party. In the present frame of mind of the leaders of parties which were to merge and their anxiey to reach a settlement at the cost of giving up our fundamental demands, I believe that it is not desirable to make further attempts to bring about a merger. Because one of the basic points of agreement for the merger was struggle for the restoration of the *status quo ante* June, 1975, and it is clear that no party other than the Socialist party is willing now to adhere to this basic objective, and the Socialist Party cannot agree to a merger unless there is agreement over this fundamental question. The political resolution adopted by the Bombay convention of the party members to address themselves to the task of "training and organisation of cadres and the widest possible mass contact for a long and sustained struggle for the restoration of democracy."

Since June 1974, I have been urging you to launch a political party, and I have committed myself, despite some reservation and a little hostility from many of my party comrades, to work for the success of that effort. At the meeting of opposition parties convened by you in November 1975 in Delhi, I had circulated a long note (which was later issued in pamphlet form) in which I had publicly appealed to you to launch a new party. I am aware of the handicaps you face because of the state of your health, but I believe that you owe it to posterity to bring under one banner all those who are pledged to fight against the dictatorship and are committed to the creation of a democratic and egalitarian society in India.

I am deliberately refraining from making any suggestions about the forms and future course of struggle. I have said enough on this during my days in the underground and done what I believed was needed and was within my capacity. I have no regrets and I can never have any reasons to revise my views. I am sure that our youth, workers and intellectuals will keep forging new and adequate instructions of struggle and succeed in overthrowing the dictatorship. There have been signs in recent weeks of restlessness and defiance in many circles, signs which should gladden your heart as they have put more hope in mine.

In the context of the negotiations that are under way and the general anxiety for a settlement that is apparent from the attitude of the leadership of most opposition parties, it is necessary to make it clear that the Socialist party cannot agree to participate in such negotiations, nor will it agree to join other parties in the move to withdraw the struggle against the dictatorship.

UNITY MOVE

New Delhi
July 9, 1976.

Dear friends,

It seems that, at least for the time being the BLD is averse to joint and coordinated functioning among our four parties, as its preference is for unification here and now. Our constant endeavour should be to persuade the BLD for joint work. In the meantime we should strive to work closely together. At district level our workers should organise activities jointly. At the State level the spokesmen of three parties should make a habit of meeting among themselves and devising common programmes for the State. We are facing a very difficult situation and unless we work unitedly the difficulties can become unsurmountable. Our joint work will also accelerate the process of unification of the democratic forces that we all favour.

The Central Offices of the parties will send out to their units appropriate, detailed directives in this matter, but this joint communication of ours should be treated as a general directive.

Pradesh Congress Committees
of Congress (O)
Bharatiya Jana Sangh and the
Socialist Party

Yours sincerely,
Sd/- (Asoka Mehta)
(N. G. Goray)
(O. P. Tyagi)

Opposition's Move for Normalcy

New Delhi,
December 23, 1976.

Dear Shri Asoka Mehta,

I have received your letters of the 12th October and 23rd November and have also read accounts of the meeting in Delhi this week of some leaders of Opposition parties. It is difficult to judge whether there was serious heart-searching at the meeting but I do hope that the efforts to understand that conditions in which normality can be restored to our politics will continue.

My party and Govenment have always been committed to parliamentary democracy which I believe as an ideal as well as practical necessity. I have repeatedly stated that a country of our diversity can hold together and prosper only through a democratic system. Unfortunately many opposition groups and parties seem to think that the rules and conventions which sustain democracy could be invoked or ignored to suit their purpose. Legislative privilege and freedom of expression were misused for personal vendetta and character assassination and to undermine national self-confidence. I need not go into all the circumstances which led to the proclamation of Emergency but surely no one would describe the earlier situation as being political normality.

It is important to recognise the changes that have taken place in the last few months. The nation has made considerable headway in the economic field, in meeting the people's aspirations and in initiating action to redress our long-term demographic and other related problems. The Constitutional amendment is by the will of the people and in their service. Once there is a genuine acceptance of the changes that have taken place, a clear disavowal of communal and separatist policies, a repudiation of the politics of violence and extra-constitutional action, and also a constructive approach to social change, then it would not be impossible to find solutions to the problems between Opposition and Government.

You have referred to Mahatma Gandhi's teaching in support

of your view that Satyagraha is integral to democracy. Doctrinal disputes will not take us far. Mahatmaji's own standards of judgment and self-examination were so exacting that he did not hesitate to call off Satyagrahas when he found them straying from the path of non-violence. Let us not misinterpret Mahatmaji and drag in his name.

State Governmets have already released a large number of political detenues and will continue to do so subject only to national security and public order.

For us the strength and growth of our nation and the welfare of our people must be the supreme consideration. If all of us and especially those elected to play a critical role in the destiny of our nation were clearly seen to subscribe to that view point, political differences would become an asset, strengthening our resolve and sharpening our policies. Without that fundamental approach they merely sap our collective energy, undermine our determination and threaten the integrity of our country.

It is my sincere desire that statesmanship and wisdom will now gain ascendancy and a more mature political awareness guide us in these important tasks.

Sri Asoka Mehta,	Yours sincerely,
President,	Sd/- Indira Gandi.
All India Congress Committee,	
7, Jantar Mantar Road,	
New Delhi.	

Patna,
30th December, 1976.

My dear Asoka,

I have a letter from Smt. Mohinder Kaur dated December 27 along with a copy of the Prime Minister's reply to your letters of October 12 and November 23.

I did not think it proper to speak on the 'phone'. So I am writing this letter which I hope will reach you in time.

Mrs. Gandhi's letter to you is full of lies and distortions. You and your collegaues will be able to spot them and deal with

16

them as you see fit. It may seem petty, but I think the Opposition would be justified in asking Mrs. Gandhi to do some heart-searching herself. This need not be put as crudely as she has done in her letter to you. But I hardly need to advise you on draftsmanship of which you are a master.

Mrs. Gandhi expects us to express some kind of repentance for our past deeds. This is impudence unworthy of the Prime Minister of a great nation. However, the Opposition document entitled 'This We Believe' is sufficient response to Mrs. Gandhi's conditions. I suggest, therefore, that in your reply you may stress the fact that the opposition has always been and will ever remain committed to the ideals, principles and methods laid down in the above document. A post-mortem of the Opposition's past will be disastrous approach to a meaningful dialogue, and you may point this out to Mrs. Gandhi. Naturally in your reply you will also stress that the Opposition is no less concerned with the progress of the nation and the decencies of democracy. If there have been lapses, both sides are to blame. So the attitude of mind with which the talks may be approached should be that of 'forgive and forget.' Otherwise, the whole thing will end up in charges and counter-charges.

As for holding talks with the Government, it seems to me that prior release of all political prisoners and withdrawal of press censorship should be essential preconditions, as I have indicated in my letter (dated Dec. 29) to you and other colleagues.

I cannot think of anything more to write in reply to Mohinderji's letter. By the way, I might point out that I feel cut off from the current events and developments and feel handicapped in telling or advising any new initiatives.

With affectionate regards,

Shri Asoka Mehta,   Yours sincerely,
New Delhi.   Sd/-Jayaprakash Narayan

P. S. : Identical letters have been sent to Atalji, Charan Sing and Surendra Mohan.

N. B. These letters were typed and circulated underground.